Knitting Counterpanes

Traditional Coverlet Patterns for Contemporary Knitters

Knitting Counterpanes

Traditional Coverlet Patterns for Contemporary Knitters

Mary Walker Phillips

The Taunton Press

TAUNTON
BOOKS&VIDEOS

...by fellow enthusiasts

©1989 by The Taunton Press, Inc.
All rights reserved

First printing: February 1989
Second printing: May 1990

International Standard Book Number: 0-918804-98-1

Library of Congress Catalog Card Number: 88-51354

Printed in the United States of America

A THREADS Book

THREADS MAGAZINE® is a trademark of The Taunton Press, Inc.,
registered in the U.S. Patent and Trademark Office.

The Taunton Press
63 South Main Street
Box 5506
Newtown, Connecticut 06470-5506

This book is dedicated to all of the wonderful knitters of the past; to the authors of needlework and knitting books who provided us with such a rich heritage; and to the knitters of the twentieth and twenty-first centuries, who will continue to enhance the world with their beautiful interpretations of this inheritance.

The Land of Counterpane

When I was sick and lay a-bed,
I had two pillows at my head,
And all my toys beside me lay
To keep me happy all the day.

And sometimes for an hour or so
I watched my leaden soldiers go,
With different uniforms and drills,
Among the bedclothes, through the hills;

And sometimes sent my ships in fleets
All up and down among the sheets;
Or brought my trees and houses out,
And planted cities all about.

I was the giant great and still
That sits upon the pillow-hill,
And sees before him, dale and plain,
The pleasant land of counterpane.

—Robert Louis Stevenson

Acknowledgments

This book was made possible in part by a Visual Artists Fellowship Grant from the National Endowment for the Arts.

It was a very solitary activity to put together this book, knit all the samples for it and write the pattern directions. But luckily, I was not alone.

In giving thanks to various people, one risks omitting some names. I hope there are no such omissions.

To all of my friends and family, thank you for your encouragement and for sharing your counterpanes, books and information. To several special people, I give a special round of thanks. Shirley and Bill Sayles have been my major backup team, starting with my first book, *Step-by-Step Knitting*, which began my writing career. In agreeing to undertake the typing and editing of my knitting directions, Sandra Morris had little idea of the task she was tackling. The intelligence and patience required to consolidate hundreds of pages of handwritten directions were considerable, and the experience was tremendously educational for both of us. Sandra's husband, C. Robert Morris, proofread every page, for which I am very grateful. Theresa Gaffey tested each pattern by working up a new set of samples from my directions. What a superb job these people have done.

To Diane M. Sabbarese, I owe thanks for the charted directions supplied with the pattern on pp. 34-35 and several on pp. 100-131.

Editors seldom receive enough praise. Christine Timmons of The Taunton Press has had the biggest job of all: coordinating the many parts of this book. Her intelligent probing, patience and personal interest in the project have kept me on track during its development, knowing that before long we would have a book in hand. Her colleagues at Taunton also deserve my thanks.

To a number of museum curators I am indebted for their generous help and support with this project, especially Gloria Seaman Allen (D.A.R. Museum), Marcia Anderson (Minnesota Historical Society), Dr. I.E. Anthony (Welsh Folk Museum), Doris M. Bohman (Smithsonian Institution), Anthea Bickley (Bradford Art Galleries), Dorothy K. Burnham (Royal Ontario Museum), Elizabeth Ann Coleman (The Brooklyn Museum), Jacqueline Fraser (Otago Early Settlers Association), Anette Flury (Gewebenmuseum), Cornelia Frisbee/Houde (Historic Cherry Hill), Frances Hinchcliffe (Victoria and Albert Museum), Dena S. Katzenberg (Baltimore Museum of Art), Robert C. Kaufmann (Metropolitan Museum of Art), Dr. Georges Klein (Musée Alsacien), Santina M. Levey (Victoria and Albert Museum), Gillian Moss (Cooper-Hewitt Museum), Frank A. Norick (Lowie Museum of Anthropology), Jane C. Nylander (Strawbery Banke), Mary-Ellen Earl Perry (Margaret Woodbury Strong Museum), Jenefer Quérée (Canterbury Museum), Milton F. Sonday, Jr. (Cooper-Hewitt Museum), Cecilia Steinfeldt (Witte Museum), Fiona Stodder (Strangers' Hall Museum) and Naeomi A. Tarrant (National Museums of Scotland).

My thanks, too, go to the New York Public Library, whose superb collection of nineteenth- and twentieth-century needlework books and pamphlets I used extensively; and to John Arnold, La Trobe Research Librarian at the State Library of Victoria in Melbourne, Australia. And to Mrs. E. Borowski of Nutley, New Jersey, whose request for instructions for a particular pattern triggered the research for this book.

Finally, a very special thank-you to a group of friends for their invaluable help: Tatsuko Akachi; Mary Elizabeth Allen; Isobel Angel; Julia Bachelder; Jean and Bruno Bisceglia; Rhett Delford Brown; Kirstie Buckland; Ellen Burton; Margery Blackman; Elizabeth Cera; Jean Downs; Jane Eschweiler; Lisa Fabietti; Betty Fogel; Phebe Fox; The Friday Knitters, St. Paul/Minneapolis, Minnesota; Christy Gade; Constance Jackson; Mary Jane Leland; Wilma Smith Leland; Susanna Lewis; James Mack; Mary Elizabeth Miles; Irene Preston Miller; Ruth Nelson; Virginia Norris; Patricia O'Connor; Elizabeth T. Page; Harriet Quimby; Janet Russell; Alma Selkirk; Yvonne Sinclair; Naomi A. E. Tarrant; Rona Warner; Antoinette Lackner Webster; Helen Webster; and Mary Anne Wells.

Preface

The title of this book could easily be *In Search of Knitted Counterpanes: The Travels and Knitting Education of Mary Walker Phillips.* For much of this education, I am indebted to a very important Englishwoman, Mary Hedges Thomas (1889-1948). In 1962, I purchased a second-hand copy of *Mary Thomas's Book of Knitting Patterns* (1943), and my life changed completely. This $1.50 investment, plus the later purchase of *Mary Thomas's Knitting Book*, which was published originally in 1938, has given me almost every bit of technical knitting advice I have ever needed. These two books are the backbone of any real knitting library.

Why another book to add to that library? Why a book on knitted counterpanes? In March, 1970, a reader of my *Step-by-Step Knitting* (1967) wrote to request directions for a counterpane from The Brooklyn Museum shown in the historical chapter of that book. When I asked the museum curators for information on the piece, they were able to give me only the donor's name. When other letters from readers arrived with the same request for directions, I knew I had to find them, and my search began in earnest.

During the early days of my research, I helped document the knitting collection at the Cooper-Hewitt Museum in New York City. This collection has outstanding knitted samplers, the source of much information in my research of knitted patterns. I searched at length for the pattern in question in the Cooper-Hewitt's collection of nineteenth-century knitting books and periodicals, but with no luck. I also routinely rummaged through boxes of incoming books, but still nothing. After months of finding more and more counterpane patterns— but still not *the* pattern—I opened a box of incoming books and found in it a copy of Butterick's *The Art of Knitting* (1892). At last, my search for the directions for The Brooklyn Museum's counterpane was over (see pp. 96-99).

Finding these directions offered just the assurance I needed to begin looking for pattern directions for other counterpanes owned by museums, historical societies and private collectors. I was convinced that an important body of design was being overlooked, and I was certain that there had been very little, if any, attempt by anyone else to research the subject and resurrect these superb old patterns.

My research led me throughout the United States and Canada and to many other parts of the world. This book records where my adventures have taken me.

In 1977, my long-time friend Mary Jane Leland sent me a copy of the magazine *Craft Australia*, which contained Hughla Davidson's article, "The Development of Knitting as a Craft." This article documents numerous counterpanes, listing private collectors and historical societies and museums with counterpane collections in Australia and New Zealand. Since I was planning to attend the World Craft Council Conference in Japan in 1978, I decided to combine this trip with one to Australia and New Zealand to see as many counterpanes as possible. As it turned out, luck was with me.

Soon after deciding to go to Australia, I received a letter from Isobel Angel of Melbourne, saying how much she was enjoying my 1971 book *Creative Knitting*. When I wrote to thank her, I told her of my plans to visit Australia and New Zealand and asked if she thought there would be any interest in my giving workshops. The affirmative reply came from Helen Webster of the Australian Wool Corporation, which made all the arrangements. In announcing these workshops, the corporation let it be known that one of the purposes of my trip was to see counterpanes and to look for nineteenth- and twentieth-century publications on knitting. At every stop, the response from knitters to my research was overwhelming.

After a hectic month in Australia and Tasmania, I went to New Zealand, where I made more new friends and continued to gather copious information on counterpanes. Constance Jackson introduced me to knitted spreads in two historic Auckland homes and in the Auckland War Memorial Museum. In Dunedin, Margery Blackman took me in hand, introducing me to local knitters and showing me more beautiful counterpanes at an exhibit entitled "Bed Spread" at the Otago Early Settlers Association Museum. (Hughla Davidson had written the catalog for the show.) In Christchurch, I found a splendid counterpane display at the Canterbury Museum. The simplicity of much of the Canterbury Museum's collection intrigued me the most. Like all the other people I met during my sojourn, Canterbury Museum curator Jenefer Quérée generously made available the museum's information on the collection.

Three years after this first trip, I was asked to be a guest speaker and exhibit my own work in connection with The New Zealand Spinning, Weaving and Woolcrafts Society's

1981 National Woolcraft Festival in Dunedin. After the conference, I traveled the length of New Zealand giving workshops, from Invergargill in the south to Kerikeri on the North Island. I was delighted to continue my counterpane research as my exhibit and I moved from city to city, and I am particularly pleased that three pieces of my own work now reside permanently in New Zealand. Throughout my travels, the New Zealanders generously shared their treasured counterpanes with me, and on this trip I finally met Hughla Davidson.

Since 1980, I have twice traveled across the Atlantic in search of counterpanes in the United Kingdom and in central Europe. And all the while, I have continued my research in various parts of the United States and Canada.

The results of my travels and years of study are contained in this book. It includes some of the counterpane patterns from the various collections I visited at home and abroad as well as other patterns I felt were significant from nineteenth-century needlework magazines and books. In the case of the former, whenever I could not find written directions for a pattern, I deciphered them from the actual counterpane (or picture of it) and supplied my own instructions. I have also supplied as much information about the patterns as I could find, and I would welcome any further information on the counterpanes readers may have. My research will continue long after this book heads off to the printer.

The patterns themselves are grouped into chapters by design effect. Within each chapter, the patterns proceed logically from the simplest to the most complex. Each pattern is accompanied by a photo of its component elements, which I knitted especially for this book. Where needed, the patterns also contain assembly diagrams and possible assembly variations. The book concludes with a list of suppliers for needles and yarn, a listing of museums and historical societies that have interesting collections of counterpanes, and a bibliography.

The patterns in this book are exquisite and will remain so no matter how you decide to use them—for a full counterpane or for curtains, a wall hanging, a panel on a garment, pillow covers or whatever else comes to mind. The lace edging patterns on pp. 144-171 can, of course, be used to trim linens, petticoats, blouses or anything in need of a handsome border. I suggest that you work the patterns as shown and then evaluate them for possible adaptations.

Whether you are an accomplished or a beginning knitter or fall somewhere in between, I hope you enjoy working these patterns and learning from them. When I first began knitting counterpane patterns I thought I was fairly knowledgeable about knitting. I soon discovered, however, that I was beginning the best self-imposed knitting education of my career. I hope these patterns serve similarly to broaden your knowledge and enjoyment of this venerable craft.

Mary Walker Phillips
New York City, February, 1989

Contents

Introduction

Unraveling the past is not always easy, and tracing the history of common objects can often be more complicated than studying the more exotic. On the surface, one would expect the history of an object as straightforward as a knitted bed covering to be easily researched. In fact, the subject of bed coverings is complicated by the history of their country of origin, individual household economics, personal taste and changing fashion. Except for the elaborately dressed beds of the wealthy and royalty, little descriptive attention has been paid historically to this most personal of all household furniture.

The terms applied to bed coverings have varied over time and locale. The word *bedspread* has been in American dictionaries for only about 100 years. If you looked up this term in the 1897 Funk & Wagnalls' *A Standard Dictionary of English Language,* for example, you would be referred to the synonyms *quilt* and *counterpane.* (The term *spread* alone was defined as "a covering for bed, table, sofa, or the like, usually of some light, fine woven fabric.")

Funk & Wagnalls' defined the term *quilt* much as we do today, as "a bed cover or coverlet made by stitching together two layers of cloth or patchwork with some soft and warm substance between." And this same source identified a *counterpane* as "an outside covering for a bed," designed to be spread over all other bed clothes. This use of the word *counterpane,* in fact, appears much earlier. In his 1803 *Cabinet Dictionary,* the great English cabinetmaker and designer Thomas Sheraton mentions the bed clothes that traditionally completed his wooden bed frame, describing the counterpane as "the utmost of bedclothes, that under which all others are concealed."

At the beginning of the nineteenth century, *counterpane* frequently implied a white covering for the bed. Sometimes quilted, it still retained its nomenclature as "counterpane." This is easy to understand since, from around 1600, the word *counterpane* had been the English-language alternative to *counterpoint,* a corruption of the Old French *coute point,* which literally meant "quilt-stabbed or stitched through." Thus the word *counterpane* really described how the cover was made, while *coverlet,* from the Old French *covrir* ("to cover") and *lit* ("bed"), describes the cover's function.

By the end of the century, the word *spread* could be applied to uses all around the house, but *counterpane* was

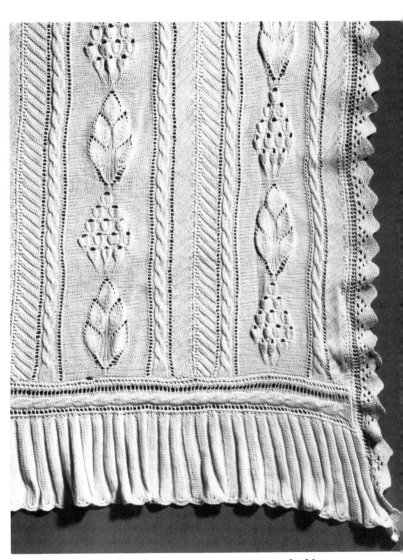

Detail of an undated, white cotton counterpane worked in strip patterns with lace and fluted borders. From the collection of The Museum of History, Berne, Switzerland.

Above: engraving accompanying printed pattern directions for a knitted counterpane square from *Weldon's Practical Knitter*. Below: nineteenth-century white cotton tidy, in the Swirls and Squares pattern (see pp. 39-41). From the collection of Antoinette Lackner Webster, East Poultney, Vermont.

restricted to use as a covering for the bed. By this time, too, counterpanes encompassed woven and knitted coverings as well as quilted spreads.

The nineteenth-century vogue in knitted counterpanes is evident in the many patterns included in the well-known domestic journals of the day—*Godey's Ladies Book*, *Peterson's*, *Harper's Bazaar* and *Demorest's* in this country *Ladies' Treasury* in England, and *La Mode Illustrée* in France. Sometimes the knitting patterns were offered in conjunction with a specific project, like making a counterpane. Oftentimes, however, the pattern alone was provided, and it was up to the knitter to decide on the design's application. The very nature of knitting patterns makes them usable for a variety of objects, and there appear to be no motifs that were uniquely associated with bed coverings.

Because piracy of designs and patterns was prevalent in the nineteenth century, it is difficult to attribute origins to most patterns. Isabella Beeton, today best remembered for *Mrs. Beeton's Book of Household Management*, published with her husband, Samuel Ochert Beeton, *The English Woman's Domestic Magazine*. Many of the fancywork projects in this magazine were acquired from Adolf Goubaud of Paris, who, likewise with his wife, published needlework, fashion and domestic-science journals.

Goubaud's business is known to have included the distribution of the latest fashion-illustration plates to other publishers. His own publications, oriented toward the ladies of the upper and middle classes, carried patterns for knitted articles and were similar to magazines published worldwide, like the German periodical *Der Moden Welt* ("The World of Fashion"), which by 1890 appeared in translation in 19 countries with a new issue every six weeks. While communication may not have been as rapid then as now, knitters around the world had access to a wide variety of new patterns and designs at almost the same time.

In addition to providing the patterns themselves, nineteenth-century magazines on household management offered counsel on the changing fashion in bed linens and treatment of the bedroom. According to the period, these journals variously reminded the reader of the benefits—or evils—of featherbeds, the cost of springs and how they cut down on bed vermin, and the need to keep the bedroom bright, cheerful, well ventilated and clear of anything that collected dust. Although knitted bed coverings certainly held dust, the surviving examples, for the most part, met one important criterion of the period: they were white. The popularity of knitted coverlets

Detail of a superb cotton counterpane, dated 1818 and signed 'R.H.,' for its maker Rebecca Hopkins of Llandyfodwg, Glamorgan, Wales. Using garter, reverse stockinette, and knit and purl stitches, the 140 squares each depict a house or object and surround a large, central rectangle showing a church or castle. From the collection of the Welsh Folk Museum, St. Fagans, Cardiff, Wales.

throughout the century can, in fact, be attributed to their ability to adjust to the shifting decorative currents.

At mid-nineteenth century, white covers topped white sheeting and blankets, which in turn sandwiched the white night clothes worn by both sexes of all ages. By the end of the century, however, color had crept into bed. Open-patterned, commercially made covers and pillow shams in Nottingham lace, darned net, appliqué, antique lace and Swiss muslin were used over unpatterned but colored silk and Silesia spreads and pillowcases. By allowing a glimpse of colorful linens underneath, the white knitted openwork counterpane adapted to the changing fashion.

For those who hadn't the time, skill or inclination to make their own open-patterned covers, the department stores and mail-order houses that sprang up in the late nineteenth century offered alternatives. Boston's great department store Jordan Marsh & Co., for example, listed "crochet" spreads in their semi-annual catalogs, pricing a single-bed spread at from 79 cents to $1.00, and a double-size spread at from $1.00 to $1.50. Because of the low cost, we must assume that these spreads were made by machine rather than by hand.

The mechanization of traditional handicraft techniques was but one aspect of the Industrial Revolution, which turned mother-and-daughter power to water-and-steam power. In the nineteenth century, many women in search of at least middle-class status left homemaking chores, including needlework, for an array of professions. Just as women began entering what had previously been an exclusively male domain, men became increasingly involved during this period in needle crafts—not a surprising development in light of the fact that historically men were the knitters in many cultures, and that they exclusively made up the populous ranks of knitting guilds in Renaissance Europe. The fact that so few known knitted counterpanes have been identified as being made by men does not necessarily mean that all the extant examples are exclusively the work of female hands. Doubtless some of these examples were actually made by men, with the credit for the work mistakenly passed on at some point over the generations to female relatives.

Today the woman—or man—who labors beyond the front door does not necessarily forego handicrafts. The scale of creativity may be as small as a knitted pair of infant

Facing page: detail of an undated, white cotton counterpane worked in Grandmother Anderson's Pattern (see pp. 60-62), with a knitted and tied-fringe border. From the collection of the National Museum of Switzerland, Zurich, Switzerland. Below, detail of a tubular sampler of knitting patterns, worked by Johanna Kofler von Walther around 1888, at about age 14 in Munich, Germany. Such samplers provided a record of patterns, which could be used alone or in combination for garments, counterpanes and any other knitted piece. From the collection of von Walther's granddaughter, Lisa Fabietti, Fresno, California.

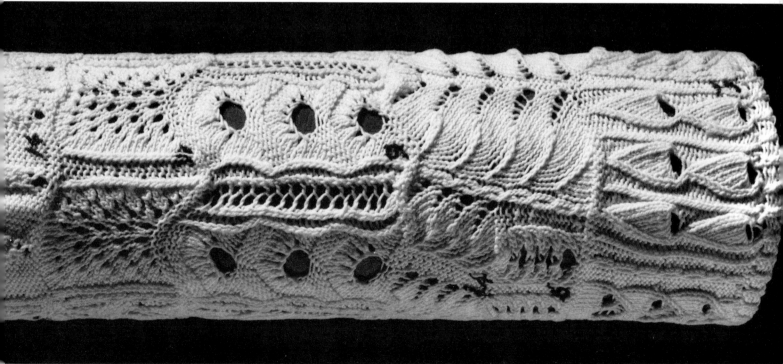

booties or as grand as a full counterpane. Yet both ends of the creative spectrum keep alive a venerable tradition.

Mary Walker Phillips has sought with this book to enliven this tradition further by bringing to light an important, but essentially overlooked body of knitted design. In the following pages she has revived many patterns from out-of-print nineteenth-century sources and has added to them patterns she deciphered from actual counterpanes studied in museums, historical societies and private collections here and abroad.

The seed for this impressive body of research and interpretation was sown in the collection of The Brooklyn Museum. Mary had included a photograph of a counterpane from the museum's collection in her 1967 book, *Step-by-Step Knitting*. Several years later, when a reader wrote to her asking for directions for that spread, Mary came to me. But I had almost no information about the piece. In the extended search for these directions that followed, Mary was unwittingly launched on a course that, almost two decades later, would yield this book.

The counterpane that initiated this book, shown on the facing page, is in fact not a stunning example of knitting. Had it been, it might not have caught Mary's eye in the first place. Rather this work spoke to her as one knitter to another—bad grammar, dropped stitches and all. The challenge she took from this single spread she now passes on to you many times over. By exploring the selection of patterns she has provided, you can help keep alive this impressive body of knitted design. And when you have finished counting stitches and casting them off, you can begin to speculate what your bedspread or coverlet or counterpane will be called one hundred years from now.

Elizabeth Ann Coleman
Curator of Costumes and Textiles,
The Brooklyn Museum, February, 1989

Detail of a white knitted crib counterpane with a crocheted border, dated 1872. From the collection of the Smithsonian Institution, National Museum of American History, Washington, D.C.

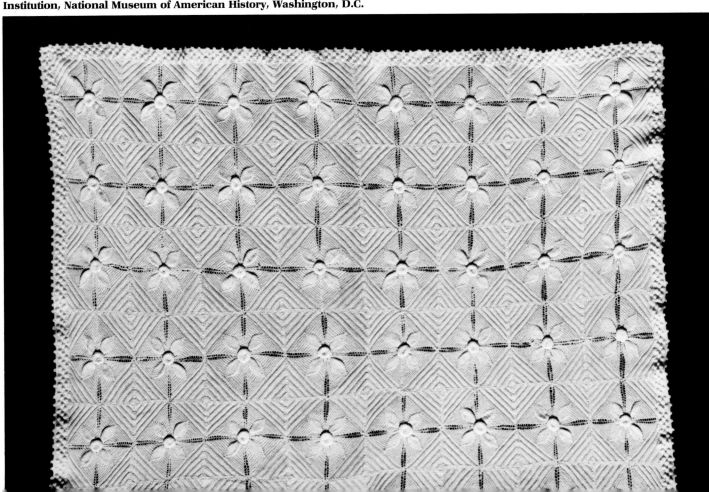

Detail of an undated, white cotton counterpane worked in an embossed pattern (see pp. 96-99) with an embossed lace border. Searching for the directions for this counterpane in 1970 initiated the research for this book. From the collection of The Brooklyn Museum, Brooklyn, New York; accession number 41.7; gift of Miss Johanna and Mr. Henry Mollenhauer.

Getting Started

The knitted spreads called counterpanes that decorated many nineteenth-century beds were traditionally worked in cotton yarn. The quality of this yarn varied widely, depending upon what was locally available. I have seen counterpanes knit in every type and grade of cotton, from grocery string to carpet warp to the finest yarns of the period. I have also seen some old counterpanes that combined strips of linen knitting with linen yardage.

Even though many old patterns recommended cotton (and some suggested a particular size and even brand of needles), only a few mentioned the weight of yarn to use. Because of this, I used my own judgment as to the suitability of yarns for the samples in this book and assembled a variety that resembled the spectrum of yarns I had seen used in many actual counterpanes. Each yarn produced slightly different results, depending on its soft or hard texture and dull or shiny finish. (Cotton yarn often undergoes mercerization, a process that treats the yarn under tension with alkaline caustic soda, giving it not only an extra-smooth surface but also a lustrous finish. This yarn is usually called perle or pearl cotton.) You will see the varying results of these yarns in the photographed samples accompanying the patterns. The yarn and needle size used are noted in the captions.

For the most part, I have specified traditional cotton yarns for the patterns in this book, but depending on the project you have in mind, other yarns could be used. Linen would make lovely curtains or placemats. Wool would be suitable for a pillow cover, a throw or garments incorporating these patterns. When choosing yarn, consider the yarn's weight, texture and finish as well as its overall appropriateness for the pattern and project you have picked and for its ultimate setting.

Some readers may wonder how to estimate the amount of yarn needed for a project. It is difficult to generalize since this amount depends on the size of the yarn and needles chosen, the kinds of stitches in the selected pattern, your gauge (that is, the tightness or looseness of your knitting) and, of course, the dimensions of the full project. Therefore, I suggest knitting up an entire ball or skein of the yarn you have chosen to see how many pattern units can be made. I found, for example, when working the Scottish Farmer's Pattern (pp. 30-31) with Parisian cotton on size 1 needles, that one ball yielded six pattern units. Yet for the Dunraven Square pattern (pp. 90-93), which I worked with Wondersheen on size 0 needles, I got 4½ pattern units per skein. And for the Corinthian Squares pattern (pp. 72-75), which I knitted in Antique Bedspread Cotton on size 0 needles, one skein produced three units.

Once you know how many pattern units can be made from one ball or skein, it is simple to calculate the amount needed for the full project. First, determine the total number of units needed by dividing the dimensions for the full project by the dimensions of a single pattern unit. Then divide the total number of units needed by the number of units produced by one ball or skein of yarn. The resulting figure will tell you the total number of balls or skeins needed for the project.

Whatever your estimate of the yarn needed, however, always buy a little more. Dye lots do run out, sometimes in a matter of weeks. Keep in mind that even white yarns are dyed. By buying more yarn than you need, you may end up with leftovers, but do not worry. It is a good idea to have some yarn on hand in case you need to mend the counterpane at a later date. If you have a lot of yarn left over, you might check with the yarn store to see if the new, unused balls or skeins can be returned.

Needles and Miscellaneous Equipment

The tools used in knitting are nominal in price and easy to come by no matter where you live. They are as near as your local shopping area or your mailbox. You may, in fact, already have some of them.

Most important is a carefully chosen selection of knitting needles. Needles greatly affect the ease and pleasure of your knitting, and it is far better to buy a few needles of good quality than many of inferior grade. The needles should be smooth, with gradually tapering points that are not sharp or blunt, but slightly rounded to avoid splitting the yarn. The need for good points is even more important when working with small needles and fine yarns that have little or no stretch, such as cotton and linen.

You will also need to consider several other things in choosing needles: the needles' size, or thickness, their length, the material they are made of, and whether you want (or need) to work with straight or circular needles. The size of needles you will need depends on the gauge you prefer for the finished piece. I knitted the samples in this book mainly on sizes 0, 1 and 2 needles, which I found best duplicated the look of the historical counterpanes.

I used both straight, double-pointed needles and circular needles in various lengths to work these samples. Circular needles are among my favorites. I find them easy to work with and ideal to travel with because they have no waving ends to catch on chair arms. And they need not be used just for circular work. They can be used for any pattern that is to be worked flat and calls for straight, single-pointed needles.

I also enjoy working on double-pointed needles, which are required for many patterns. These needles also offer an advantage when working on medallion units. The needles conveniently serve as "stretchers" for the work, allowing me to stretch the work out flat, check my progress and spot any errors. In the end, the choice of needles is a matter of personal taste. By all means, use whichever needles you feel most comfortable with. But whatever your choice, always buy the best available.

Since cable needles for turning a cable do not come in sizes small enough for the pieces in this book, I use an extra double-pointed needle for this purpose. It does not have the bend of a regular cable needle, but it nonetheless securely holds the stitches being moved for the cable. Some companies package double-pointed needles in sets of five, but more often they are sold in sets of four. If you plan to work on more than one piece at a time and prefer a particular brand of needle, I suggest buying several packages of double-pointed needles.

Another matter of personal taste involves needle finish. The most common needles in sizes small enough for counterpane knitting are made of aluminum or plastic, but there are also other types of metal needles and some made of natural materials like bamboo. If you have not already found your own preference of finish, try out a variety of needles. You will soon find one that feels just right to you.

Needle weight is another consideration for some, and I include myself among them. I find that I work best with needles that are light in weight. I suggest again that you experiment to find your preference. After all, a counterpane is a time-consuming project, and it pays to work with tools that you find really comfortable.

In addition to needles, you will also need crochet hooks and tapestry needles. Crochet hooks are frequently used to join seams, finish edges or add borders; and they are invaluable for picking up dropped stitches. Match the size of the crochet needle to the size of the knitting needle you are using, and choose them as carefully as you do knitting needles. I used sizes 2.0 mm and 2.5 mm to join some of the multipart pieces in this book (see Assembling and Finishing Counterpanes on p. 14). Some other several-part patterns were joined by sewing with a tapestry needle. This needle has a blunt point with an elongated eye and is also used for weaving in yarn ends. You will want tapestry needles in sizes 13 to 16 for a range of yarn sizes.

Besides these necessary tools, there are others that make certain tasks easier. Ring markers (in small sizes for the pieces in this book) help designate where patterns begin and end, and where increases or decreases are to be made. A needle-size gauge (use one for your particular brand of needle), a stitch counter, scissors and a thimble are all useful additions to your tool box. A tape measure or ruler, T-pins or other strong straight pins, and a blocking board are important for blocking the finished piece.

I recommend tagging samples so that you will have an accurate record of your work for future reference. String tags are perfect for this purpose. Record all the relevant information about the swatch: the type of yarn, its weight and dye lot; the size of needle; the pattern name and source; and the date the sample is knitted.

A small box, approximately 5 in. by 3½ in. by 5 in., makes an excellent spool holder, but any box about that size will do. The spool holder allows the yarn to be drawn off the spool in the direction of the twist—that is, in the direction in which it was spun and wound. If the yarn is drawn off in another direction, an extra twist will be added to it, causing it to kink and tangle.

To make a spool holder, punch holes through two opposite sides of the box. Insert a long knitting needle, a chopstick or a thin dowel through the holes and through the center of the spool to hold it steady. An empty coffee can or container of a similar size will hold a coned yarn steady.

Finally, here is one last bit of "equipment" to add to your kit. Since yarn can be snagged by rough fingernails or skin, I suggest keeping handy an emery board and hand cream.

Making Swatches

Before settling down to knit a project, it is important to knit pattern samples to determine your gauge. This is a vital and valuable exercise for all types of knitting, and in the case of clothing, where exact fit is required, determining exact gauge is crucial. In the case of counterpanes, however, gauge is less crucial and need not be exactingly determined—a counterpane, after all, must only approximate certain dimensions to cover a bed.

Yet while there is some leeway with gauge in counterpane knitting, making sample pattern units is still important. These samples provide an opportunity to experiment with various yarns and needle sizes and let you see the pattern worked in different gauges. I suggest beginning with the yarns and needle sizes I used for a given pattern. Then if you find the sample too loosely or tightly knit,

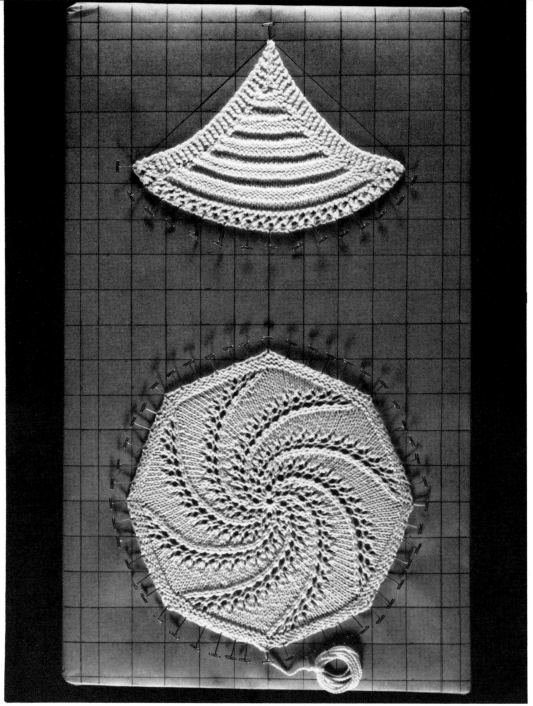

Counterpane units should be blocked on a blocking board when finished to flatten them and bring them to their final size and shape. In the photo here, a unit of Wilma's Pattern (see p. 141) is being blocked as a fan shape and a Swirls and Squares medallion (see p. 40) is pinned for blocking as an octagon. After being dampened with water and air-dried, the units will retain their shape when removed from the board.

change yarns or needles or both until you produce a fabric that pleases you.

Once you become familiar with a pattern as written, you may want to try changing it a bit. Making sample pattern units enables you to experiment with new combinations of stitches and see how patterns interact with one another. You will find that even slight variations in an element of the existing pattern can alter the appearance of the knitting. This is the time to discover that a pattern combination or a particular yarn is the right—or wrong—choice for the piece you plan to make.

Blocking

An unblocked piece of knitting is in a limp, unfinished state. The blocking process makes the knitting lie smooth and flat and form to its final shape and size. Block the pieces as you finish them, and always block before joining pieces together.

For blocking you will need a surface that is flat and rigid, yet porous enough to insert pins easily. Half-inch fiberboard sheathing, a lightweight insulating material that is available at most lumberyards (I use Celotex brand), makes an excellent blocking surface. It comes in 4-ft. by 8-ft. sheets and can be cut by the lumberyard to any size you want. For my purposes, I find a 12-in. by 24-in. rectangle convenient. If you cannot find fiberboard sheathing, use a cork-faced bulletin board. You will also need heavy brown wrapping paper, several inches larger on all sides than the fiberboard or bulletin board, 1¼-in. T-pins or some other rustproof pins strong enough to be held under tension, sturdy tape and a spray bottle of water.

Cover the top of the board with the brown paper, pulling the paper tightly over the edges and taping it on the underside. With a pencil and ruler, mark off 1-in. squares with a series of parallel horizontal and vertical lines set 1 in. apart. (If you use a #2½ pencil, the pencil marks will not come off on your knitting.) These lines will be the measuring guides for the length and width of the piece being blocked and will also serve to keep it straight while it is being stretched. A ½-in. grid can be added if the size of the pattern units requires it.

It is the edge of the pattern unit with the least amount of stretch that will establish the blocked size of the piece. For strip and rectangular patterns, the cast-on edge is the one with the least amount of stretch. For squares, triangles and fan patterns, another edge may be the least elastic. And in the case of medallion patterns, all the edges will

have the same amount of stretch, which means that any side can serve to establish the blocked size of the piece.

Begin blocking by placing the finished piece face up in the center of the blocking board. Position the square or rectangular units so that the edge with the least amount of stretch sits on a horizontal line and another side of the piece sits on a vertical line. For a medallion unit, position any one of its sides on a grid line, or align the points on opposite sides along a grid line, as I have done in the photo on the facing page. For a shell or fan pattern, decide first how you want to assemble the units, since they will be blocked differently for the two possible assembly methods. To join the units as a series of cascading fan shapes (see the diagram below), each unit should be blocked as a fan, as shown in the top of the photo on the opposite page. To assemble the pieces as four-unit squares,

Assembly Options for Shell and Fan Patterns

Any of the fan or shell patterns (pp. 132-143) can be assembled in one of two ways: as a series of cascading fans or shells, or as four-unit squares. For the first method of assembly, the unit must be blocked as a fan shape, as shown in the photo on the facing page. For the second method, the unit should be blocked as a right triangle.

 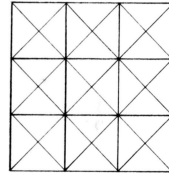

each unit should be blocked as a triangle. In the latter case, the two short sides of the unit will be blocked as a right triangle. The side with the least amount of stretch should be positioned along a horizontal grid line, and the adjoining side along a vertical line.

When working with squares or rectangles, pin one corner of the horizontal edge, pull the edge taut and pin the other corner. Then place pins at 1-in. intervals along this edge, angling the pins away from the knitting. Next, pin the top corners of the piece. Then return to the bottom edge and begin working your way up each side, pinning at ½-in. intervals and alternating from side to side. Stretch each side to its maximum as you work up the length of the piece, and be careful to keep it hugging the vertical lines and undistorted in shape. Make sure that the opposite sides are stretched equally in length, and repin them if necessary.

Work similarly with a triangle, pinning first the side you have positioned on a horizontal grid line, then the adjacent side positioned on a vertical grid line and finally the diagonal edge. Be sure to stretch and pin all edges taut, and keep the triangle undistorted. Do not rush the blocking process. Instead, be patient in order to do a good job. You are, after all, establishing the finished size of the piece and ultimately the size of the counterpane. If the pieces are blocked properly at the outset, chances are that you will not need to block them again after cleaning the counterpane.

With a spray bottle and warm water, dampen the piece well and press it with your hand so that the water penetrates the knitting. Then let the piece air-dry completely before removing the pins. Once removed from the blocking board, the piece will collapse slightly.

Assembling and Finishing Counterpanes

Counterpane pieces are joined by crocheting or sewing them together, no matter what their configuration is to be. When crocheted together, the pieces can be positioned back to back or face to face. The former produces a raised seam on the front of the fabric, which can be an interesting design element. The latter yields an invisible seam. When sewn together, the pieces are placed face to face or side to side, with the resulting seam invisible in both cases.

Crocheting Units Together

When crocheting units together, they can be positioned either back to back or face to face. To join units, insert crochet hook through edge stitch on one unit and corresponding stitch on other unit (1). You can pick up both loops of edge stitch, as shown, or just inside loop if working with pieces back to back. In latter case, strengthen seam by also picking up on back, inside loop of stitch below and corresponding pair of inside loops on other unit.

With crochet hook inserted, throw yarn over hook (1) and pull a loop through (2). Then insert hook into next pair of edge stitches, throw yarn over hook (3) and draw a second loop through. Finally, throw yarn over hook (4) and draw a single loop through the two loops (5). Continue in this fashion across edges being joined.

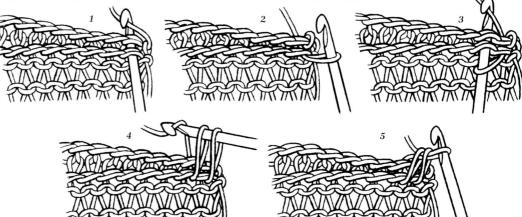

In order to crochet the pieces together, you will need a fresh length of matching yarn and a crochet hook the same size as your knitting needle. You can weave in the tail ends of the yarn in the knitting with a tapestry needle before joining the pieces, as you come to them or after joining them. Place the two pieces together, back to back or front to front, and make sure that the edges meet evenly and that the corresponding rows match. Work from right to left and insert the crochet hook through the end stitch of one piece and through the corresponding stitch of the other piece. Begin working a single crochet stitch by throwing the yarn over the hook and drawing it through the stitch, producing one loop on the hook, as shown in the drawing at the bottom of the facing page. Then insert the hook into the next pair of stitches, as before. Again throw the yarn over the hook and draw it through the stitch. Then throw the yarn over the hook again and draw it through the two loops on the hook, producing a single loop. Continue working in this fashion across the two edges being joined. Finish off by pulling the yarn through the final loop, knotting it and weaving in the tail end.

To sew units together, position them face to face, with the edges meeting evenly and corresponding rows matching, or lay them face down, side by side. Then thread a tapestry needle with the tail end from the original cast-on stitch on one of the two pieces and carefully pick up the end stitch on one of the pieces, as shown in the drawing below. (With the pieces held face to face, you can pick up either the inside or outside loop of the stitch. With the pieces laid side by side, pick up the head of the stitch.). Then direct the needle through the end stitch of the other piece. Next sew through the second stitch in the first piece, and through the corresponding stitch in the other piece. Continue working back and forth in this fashion across the two pieces. You can sew from left to right or from right to left, as you like. With medallion and fan or shell patterns, you can start sewing anywhere. When assembling multipart patterns, it is easiest to sew the appropriate parts together into strips the length of the counterpane and then join one full-length strip to the next.

Do not pull the yarn too tightly as you sew pieces together. Most of the antique counterpanes that I have seen in disrepair had their seams sewn too tightly. When you finish sewing across the edge, secure the yarn and weave in the tail end.

Sewing Units Together

When sewing counterpane units together, use a tapestry needle threaded with a tail end of yarn from one unit and position the pieces either face to face (1), or side by side, face down (2).

1. With pieces held face to face, sew through edge stitch on one unit and corresponding stitch on other unit. Needle can pick up inside loop of stitches, as shown below, or outside loop.

2. With pieces laid face down, side by side, sew alternately through edge stitch on one unit and then other unit.

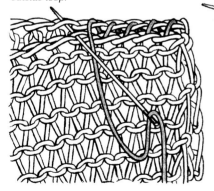
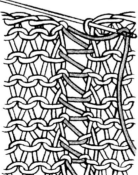

Working New Patterns

There is much to be learned, even by the accomplished knitter, from trying out new patterns. The construction of each pattern is a fascinating challenge, and the process itself stimulates ideas and encourages acquiring further knowledge. The more new patterns you work and the more you extend the possibilities of yarn and stitches, the more familiar you become with the medium and its techniques.

I approach a new pattern that interests me with a pencil and pad of yellow lined paper in hand. At the top of the sheet, I write the date, the name of the pattern and its source—a book, magazine or friend. (For the pieces in this book, I included the name of the counterpane, its source—museum, historical society, restored historical site or private collection—and, if known, the name of the person who knitted the original example. If there were no written directions, I noted that too.)

Next I carefully write down and knit each row before moving on to write down and knit the next row. After knitting the row, I check it against the written instructions and correct any mistakes I find in the original. As elementary as it may seem, this procedure is valuable because it helps familiarize me with the pattern, and I recommend it.

After I have completed and blocked a sample, I may be perfectly satisfied with the pattern as knitted, or I may decide to make some changes. On the other hand, I may decide to use the pattern as a take-off point to experiment with or shape new ideas—something you too can do.

You can make changes in the rows as written. For example, if there are two rows of a pattern stitch within the design, you might increase them to four, six or eight rows. You can also isolate a section of the pattern and adapt it as a repeat design. In the counterpane, you can incorporate a separate border pattern within the body of the piece, running it horizontally or vertically, enlarging or reducing it or using it as a repeat pattern in some areas.

Also try experimenting with different yarns. You can enlarge the scale of the work with a heavy yarn or a doubled strand or refine it with a thin yarn. The yarn weight also changes the proportion of the stitch, making it variously longer, shorter, wider or narrower.

Next, if a pattern calls for decreases, try changing the direction of those decrease stitches, to give a crisper, more defined line to the motif. Depending on how you work the decrease (there are numerous methods, many of them included in the annotated glossary of knitting terms on pp. 20-27), it can slant to the left or right or produce a central vertical ridge. By experimenting with various decreases, you will soon see how each can affect a pattern.

In fact, you will soon discover that a stitch acquires quite a different look every time a variation is introduced. Note the texture created by the different stitches—some are flat, others raised. Texture is as dependent on the nature of the stitches as it is on the character of the yarn.

Keep a record of the discoveries you make when changing a pattern. If you are dissatisfied with what you have done, rip it out and start over. I do it all the time.

Analyzing Patterns

The more patterns you are familiar with from the vast universe of knitting patterns, the better able you will be to take the first step toward analyzing a pattern's construction. Venturing into the field of deciphering—or creating—patterns is a difficult task without a sound knowledge of how patterns are designed.

When I started research in counterpanes in the early 1970s, I had not the slightest suspicion that I was about to undertake the finest self-imposed knitting course available. Some of the nineteenth-century pattern directions I found were well written. Others were impossible to follow or frustratingly incomplete (the latter occasionally ended with a terse, cryptic direction like "Finish off in a hurry!"). And for still other counterpanes, I could find no instructions at all.

I turned to *Mary Thomas's Knitting Book* and *Mary Thomas's Book of Knitting Patterns* (see the bibliography on pp. 176-177) for almost every technical question. Without the help of these books, it is possible that many of the directions in this book could not have been written. I worked all the samples in the pattern book in the section "Medallion Knitting: Building Units—Increases or Decreases." It was while doing this that I realized the importance of the direction of decreases.

With such information as part of my knitting vocabulary, I had the means to analyze a new piece and, by knitting and ripping, to produce directions from a photograph or actual example. To do this, I carefully scrutinize the photo or the piece and then begin the trial-and-error process of knitting. For patterns I am unfamiliar with and cannot locate in my pattern dictionaries or old knitting books, I knit a trial sample, coming as close as I can to what I guess are its component stitches. Just as when I knit any other new pattern, I work row by row, writing down a tentative guess of a row's instructions and knitting it before moving on to the next row. I carefully compare my sample as it progresses to the photo or example. If need be—which happens more often than not—I rip out the knitting to the point of misinterpretation and re-knit, trying out new ways to produce the pattern's various elements. I keep at this as long as it takes to arrive at the pattern I want to reproduce.

I also make changes in pattern directions when I feel that they will enhance the original. The changes usually involve the relationship of yarn-overs to increasing and decreasing stitches. The direction of decreases and the relationship of yarn-overs to both decreases and increases, after all, is what pattern knitting is all about.

Sometimes the changes I make in design come about by chance. Occasionally my mind wanders when I am knitting, and in many cases these attention lapses are rewarded. When I was working on the sample for the Sawtooth Edgings below (see p. 149 for instructions), for example, my mind began to skip about. Instead of knitting a second pattern row, as the directions called for, I purled it, reversing the decrease edge—a happy result since it produced a new pattern.

I find the process of analyzing patterns fascinating. Sometimes I will be stumped for quite a while by a particular element of a pattern. Then after a lot of knitting and ripping, I suddenly find the combination of stitches or moves that I am after.

The original Sawtooth lace border pattern (shown at top in the photo below) and my inadvertent variation on it, shown at bottom (see p. 149 for instructions).

In the case of the Bassett coverlet, below left, (see also pp. 82-86), I had difficulty with the yarn-overs, the basic pattern unit for all three of the counterpane's component pieces. The faggot stitch is usually worked with a yarn-over and a decrease on the face of the knitting and purling across the back. These patterns were different, however, and unlike any I had ever seen. Still, I knew that they were based on some combination of yarn-over and decrease.

Since I knew of no written instructions, I tried as many variations as possible of yarn-overs and decreases. The solution turned out to be knitting the face side and working a yarn-over and decrease on the back. This produced the unusual, very dimensional faggotting stitch of the original counterpane.

Usually there is a logic to the way patterns are written. For example, when a pattern starts with a single stitch, increases evenly to the halfway point, repeats the same

pattern in reverse and decreases back to one stitch, a mirror-image square is formed. The original example of the Bisceglia counterpane, below right (see also pp. 76-79) looked as if it should have conformed to this logic. Yet, when I knitted what I thought I saw, I realized the original pattern was not a mirror image.

I went back to the original counterpane, studied it further and soon discovered the snag. In order to have created a mirror image, the central "checked" band would have needed to be positioned at the exact midpoint of the pattern. Instead it began at the midpoint and was worked completely in the decreasing section of this pattern. I isolated the band's pattern and knitted what should have been the center section to establish the row count. I then decided to alter the pattern to make it symmetrical, and with repeated counting of rows and stitches, divided the pattern in half, made allowances for increases and

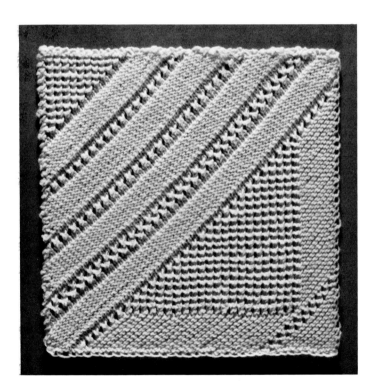

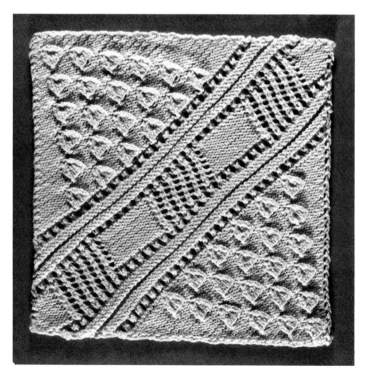

decreases and produced the final set of instructions presented on pp. 56-99.

The Larnach Castle Pattern, below, (see also pp. 66-69) was somewhat easier to decipher. I worked from a fellow traveler's photographs and my own badly drawn sketches and notes to analyze the pattern's four main elements: the large leaf design, the bands of faggotting and slip-knit patterns, and the center band of raised leaves. The first pattern was similar to that of the well-known counterpane pattern, the Garden Plot Square, which uses the same center increases. Thus all I had to do was count the number of these increases and then finish off the leaf with paired decreases.

The second and third patterns were ones I was already familiar with. The fourth pattern, the raised leaf band, occurred at the midpoint of the pattern. It had its increases worked at the outer edges and its D3 decreases (see p. 24) positioned in the center. I figured out the decrease pattern by counting a lot of stitches, and knitting and ripping to place the decreases correctly. I did not perfect the full pattern until I had knitted several samples and checked and rechecked my work with additional photos of the piece sent to me by friends.

As you can see, analyzing a pattern is not a mysterious process, but rather a time-consuming procedure of counting rows and stitches, and knitting and ripping, which requires some real knitting knowledge. If you are curious about trying your analytical abilities, you might begin with the historical counterpanes that illustrate the Introduction (pp. 1-7). If you do not recognize a pattern element or if you are puzzled by a particular design, look through pattern and reference books on knitting to see if you can find some clues. Then get out your needles and yarn, and start knitting—and be ready to rip!

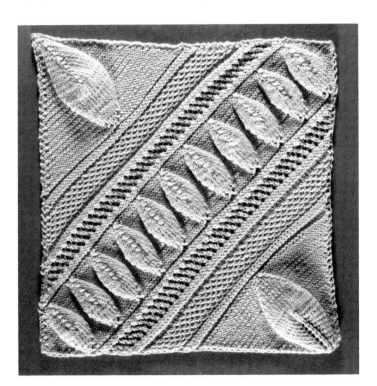

Far left: main pattern of the Bassett coverlet (see pp. 82-86 for instructions); center photo: the Bisceglia Pattern (see pp. 76-79 for instructions); and left: Larnach Castle Pattern (see pp. 66-69 for instructions).

A Glossary of Knitting Terms

There are several methods of knitting, and you may be accustomed to one that is different from that shown in this book. For the best results in working these patterns, however, it is important to follow the direction of the stitches as shown in the drawings.

General

Cast on   *Putting stitches on the needle to form the foundation row.*

There are various ways to cast on, but this method works for most uses: Allow about ½ in. of yarn for each stitch to be cast on. Make a slipknot as shown in the drawing below, a couple of inches beyond the measured length. Place the loop for the slipknot on the needle and pull it taut.

Wrap the short end of yarn around the left thumb and the yarn from the ball over the left forefinger. Hold both ends of yarn taut in the back fingers. Insert the needle up through the loop on the thumb, then over the yarn on the forefinger, catching the yarn on the forefinger and pulling it down through the loop on the thumb. Drop the thumb from the new stitch to catch the short end of yarn and pull the new stitch taut on the needle. Repeat as many times as needed, taking care not to cast on too tightly. (*See also* LCO.)

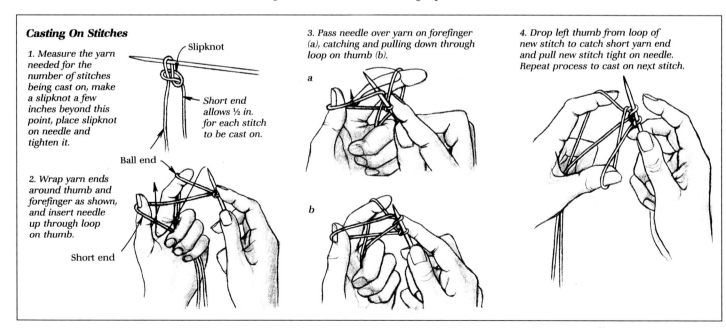

Casting On Stitches

1. Measure the yarn needed for the number of stitches being cast on, make a slipknot a few inches beyond this point, place slipknot on needle and tighten it.

Slipknot

Short end allows ½ in. for each stitch to be cast on.

Ball end

2. Wrap yarn ends around thumb and forefinger as shown, and insert needle up through loop on thumb.

Short end

3. Pass needle over yarn on forefinger (a), catching and pulling down through loop on thumb (b).

a

b

4. Drop left thumb from loop of new stitch to catch short yarn end and pull new stitch tight on needle. Repeat process to cast on next stitch.

Cast off   *Taking stitches off the needle and binding them to close the loops and prevent the knitting from unraveling.*

There are several ways to cast off. I like the following method: Knit the first two stitches. Insert the left needle into the stitch knit first and pull it over the stitch knit second and off the right needle. Knit the next stitch on the left needle and repeat the pull-over process, being careful not to cast off too tightly. Continue in this fashion until all the stitches have been cast off the left needle. Cut the yarn, leaving a length triple that of one side of the counterpane unit which can later be used for sewing or crocheting units together. Pull the end of the yarn through the one stitch remaining on the right needle, and fasten it securely.

DL   *Drop loop* (see also *O2*).

K   *Knit.*

K1B   *Knit into the back of the stitch.*

LCO   *Loop cast-on.* As shown in the drawing below, loop the yarn around the left thumb. Insert the right needle into the loop as if to knit. Slip the loop off the thumb and onto the needle. Repeat as many times as required.

P   *Purl.*

PSSO   *Pass slipped stitch(es) over.* In addition to being a method of decreasing, PSSO is also often used with yarn-over (O) to create patterns.

Loop Cast-On (LCO)

Loop yarn around left thumb (1). Insert right needle into loop as if to knit and transfer loop to needle (2).

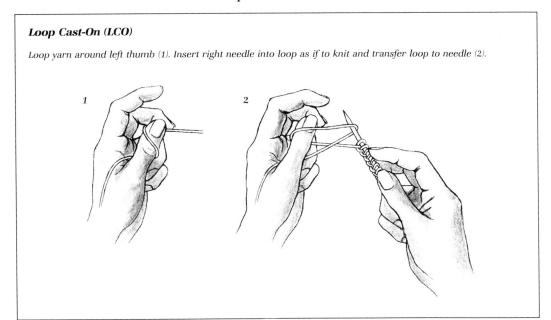

Sl	*Slip stitch knitwise.*
Slp	*Slip stitch purlwise.*
st	*Stitch.*
sts	*Stitches.*
tog	*Together.*

Increases

B1	*Bar increase.* As shown in the drawing below left, knit into the front, then into the back, of the same stitch. This increase forms a bar across the base of the second stitch.
B1p	Similar to B1, except purl into the back, then into the front, of the same stitch, as shown in the drawing below right.
KP1	*Knit and purl into the same stitch.*
PK1	*Purl and knit into the same stitch.*

Bar Increase in Knit Stitch (B1)

To make a bar increase in a knit stitch, knit into front, then into back of same stitch.

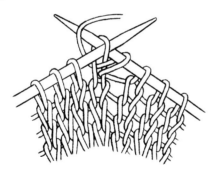

Stockinette fabric with bar increases on face

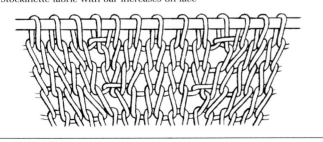

Bar Increase in Purl Stitch (B1p)

To make a bar increase in a purl stitch, purl into back, then front of same stitch.

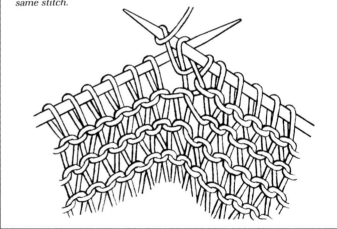

M1L   *Make a left increase.* Insert the left needle under the yarn joining the two stitches on opposite needles, from front to back, as shown at the top in the drawing below left. Insert the right needle into the back of this new stitch and knit it from this position.

M1R   *Make a right increase.* Insert the left needle under the yarn joining the two stitches on the opposite needles, from back to front, as shown in the drawing below right. Insert the right needle into the front of this new stitch and knit it from this position.

O   *Throw yarn over the needle.*

O2   *Throw yarn over the needle twice.* The two loops are treated in various ways on the next row. In some patterns, DL indicates that one of the loops is dropped, forming a long stitch (one increase). In other patterns, each of the two loops is considered a separate stitch (two increases). Every pattern that uses the O2 increase specifies how the loops are to be treated on subsequent rows.

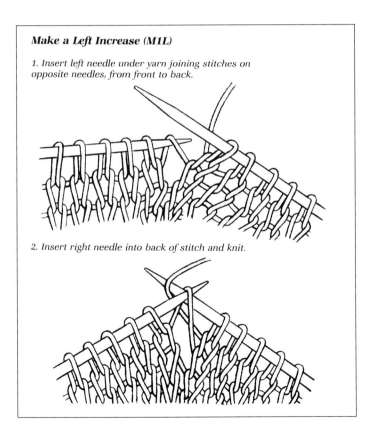

Make a Left Increase (M1L)

1. Insert left needle under yarn joining stitches on opposite needles, from front to back.

2. Insert right needle into back of stitch and knit.

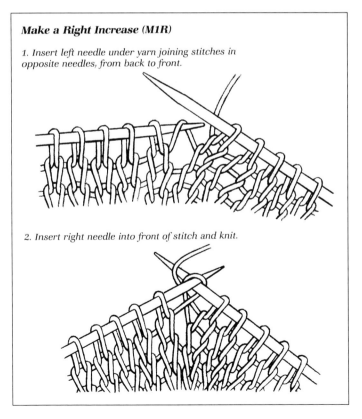

Make a Right Increase (M1R)

1. Insert left needle under yarn joining stitches in opposite needles, from back to front.

2. Insert right needle into front of stitch and knit.

Decreases

D3   *Right-left double decrease.* Slip the first stitch, then work a left-right decrease (LRD) and pass the slipped stitch over the stitches just knitted (two decreases), as shown in the drawing below left . This decrease slants from right to left on the face of the fabric.

D3C   *Central double decrease.* To produce this decrease, which creates a vertical ridge, slip the first two stitches together knitwise onto the right needle, as shown in the drawing below right. Knit the next stitch. Pass the two slipped stitches over the knitted stitch (two decreases).

D3LR   *Left-right double decrease.* To produce this decrease, work a right-left decrease (RLD), then return the remaining stitch to the left needle, and pass the second stitch on the left needle over the returned stitch. Transfer this stitch to the right needle (two decreases).

K3tog   *Knit three stitches together.* This decrease slants from left to right (two decreases).

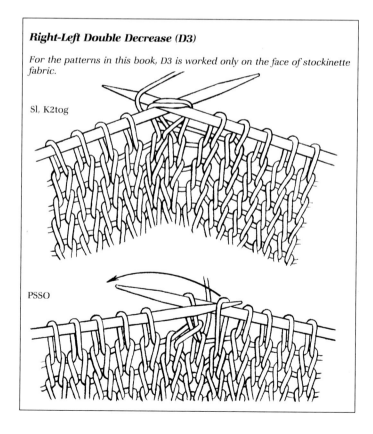

Right-Left Double Decrease (D3)

For the patterns in this book, D3 is worked only on the face of stockinette fabric.

Sl, K2tog

PSSO

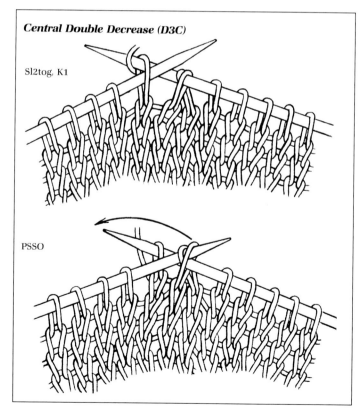

Central Double Decrease (D3C)

Sl2tog, K1

PSSO

LRD *Left-right decrease.* To produce this decrease, which slants from left to right, knit two stitches together as one (one stitch decreased), as shown in the drawing below left.

P2tog *Purl two stitches together.* This decrease slants from left to right on the face of the fabric (one decrease).

PRD *Purl reverse decrease.* To produce this decrease, which slants from right to left on the face of the fabric, begin by purling one stitch. Slip the next stitch on the left needle knitwise to the right needle and transfer it back to the left needle, as shown in the drawing below right. Then return the newly purled stitch to the left needle, as shown. Next pull the second stitch on the left needle over the first (purled) stitch and return the first stitch to the right needle (one decrease).

PRD3 *Purl reverse double decrease.* Similar to PRD, this decrease calls for purling two stitches together as the first step (two decreases).

Left-Right Decrease (LRD)

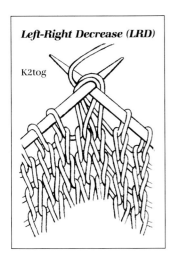

K2tog

Purl Reverse Decrease (PRD)

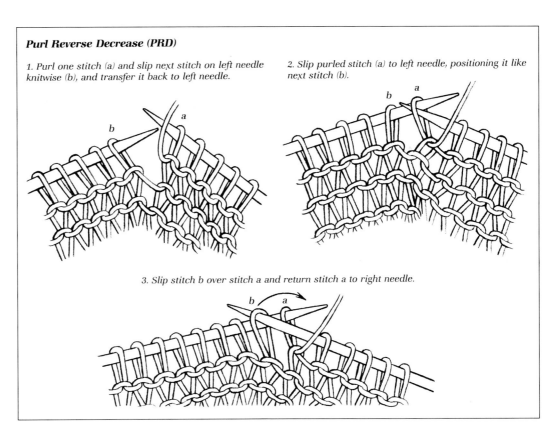

1. Purl one stitch (a) and slip next stitch on left needle knitwise (b), and transfer it back to left needle.

2. Slip purled stitch (a) to left needle, positioning it like next stitch (b).

3. Slip stitch b over stitch a and return stitch a to right needle.

RLD   *Right-left decrease.* There are two methods of producing this decrease, which slants from right to left, and both are shown in the drawings below. In the first method, slip the first stitch, knit the second stitch and pass the slipped stitch over the knitted stitch (Sl, K1, PSSO). A preferred method (Sl, Sl, K2tog) is to slip two stitches, one at a time, knitwise, return them to the left needle and knit them together (one stitch decreased).

Cables, Bobbles, Knobs and Related Techniques

Bobble   A bobble is built up and completed in a single stitch before moving on to the next stitch. Work a bobble as follows, turning after every row: Cast on four new stitches (or more if you want a larger bobble) in one stitch, as shown in the drawing at right, and turn the work.
Row 1: K4
Row 2: (K2togB)2x
Row 3: PSSO

CB6   *Cable worked on six stitches, held at back.* Slip the first three stitches onto an extra needle and hold in back of the work. Knit the next three stitches and then knit the stitches from the extra needle.

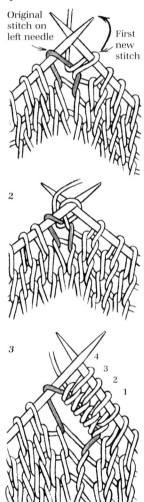

Casting On Stitches for a Bobble

Knit into one stitch, and, without slipping base stitch off left needle, slip new stitch onto left needle (1). Knit into this new stitch and slip it onto right needle (2). Repeat these two steps until required number of stitches has been cast on (3) and slip base stitch off left needle.

1

Original stitch on left needle

First new stitch

2

3

Right-Left Decrease (RLD)

There are two methods of working a RLD:

Method 1

Sl, K1

Method 2

Sl, Sl, K2tog

A general note about cables: Any convenient number of stitches can be used for cables, whether even (two over two, three over three, etc.) or uneven (three over two). Nineteenth-century patterns generally used an uneven number of stitches for cables, making one less stitch on the extra cable needle, lessening the pull and allowing the twist to lie flatter than when worked on an even number of stitches. When you are knitting with inelastic cotton yarns, this pull is an important consideration.

CF6　　Cable worked on six stitches, held at front. Slip the first three stitches onto an extra needle and hold in front of the work. Knit the next three stitches. Knit the stitches from the extra needle. (See "A general note about cables" in CB6 above.)

Knob　　A knob is built up and completed in a single stitch before moving on to the next stitch. Work a knob as follows, turning the work after each row:
Row 1: (O, K1)3x in the same stitch
Row 2: Slp, P5
Row 3: Sl, K5
Row 4: Slp, P5
Row 5: Sl, K5
Row 6: (P2tog)3x
Row 7: D3
　　　　One stitch remains, as shown in the drawing below.

Repeats

AP1 (AP2, AP3, etc.)　　Abbreviated Pattern #1 (#2, #3 and so on) identifies a stitch combination used frequently throughout one given set of knitting instructions.

x　　*Times.*

(...)　　Parentheses are used with the symbol x to identify the stitches to be repeated. An empty set of parentheses, ( ), means to repeat the material in parentheses in the same row or round.

[...]　　Brackets are used with the symbol x to identify a group of stitches to be repeated.

...　　Stitches between single asterisks are worked in more than one place in a given row or round. When * - * appears in a line of instruction, repeat the stitch pattern previously written between asterisks.

...　　Stitches between double asterisks are worked in more than one place in a given row or round. When ** - ** appears in a line of instruction, repeat the stitch pattern previously written between asterisks.

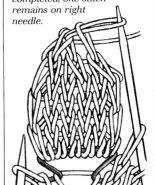

Completed Knob

To form a knob, extra stitches are cast on, worked and then decreased in a single stitch (shown shaded). When knob is completed, one stitch remains on right needle.

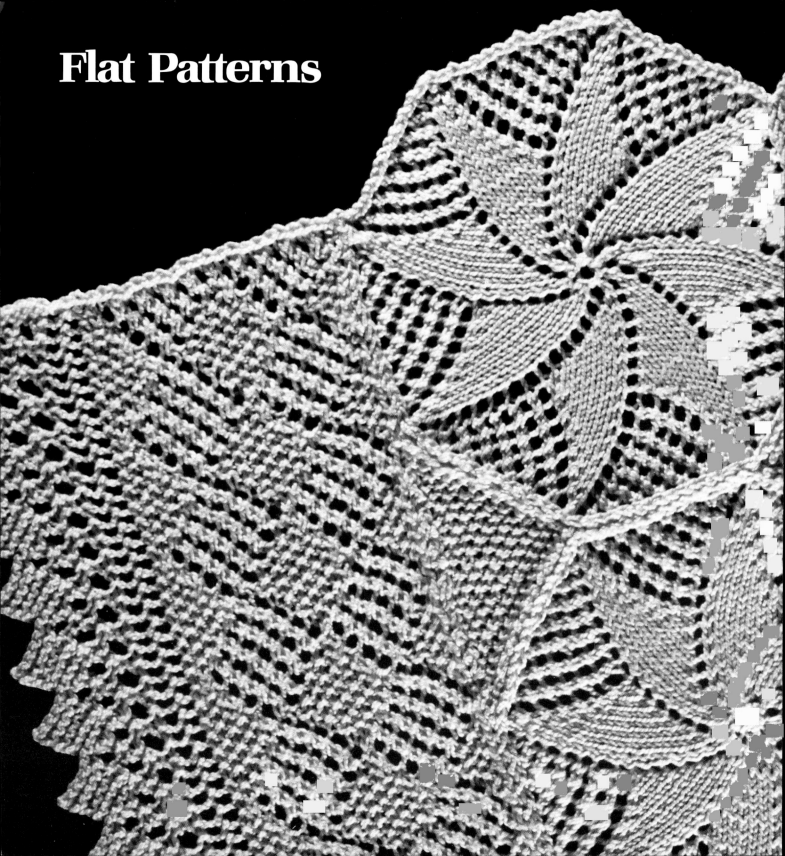

Flat Patterns

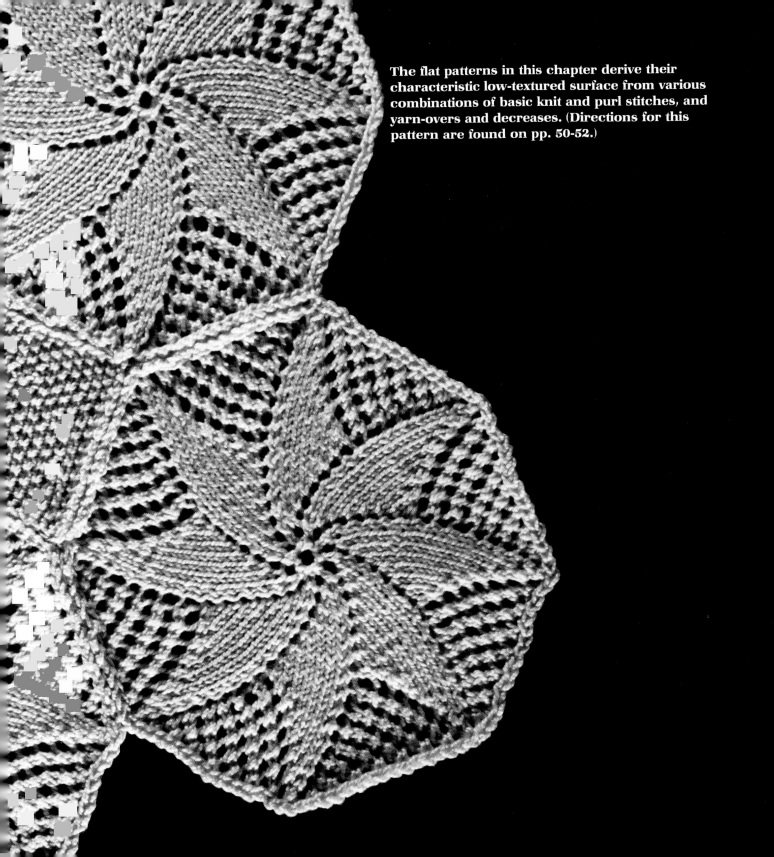

The flat patterns in this chapter derive their
characteristic low-textured surface from various
combinations of basic knit and purl stitches, and
yarn-overs and decreases. (Directions for this
pattern are found on pp. 50-52.)

Scottish Farmer's Pattern

I first came across this pattern when visiting New Zealand in 1978. It appeared in a nineteenth-century British publication I was shown several times during my stay, The Young Ladies Journal: Complete Guide to the Worktable. *I later found the pattern in another book of the same period,* Needles and Brushes, *and then saw an example of this counterpane in a 1977 article in the magazine* Craft Australia. *The example in the article had been knitted by a Mr. Mason, a Scottish farmer who had emigrated to New Zealand in the 1870s. I have reproduced the pattern under the moniker Scottish Farmer's Pattern in honor of Mr. Mason.*

This is a very simple, two-needle pattern. It combines knit and purl stitches with a three-stitch decrease to produce a six-pointed medallion. I suggest adding a tied fringe border (see pp. 150-151) to complete the counterpane.

Cast on 37 stitches.

Row 1: Purl.
Row 2: Knit.
Row 3: K2, (O, LRD)8x, O, K3tog, ( )7x, O, K2.
Row 4: Knit.
Row 5: K2, O, LRD, (K2, P2)3x, K2, P1, ( )3x, K6.
Row 6: K2, O, LRD, (P2, K2)3x, P1, K3tog, P1, (K2, P2)3x, K4.
Row 7: K2, O, LRD, (K2, P2)3x, K3, (P2, K2)3x, K4.
Row 8: K2, O, LRD, (P2, K2)3x, P3tog, (K2, P2)3x, K4.
Row 9: K2, O LRD, (K2, P2)3x, K1, (P2, K2)2x, P2, K6.
Row 10: K2, O, LRD, (P2, K2)2x, P2, K1, K3tog, K1, ( )2x, P2, K4.
Row 11: K2, O, LRD, (K2, P2)2x, K2, P3, ( )2x, K6.

Row 12: K2, O, LRD, (P2, K2)2x, P2, K3tog, ( )2x, P2, K4.
Row 13: K2, O, LRD, (K2, P2)2x, K2, P1, ( )2x, K6.
Row 14: K2, O, LRD, (P2, K2)2x, P1, P3tog, P1, (K2, P2)2x, K4.
Row 15: K2, O, LRD, (K2, P2)2x, K3, P2, K2, P2, K6.
Row 16: K2, O, LRD, (P2, K2)2x, P3tog, (K2, P2)2x, K4.
Row 17: K2, O, LRD, (K2, P2)2x, K1, P2, K2, P2, K6.
Row 18: K2, O, LRD, P2, K2, P2, K1, K3tog, K1, P2, K2, P2, K4.
Row 19: K2, O, LRD, K2, P2, K2, P3, K2, P2, K6.
Row 20: K2, O, LRD, P2, K2, P2, K3tog, P2, K2, P2, K4.
Row 21: K2, O, LRD, K2, P2, K2, P1, K2, P2, K6.
Row 22: K2, O, LRD, P2, K2, P1, P3tog, P1, K2, P2, K4.

Row 23: K2, O, LRD, K2, P2, K3, P2, K6.
Row 24: K2, O, LRD, P2, K2, P3tog, K2, P2, K4.
Row 25: K2, O, LRD, K2, P2, K1, P2, K6.
Row 26: K2, O, LRD, P2, K1, K3tog, K1, P2, K4.
Row 27: K2, O, LRD, K2, P3, K6.
Row 28: K2, O, LRD, P2, K3tog, P2, K4.
Row 29: K2, O, LRD, K2, P1, K6.
Row 30: K2, O, LRD, P1, P3tog, P1, K4.
Row 31: K2, O, LRD, K7.
Row 32: K2, O, LRD, P3tog, K4.
Row 33: K2, O, LRD, K5.
Row 34: K2, O, LRD, K1, LRD, K2.

Row 35: K2, O, K3tog, K3.
Row 36: K2, O, K3tog, K2.
Row 37: K2, O, K3tog, K1.
Row 38: K1, K3tog, K1.
Row 39: K3tog; fasten off.

When sewing pieces together, work from the center of the counterpane to its edges.

Scottish Farmer's Pattern was knit with Parisian Cotton on size 1 needles.

Ribbed Squares

This pattern is my own variation on one I saw in a four-square panel in the Witte Museum in San Antonio, Texas. To enhance the original pattern, I added the diagonal cross rib, but there are many variations that could be worked with this very simple pattern. For example, I have seen a fan pattern that begins with a six-row rib pattern and then progressively eliminates two rows of the rib with each completion of the pattern. The visual tension created by gradually condensing the pattern is relieved after the last two purl rows with a series of eyelet rows. The ribbed square, the simplest five-needle pattern in this book, offers endless possibilities for experimentation.

Special Instructions:
The O's should be knit or purled closed on the following round. Each line of instruction should be repeated 4 times, once on each needle.

Cast on 8 stitches and distribute evenly on 4 needles. Knit with a 5th needle.

Round 1: K1, O, K1.
Round 2: K3.
Round 3: K1, (O, K1)2x.
Round 4: K5.
Round 5: K1, O, K3, O, K1.
Round 6: K7.
Round 7: K1, O, P5, O, K1.
Round 8: K1, P7, K1.
Round 9: K1, O, P7, O, K1.
Round 10: K1, P9, K1.
Round 11: K1, O, K9, O, K1.
Round 12: K13.
Round 13: K1, O, K11, O, K1.
Round 14: K15.
Round 15: K1, O, P13, O, K1.
Round 16: K1, P15, K1.
Round 17: K1, O, P15, O, K1.
Round 18: K1, P17, K1.
Round 19: K1, O, K17, O, K1.
Round 20: K21.
Round 21: K1, O, K19, O, K1.
Round 22: K23.

Round 23: K1, O, P21, O, K1.
Round 24: K1, P23, K1.
Round 25: K1, O, P23, O, K1.
Round 26: K1, P25, K1.
Round 27: K1, O, K25, O, K1.
Round 28: K29.
Round 29: K1, O, K27, O, K1.
Round 30: K31.
Round 31: K1, O, P29, O, K1.
Round 32: K1, P31, K1.
Round 33: K1, O, P31, O, K1.
Round 34: K1, P33, K1.
Round 35: K1, O, K33, O, K1.

Round 36: K37.
Round 37: K1, O, K35, O, K1.
Round 38: K39.
Round 39: K1, O, P37, O, K1.
Round 40: K1, P39, K1.
Round 41: K1, O, P39, O, K1.
Round 42: K1, P41, K1.

Cast off or, if larger square is desired, continue in established pattern.

The Ribbed Squares sample was knit with Parisian Cotton on size 1 needles.

Madame Weigel's Pattern

I found this pattern in an old issue of a periodical called Madame Weigel, *published from 1880 to 1950 in Melbourne, Australia, by a needleworker of the same name. Madame Weigel emigrated "Down Under" from Poland via the United States in the 1870s. The patterns she dispensed in Australia through her magazine were probably brought with her from Europe.*

This pattern is an excellent one for a beginning knitter. A simple, two-needle pattern, it uses a three-stitch rib that moves to the left and right to create a radiating diamond effect.

Madame Weigel's Pattern (shown three-quarter size) was knit with carpet warp on size 1 needles.

Legend for chart
(facing page):
☐ = Knit on front of
fabric, purl on back.
■ = Purl on front side of
fabric, knit on back.

Chart represents front side
of fabric, with one square
being one stitch. Begin at
lower right corner, working
odd-numbered rows on
front side of fabric and even-
numbered rows on back.

Rib Pattern

For all its simplicity, this pattern has long fascinated me. The two examples I have seen of this pattern were in snapshots sent by friends, one from Austria, the other from Greece. The two counterpanes were assembled differently, as shown in the diagrams on p. 38, and the distinctive illusions they create are remarkable.

The pattern itself is utterly simple. Based on six rows of stockinette stitch and six rows of reverse stockinette, it increases regularly from two cast-on stitches to the widest point, and then decreases to fashion the other half as a mirror image of the first. Any of the lace borders (pp. 144-171) would nicely complete this counterpane.

Knit (or purl) the O's closed on the following row.

Cast on 2 stitches.

Row 1: Slp, O, P1.
Row 2: Sl, K2.
Row 3: Slp, (O, P1)2x.
Row 4: Sl, K4.
Row 5: Slp, O, P3, O, P1.
Row 6: Sl, K6.
Row 7: Sl, O, K5, O, K1.
Row 8: Slp, P8.
Row 9: Sl, O, K7, O, K1.
Row 10: Slp, P10.
Row 11: Sl, O, K9, O, K1.
Row 12: Slp, P12.
Row 13: Slp, O, P11, O, P1.
Row 14: Sl, K14.
Row 15: Slp, O, P13, O, P1.
Row 16: Sl, K16.
Row 17: Slp, O, P15, O, P1.
Row 18: Sl, K18.
Row 19: Sl, O, K17, O, K1.

Row 20: Slp, P20.
Row 21: Sl, O, K19, O, K1.
Row 22: Slp, P22.
Row 23: Sl, O, K21, O, K1.
Row 24: Slp, P24.
Row 25: Slp, O, P23, O, P1.
Row 26: Sl, K26.
Row 27: Slp, O, P25, O, P1.
Row 28: Sl, K28.
Row 29: Slp, O, P27, O, P1.
Row 30: Sl, K30.
Row 31: Sl, O, K29, O, K1.
Row 32: Slp, P32.
Row 33: Sl, O, K31, O, K1.
Row 34: Slp, P34.
Row 35: Sl, O, K33, O, K1.
Row 36: Slp, P36.
Row 37: Slp, O, P35, O, P1.
Row 38: Sl, K38.
Row 39: Slp, O, P37, O, P1.
Row 40: Sl, K40.
Row 41: Slp, O, P39, O, P1.
Row 42: Sl, K42.
Row 43: Sl, O, K41, O, K1.
Row 44: Slp, P44.

Row 45: Sl, O, K43, O, K1.
Row 46: Slp, P46.
Row 47: Sl, O, K45, O, K1.
Row 48: Slp, P48.
Row 49: Slp, O, P47, O, P1.
Row 50: Sl, K50.
Row 51: Slp, O, P49, O, P1.
Row 52: Sl, K52.
Row 53: Slp, O, P51, O, P1.
Row 54: Sl, K54.
Row 55: Sl, O, K53, O, K1.
Row 56: Slp, P56.
Row 57: Sl, O, K55, O, K1.
Row 58: Slp, P58.
Row 59: Sl, O, K57, O, K1.
Row 60: Slp, P60.
Row 61: Slp, O, P59, O, P1.
Row 62: Sl, K62.
Row 63: Slp, O, P61, O, P1.
Row 64: Sl, K64.
Row 65: Slp, O, P63, O, P1.
Row 66: Sl, K66.
Row 67: Sl, O, K65, O, K1.

Row 68: Slp, P68.
Row 69: Sl, O, K67, O, K1.
Row 70: Slp, P70.
Row 71: Sl, LRD, K65, LRD, K1.
Row 72: Slp, P68.
Row 73: Slp, P2tog, P63, P2tog, P1.
Row 74: Sl, K66.
Row 75: Slp, P2tog, P61, P2tog, P1.
Row 76: Sl, K64.
Row 77: Slp, P2tog, P59, P2tog, P1.
Row 78: Sl, K62.
Row 79: Sl, LRD, K57, LRD, K1.
Row 80: Slp, P60.
Row 81: Sl, LRD, K55, LRD, K1.
Row 82: Slp, P58.
Row 83: Sl, LRD, K53, LRD, K1.
Row 84: Slp, P56.

The Rib Pattern was worked with size 3 perle cotton on size 1 needles.

Row 85: Slp, P2tog, P51, P2tog, P1.
Row 86: Sl, K54.
Row 87: Slp, P2tog, P49, P2tog, P1.
Row 88: Sl, K52.
Row 89: Slp, P2tog, P47, P2tog, P1.
Row 90: Sl, K50.
Row 91: Sl, LRD, K45, LRD, K1.
Row 92: Slp, P48.
Row 93: Sl, LRD, K43, LRD, K1.
Row 94: Slp, P46.
Row 95: Sl, LRD, K41, LRD, K1.

Row 96: Slp, P44.
Row 97: Slp, P2tog, P39, P2tog, P1.
Row 98: Sl, K42.
Row 99: Slp, P2tog, P37, P2tog, P1.
Row 100: Sl, K40.
Row 101: Slp, P2tog, P35, P2tog, P1.
Row 102: Sl, K38.
Row 103: Sl, LRD, K33, LRD, K1.
Row 104: Slp, P36.
Row 105: Sl, LRD, K31, LRD, K1.
Row 106: Slp, P34.

Row 107: Sl, LRD, K29, LRD, K1.
Row 108: Slp, P32.
Row 109: Slp, P2tog, P27, P2tog, P1.
Row 110: Sl, K30.
Row 111: Slp, P2tog, P25, P2tog, P1.
Row 112: Sl, K28.
Row 113: Slp, P2tog, P23, P2tog, P1.
Row 114: Sl, K26.
Row 115: Sl, LRD, K21, LRD, K1.
Row 116: Slp, P24.
Row 117: Sl, LRD, K19, LRD, K1.
Row 118: Slp, P22.
Row 119: Sl, LRD, K17, LRD, K1.
Row 120: Slp, P20.
Row 121: Slp, P2tog, P15, P2tog, P1.
Row 122: Sl, K18.
Row 123: Slp, P2tog, P13, P2tog, P1.
Row 124: Sl, K16.
Row 125: Slp, P2tog, P11, P2tog, P1.
Row 126: Sl, K14.
Row 127: Sl, LRD, K9, LRD, K1.
Row 128: Slp, P12.
Row 129: Sl, LRD, K7, LRD, K1.
Row 130: Slp, P10.
Row 131: Sl, LRD, K5, LRD, K1.
Row 132: Slp, P8.
Row 133: Slp, P2tog, P3, P2tog, P1.
Row 134: Sl, K6.
Row 135: Slp, (P2tog, P1)2x.
Row 136: Sl, K4.
Row 137: Slp, (P2tog)2x.
Row 138: D3, fasten off.

Alternate Assembly Diagrams

For the top assembly the pieces are blocked as diamonds; for the bottom assembly, as squares (for information on blocking, see pp. 13-14). Half of the pattern can be worked to fill in the triangular spaces along the edges.

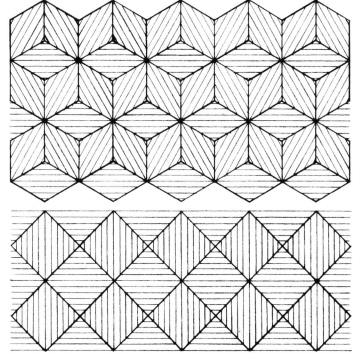

Swirls and Squares

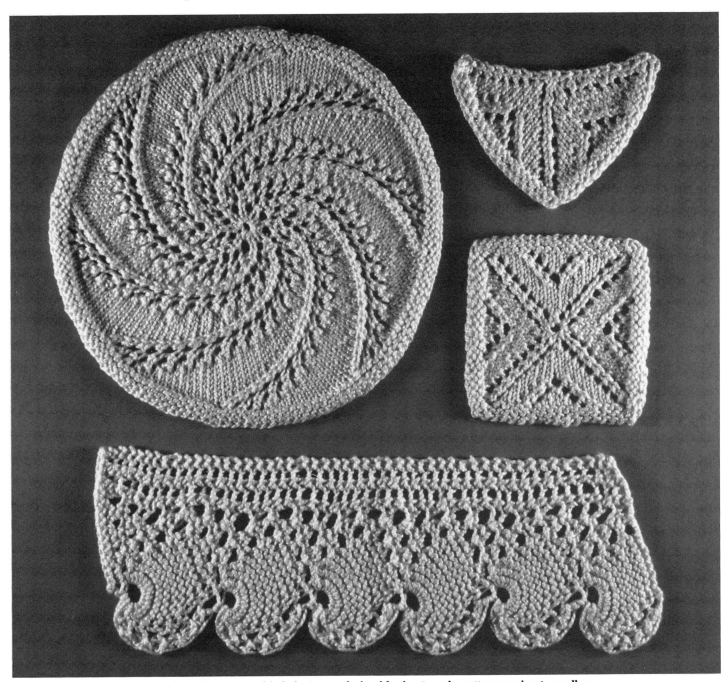

The Swirls and Squares samples (shown two-third size) were knit with size 3 perle cotton on size 1 needles.

The Swirls and Squares pattern is a very old one. I have seen instructions for it in several nineteenth-century needlework periodicals and four examples of it worked in varying sizes. The Witte Museum in San Antonio, Texas, has a lovely full counterpane. A friend of long-standing, Antoinette Lackner Webster, has a tidy (a protective covering for a piece of furniture) knit by her German grandmother, Emma Wolff Münch. There is also an example in a private collection in Bozen, Italy (I have only seen a photograph of this one). Finally, there is one covering a bed at Hillwood, Mrs. Merriweather Post's home in Washington, D.C., which was once one of a pair that covered twin beds on Mrs. Post's private yacht, Sea Cloud.

This five-needle pattern is moderately difficult. It is worked from the center outward, using a series of yarn-over increases to produce the circle. The medallion and its accompanying square can, of course, be enlarged if the knitter wishes.

The border pattern I have provided is the one used on Mrs. Münch's tidy. To use this border—or another one from pp. 144-171—you will need to complete the edge of the counterpane with triangle filler pieces. You might also use a fringed border (see pp. 150-151) to complete this counterpane. With fringe, you need not use the triangular pieces. And with either a knit or fringe border, the corners can be left unfilled and "rounded."

Medallion

Special Instructions:
AP1   Abbreviated Pattern #1 is worked as follows:
(O, K1)2x, O.
Each line of instruction below should be repeated 8 times, 2 times on each needle.

Cast on 8 stitches and distribute evenly on 4 needles. Knit with a 5th needle.

Rounds 1-2: Knit.
Round 3: O, K1.
Round 4: Knit.
Round 5: (O, K1)2x.
Round 6: K2, LRD.
Round 7: O, K1, O, LRD.
Round 8: Knit.
Round 9: AP1, LRD.
Round 10: K4, LRD.
Round 11: AP1, K1, LRD.
Round 12: K5, LRD.
Round 13: AP1, K2, LRD.
Round 14: K6, LRD.
Round 15: AP1, K3, LRD.

Round 16: K7, LRD.
Round 17: AP1, K4, LRD.
Round 18: K8, LRD.
Round 19: AP1, K5, LRD.
Round 20: K9, LRD.
Round 21: AP1, K6, LRD.
Round 22: K10, LRD.
Round 23: AP1, K7, LRD.
Round 24: K11, LRD.
Round 25: AP1, K8, LRD.
Round 26: K12, LRD.
Round 27: AP1, K9, LRD.
Round 28: K13, LRD.
Round 29: AP1, K10, LRD.

Round 30: K14, LRD.
Round 31: AP1, K11, LRD.
Round 32: K15, LRD.
Round 33: AP1, K12, LRD.

Round 34: K16, LRD.
Round 35: AP1, K13, LRD.
Round 36: K17, LRD.
Round 37-39: Purl.
Cast off, knitting.

Square

Special Instructions:
Each line of instruction should be repeated 4 times, once on each needle.

Cast on 8 stitches and distribute evenly on 4 needles. Knit with a 5th needle.

Round 1 and all odd-numbered rounds through 15: Knit.
Round 2: (O, K1)2x.
Round 4: O, K3, O, K1.

Round 6: O, K5, O, K1.
Round 8: O, K7, O, K1.
Round 10: O, K4, O, RLD, K3, O, K1.
Round 12: O, K3, LRD, O, K1, O, RLD, K3, O, K1.
Round 14: O, K3, LRD, O, K3, O, RLD, K3, O, K1.
Round 16: O, K3, LRD, O, K5, O, RLD, K3, O, K1.
Purl 2 rounds. Cast off, purling.

Half-Square

Cast on 4 stitches, placing marker after 2nd stitch.

Row 1 and all odd-numbered rows: Purl.

Follow directions for Square Pattern for rows 2-16, repeating directions twice for each row.

Row 17: Knit.

Row 18: Purl.

Transfer half of the stitches to a second needle and, using a 3rd needle, pick up 19 stitches along the two outer edges (this will give a strong, neat edge to which to attach the border pattern or fringe).

Cast off the 3 sides, knitting.

Assembly Diagram

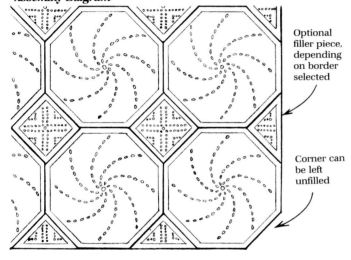

Optional filler piece, depending on border selected

Corner can be left unfilled

Shell Lace Border

Special Instructions:
AP1 *Abbreviated Pattern #1 is worked as follows:*
O2, LRD, K1.
AP2 *Abbreviated Pattern #2 is worked as follows:*
Sl, K1, (O, RLD)2x.
O2 is the basis for 2 stitches on following row, unless otherwise indicated by drop loop (DL).

Cast on 18 stitches.

Row 1: Sl, K1, (O, RLD)3x, O, LRD, K7, O2, K1.

Row 2: AP1, P1, K9, (P1, K1)2x, P1, K2.

Row 3: AP2, K11, O2, LRD, K1, DL.

Row 4: AP1, P1, K12, P1, K1, P1, K2.

Row 5: AP2, (O2, LRD)2x, K8, O2, LRD, K1, DL.

Row 6: AP1, P1, K10, P1, K2, (P1, K1)2x, P1, K2.

Row 7: AP2, O, K15, O2, LRD, K1, DL.

Row 8: AP1, DL, P1, K16, P1, K1, P1, K2.

Row 9: AP2, (O2, LRD)3x, K10, O2, LRD, K1, DL.

Row 10: AP1, P1, K12, (P1, K2)2x, (P1, K1)2x, P1, K2.

Row 11: AP2, K20, O2, LRD, K1, DL.

Row 12: AP1, P1, K21, P1, K1, P1, K2.

Row 13: AP2, (O2, LRD)4x, K13, O2, LRD, K1, DL.

Row 14: AP1, P1, K15, (P1, K2)3x, (P1, K1)2x, P1, K2.

Row 15: AP2, K12, return last stitch to left needle. Draw next 18 stitches over the one just returned (O2 considered 2 stitches). Knit stitch remaining on left needle.

Row 16: K13, P1, K1, P1, K2.

Repeat rows 1-16 for desired length.

Beeton's Flower

Directions for Beeton's Flower were included in several nineteenth-century English publications, the first of them Beeton's Needlework, *published in 1870. The same pattern appears in an 1887 booklet on the use of Scottish linen, published in Boston by the linen company's agent. This booklet credits the pattern to a Mme Goubaud, co-publisher with her husband of needlework, fashion and domestic science journals in France. It is known that Mrs. Beeton, of* Beeton's Needlework, *occasionally purchased patterns and engravings from Mme Goubaud for her publication, and the genuine author of these instructions remains a mystery.*

I have never seen an example of a full counterpane worked in this pattern, but I have come across handsome examples of placemats and a tablecloth using Beeton's Flower. It would also make a dandy pillow cover.

This pattern is appropriate for the intermediate knitter. Worked on five needles from the center outward, it is made up of increases, yarn-overs and decreases, with the solid pattern areas created by paired decreasing in the center. Many of the border patterns (pp. 144-171) would nicely complete this counterpane.

Special Instructions:
Each line of instruction should be repeated 4 times, once on each needle.

Cast on 8 stitches and distribute evenly on 4 needles. Knit with a 5th needle.

Round 1 and all odd-numbered rounds: Knit.
Round 2: K1, O, K1.
Round 4: (K1, O)2x, K1.
Round 6: K1, O, K3, O, K1.
Round 8: K1, O, K5, O, K1.
Round 10: K1, O, K7, O, K1.
Round 12: K1, O, K9, O, K1.
Round 14: K1, O, K11, O, K1.

Round 16: K1, O, K13, O, K1.
Round 18: K1, O, K15, O, K1.
Round 20: (K1, O)2x, K5, RLD, K1, LRD, K5, (O, K1)2x.
Round 22: (K1, O)2x, RLD, O, K4, RLD, K1, LRD, K4, O, LRD, (O, K1)2x.
Round 24: (K1, O)2x, (RLD, O)2x, K3, RLD, K1, LRD, K3, (O, LRD)2x, (O, K1)2x.
Round 26: (K1, O)2x, (RLD, O)3x, K2, RLD, K1, LRD, K2, (O, LRD)3x, (O, K1)2x.
Round 28: (K1, O)2x, (RLD, O)4x, K1, RLD, K1, LRD, K1, (O, LRD)4x, (O, K1)2x.
Round 30: (K1, O)2x, (RLD, O)5x, RLD, K1, LRD, (O, LRD)5x, (O, K1)2x.

Round 32: (K1, O)2x, (RLD, O)6x, D3, (O, LRD)6x, (O, K1)2x.
Round 34: (K1, O)2x, (RLD, O)6x, RLD, K1, LRD, (O, LRD)6x, (O, K1)2x.
Round 36: (K1, O)2x, (RLD, O)7x, D3, (O, LRD)7x, (O, K1)2x.
Round 38: (K1, O)2x, (RLD, O)7x, RLD, K1, LRD, (O, LRD)7x, (O, K1)2x.
Round 40: (K1, O)2x, (RLD, O)8x, D3, (O, LRD)8x, (O, K1)2x.
Round 41: Knit.

Cast off.

Beeton's Flower (shown three-quarter size) was worked with 10/2 linen on size 2 needles.

Double Star

On my visit to Tasmania in 1978, a friend gave me directions for the Double Star pattern. Several weeks later, when I went on to New Zealand, I was delighted to find a wonderful collection of counterpanes in the War Memorial Museum in Auckland. One particularly striking counterpane in the collection used this Double Star.

The pattern is moderately difficult to work. Knit on five needles and begun in the center, it is made up of increases, yarn-overs and decreases. The connecting square is knit at the same time as the main unit, and its simple pattern is the double-moss stitch. Other patterns could, of course, be worked in this connecting piece.

Handsome table mats could be made with four medallions. They could either be joined with the connecting square I present, or, like the New Zealand example I saw, with crochet filling the empty areas between the units.

When making a full counterpane with this pattern, knit the wedge-shaped filler pieces to complete the sides of the spread. The corners can be left unfilled. One of the lace borders from pp. 144-171 or a simple tied-fringe border (see pp. 150-151) can be used to finish the counterpane.

Assembly Diagram

The easiest way to assemble this counterpane is to sew the units into strips the length of the spread. Then alternate the direction of the strips, as shown below, and sew them together. The outer edge may be completed with the wedge-shaped pieces or left unfilled and 'scalloped.' The corners can also be left unfilled.

Special Instructions:
Each line of instruction should be repeated 8 times, 2 times on each needle.

Cast on 8 stitches and distribute evenly on 4 needles. Knit with a 5th needle.

Round 1 and all odd-numbered rounds: Knit.
Round 2: O, K1.
Round 4: O, K2.
Round 6: O, K3.
Round 8: O, K4.
Round 10: O, K5
Round 12: O, Kl, O, K3, LRD.
Round 14: O, K3, O, K2, LRD.
Round 16: O, K5, O, K1, LRD.
Round 18: O, K7, O, LRD
Round 20: O, K1, O, K5, LRD, O, LRD.
Round 22: O, LRD, O, K1, O, K4, LRD, O, LRD.
Round 24: (O, LRD)2x, O, K1, O, K3, LRD, O, LRD.
Round 26: (O, LRD)3x, O, K1, O, K2, LRD, O, LRD.
Round 28: (O, LRD)4x, (O, K1)2x, LRD, O, LRD.
Round 30: (O, LRD)5x, O, K1, (O, LRD)2x.
Round 32: Cast off until 18 stitches remain.

The following directions are worked in rows on the 18 remaining stitches:

Row 1: (K2, P2)4x, K2.
Row 2: (P2, K2)4x, P2.
Row 3: (K2, P2)4x, K2.

Repeat rows 1-3 six more times. Then repeat rows 1 and 2.

Cast off on next row, knitting the knit stitches and purling the purl stitches.

Trapezoid

Cast on 17 stitches.

Row 1 and all odd-numbered rows: Purl.
Row 2: K1, (O, LRD)7x, (O, K1)2x.
Row 4: K1, (O, LRD)8x, (O, K1)2x.
Row 6: K1, (O, LRD)9x, (O, K1)2x.
Row 8: K1, (O, LRD)10x, (O, K1)2x.
Row 10: K1, (O, LRD)11x, (O, K1)2x.
Row 12: K1, (O, LRD)12x, (O, K1)2x.
Row 14: K1, (O, LRD)13x, (O, K1)2x.
Row 15: Purl.

Cast off.

Double Star and Trapezoid were knit with Parisian cotton on size 1 needles.

Lily

The Lily pattern is a wonderful but little-known pattern. Among nineteenth-century publications, I found directions for it only in Weldon's Practical Needlework. When I chanced upon a counterpane in a New York City antique shop in 1985, I was delighted to find that it was worked primarily in this pattern. The design of the counterpane was stunning: it used the Lily pattern as its main design and the Star Tidy pattern (see pp. 50-52) for its border.

This pattern is moderately difficult, but a good one for knitters learning to work on five needles. Knit from the center out, the Lily pattern is composed of nothing more than stockinette stitch, increases and decreases, and rows of purling. This pattern is also a good one for experimenting with design changes. For example, one or several of the purled bands in each purled "petal" could be extended across the neighboring flat petals. Many of the borders on pp. 144-171 can be used to complete a counterpane in this pattern.

Special Instructions:
Each line of instruction should be repeated 4 times, once on each needle.

Cast on 8 stitches and distribute evenly on 4 needles. Knit with a 5th needle.

Knit 2 rounds.

Round 1: (O, K1)2x.
Round 2: K4.
Round 3: (O, K2)2x.
Round 4: K6.
Round 5: (O, RLD, O, K1)2x.
Round 6: K8.
Round 7: *O, RLD, O*, P2, *-*, K2.
Round 8: K3, P2, K5.
Round 9: (O, RLD, O, K3)2x.
Round 10: K12.
Round 11: *O, RLD, O*, P4, *-*, K4.
Round 12: K3, P4, K7.
Round 13: (O, RLD, O, K5)2x.
Round 14: K16.
Round 15: *O, RLD, O*, P6, *-*, K6.
Round 16: K3, P6, K9.
Round 17: (O, RLD, O, K7)2x.
Round 18: K20.
Round 19: *O, RLD, O*, P8, *-*, K8.
Round 20: K3, P8, K11.

Round 21: (O, RLD, O, K9)2x.
Round 22: K24.
Round 23: *O, RLD, O*, P10, *-*, K10.
Round 24: K3, P10, K13.
Round 25: (O, RLD, O, K11)2x.
Round 26: K28.
Round 27: *O, RLD, O*, P12, *-*, K12.
Round 28: K3, P12, K15.
Round 29: (O, RLD, O, K13)2x.
Round 30: K32.
Round 31: *O, RLD, O*, P14, *-*, K14.

Round 32: K3, P14, K17.
Round 33: (O, RLD, O, K15)2x.
Round 34: K36.
Round 35: *O, RLD, O*, P16, *-*, K16.
Round 36: K3, P16, K19.
Round 37: (O, RLD, O, K17)2x.
Round 38: K40.
Round 39: *O, RLD, O*, P18, *-*, K18.
Round 40: K3, P18, K21.
Round 41: (O, RLD, O, K19)2x.
Round 42: K44.
Round 43: *O, RLD, O*, P20, *-*, K20.
Round 44: K3, P20, K23.

Begin working in rows to complete the corner shaping.

Row 45: Cast off 3 stitches, K17 (18 stitches on right needle), LRD, turn.

Row 46: Sl, P16, P2tog, continue to turn at the end of each row.

Row 47: Sl, P15, P2tog.

Row 48: Sl, K14, LRD.

Row 49: Sl, K13, LRD.

Row 50: Sl, P12, P2tog.

Row 51: Sl, P11, P2tog.

Row 52: Sl, K10, LRD.

Row 53: Sl, K9, LRD.

Row 54: Sl, P8, P2tog.

Row 55: Sl, P7, P2tog.

Row 56: Sl, K6, LRD.

Row 57: Sl, K5, LRD,.

Row 58: Sl, P4, P2tog.

Row 59: Sl, P3, P2tog.

Row 60: Sl, K2, LRD.

Row 61: Sl, K1, LRD.

Row 62: Sl, P2tog.

Row 63: LRD, fasten off.

Attach yarn to the stitches remaining on the first needle and cast them off. Repeat rows 45-63 three more times.

The Lily pattern (shown three-quarter size) was worked with Parisian Cotton on size 1 needles.

Theresa's Pattern

Theresa's Pattern (shown three-quarter size) was knit with size 3 perle cotton on size 1 needles.

This pattern is one I varied slightly from similar patterns I found in Thérèse de Dillmont's Knitting, 5th Series *and James Norbury's* Traditional Knitting Patterns. *Similar to* A Bit of Italy *(see p. 53-55), this pattern can be combined with its fancier counterpart for an interesting effect. The pair can even be worked with any number of other different patterns and tied together with a wide border, as they were in a superb counterpane I saw in a December, 1981, issue of* Architectural Digest.

This moderately difficult pattern is knit on five needles. Begun in the center and worked outward, the flower motif is produced with simple increases and decreases, and the border with rows of purling and faggoting.

Special Instructions:
Each line of instruction should be repeated 4 times, once on each needle.

Cast on 8 stitches and distribute evenly on 4 needles. Knit with a 5th needle.

Round 1 and all odd-numbered rounds through Round 43: Knit.
Round 2: (O, K1)2x.
Round 4: O, K1, O, RLD, O, K1.
Round 6: O, LRD, O, K1, O, RLD, O, K1.
Round 8: O, K2, O, P3tog, O, K2, O, K1.
Round 10: O, K1, LRD, O, K3, O, RLD, K1, O, K1.
Round 12: O, K3, O, K1, P3tog, K1, O, K3, O, K1.

Round 14: O, K2, LRD, O, K5, O, RLD, K2, O, K1.
Round 16: O, K4, O, K2, P3tog, K2, O, K4, O, K1.
Round 18: O, K3, LRD, O, K7, O, RLD, K3, O, K1.
Round 20: O, K5, O, K3, P3tog, K3, O, K5, O, K1.
Round 22: O, K4, LRD, O, K9, O, RLD, K4, O, K1.
Round 24: O, K6, O, K4, P3tog, K4, O, K6, O, K1.
Round 26: O, K5, LRD, O, K11, O, RLD, K5, O, K1.
Round 28: O, K7, O, K5, P3tog, K5, O, K7, O, K1.

Round 30: O, K6, *LRD, O, K1, O, RLD*, K7, *-*, K6, O, K1.
Round 32: O, K6, *LRD, O, K3, O, RLD*, K5, *-*, K6, O, K1.
Round 34: (*O, K1, O, RLD, K3, LRD, O, K1, O*, D3)2x, *-*, K1.
Round 36: O, K3, O, (RLD, K1, LRD, O, K3, O, RLD, K2, O)2x, RLD, K1, LRD, O, K3, O, K1.
Round 38: (O, K1, O, D3)9x, (O, K1)2x.
Round 40: O, K3, (O, RLD, K2)9x, O, K1.
Round 42: (O, K1, O, D3)10x, (O, K1)2x.
Round 44: O, K43, O, K1.

Round 45: P45, K1.
Round 46: O, P45, O, K1.
Round 47: K48.
Round 48: O, K1, (O, RLD)23x, O, K1.
Round 49: K50.
Round 50: O, P49, O, K1.
Round 51: P51, K1.
Round 52: O, K51, O, K1.
Round 53: K1, (O, RLD)26x, K1.
Round 54: O, K53, O, K1.
Round 55: P55, K1.
Round 56: O, P55, O, K1.
Round 57: P57, K1.

Cast off.

Star Tidy

This pattern has turned up on counterpanes in numerous places: the War Memorial Museum in Auckland, New Zealand; the Royal Ontario Museum in Toronto, Canada; the Witte Museum in San Antonio, Texas; the Shelburne Museum in Shelburne, Vermont; the Smithsonian Institution, National Museum of American History in Washington, D.C.; the Bradford Industrial Museum in Bradford, England; and in a personal collection I saw in Australia. The directions for this deservedly popular pattern appeared in several nineteenth-century sources, and I have included the earliest version of them from Cornelia Mee's Manual of Needlework, self-published in 1845.

This is a relatively easy pattern to work. It is knit on five needles, beginning in the center. Unlike the similar Double Star (see pp. 44-45), the octagon and the square are worked separately. The square and the half-square are knit in seed stitch. The lace border is also from Mrs. Mee's manual. (See also pp. 28-29.)

Octagon

Special Instructions:
Each line of instruction should be repeated 8 times, that is, 2 times on each needle.

Cast on 8 stitches and distribute evenly on 4 needles. Knit with a 5th needle.

Round 1: Knit working into the back of each stitch.
Round 2: O, K1.
Round 3 and all odd-numbered rounds: Knit.
Round 4: O, K2.
Round 6: O, K3.
Round 8: O, K4.
Round 10: O, K5.
Round 12: O, K6.
Round 14: O, K7.
Round 16: O, K8.
Round 18: O, K1, O, LRD, K6.

Round 20: O, K1, (O, LRD)2x, K5.
Round 22: O, K1, (O, LRD)3x, K4.
Round 24: O, K1, (O, LRD)4x, K3.
Round 26: O, K1, (O, LRD)5x, K2.
Round 28: O, K1, (O, LRD)6x, K1.
Round 30: O, K1, (O, LRD)7x.

Cast off.

Assembly Diagram

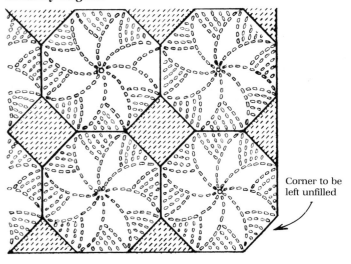

Corner to be left unfilled

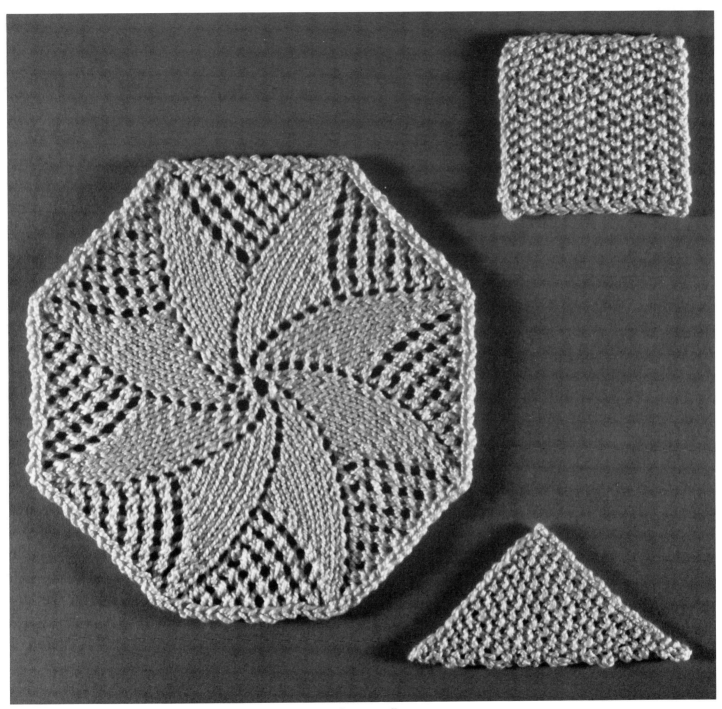

The Star Tidy samples were knit with size 5 perle cotton on size 0 needles.

Square

Cast on 17 stitches.

Row 1: (K1, P1)8x, K1.

Repeat this row 25 more times.

Cast off in pattern.

Half-Square

Cast on 17 stitches.

Row 1: (K1, P1)8x, K1.
Row 2: LRD, (K1, P1)7x, K1.
Row 3: LRD, (K1, P1)7x.
Row 4: LRD, (P1, K1)6x, P1.
Row 5: LRD, (P1, K1)6x.
Row 6: LRD, (K1, P1)5x, K1.
Row 7: LRD, (K1, P1)5x.
Row 8: LRD, (P1, K1)4x, P1.
Row 9: LRD, (P1, K1)4x.
Row 10: LRD, (K1, P1)3x, K1.
Row 11: LRD, (K1, P1)3x.
Row 12: LRD, (P1, K1)2x, P1.
Row 13: LRD, (P1, K1)2x.
Row 14: LRD, K1, P1, K1.
Row 15: LRD, K1, P1.
Row 16: LRD, P1.
Row 17: LRD, fasten off.

Star Tidy Border

Special Instructions:
O2 is the basis for 2 stitches on the following row.

Cast on 33 stitches.

Row 1: [K1, P1, (O, LRD)4x]2x, P1, K1, O, P2tog, K1, (O2, LRD)2x, K4.
Row 2: K6, P1, K2, P1, K1, O, P2tog, K1, P1, K1, P8, K1, P10.
Row 3: K1, P1, K1, (O, LRD)3x, (P1, K1)2x, (O, LRD)3x, K1, P1, K1, O, P2tog, K11.
Row 4: K11, O, P2tog, K1, P1, K1, P6, (K1, P1)2x, K1, P5, K1, P2.

Row 5: (K1, P1)2x, (O, LRD)2x, (K1, P1)3x, (O, LRD)2x, (P1, K1)2x, O, P2tog, K1, (O2, LRD)3x, K4.
Row 6: K6, (P1, K2)2x, P1, K1, O, P2tog, (K1, P1)2x, K1, P4, (K1, P1)2x, K1, P5, K1, P2.
Row 7: (K1, P1)2x, K1, O, LRD, (P1, K1)4x, O, LRD, (K1, P1)2x, K1, O, P2tog, K14.
Row 8: Cast off 5, K8, O, P2tog, (K1, P1)2x, K1, P2, (K1, P1)6x, K1, P2.
Row 9: (K1, P1)2x, (O, LRD)2x, (K1, P1)3x, (O, LRD)2x, (P1, K1)2x, O, P2tog, K1, (O2, LRD)2x, K4.

Row 10: K6, P1, K2, P1, K1, O, P2tog, (K1, P1)2x, K1, P4, (K1, P1)2x, K1, P5, K1, P2.
Row 11: K1, P1, K1, (O, LRD)3x, (P1, K1)2x, (O, LRD)3x, K1, P1, K1, O, P2tog, K11.
Row 12: K11, O, P2tog, K1, P1, K1, P6, (K1, P1)2x, K1, P5, K1, P2.
Row 13: K1, P1, (O, LRD)4x, K1, P1, (O, LRD)4x, P1, K1, O, P2tog, K1, (O2, LRD)3x, K4.
Row 14: K6, P1, (K2, P1)2x, K1, O, P2tog, K1, P1, K1, P8, K1, P10.
Row 15: K1, (O, LRD)10x, K1, O, P2tog, K14,
Row 16: Cast off 5 stitches, K8, O, P2tog, K1, P21.

Repeat rows 1-16 for desired length.

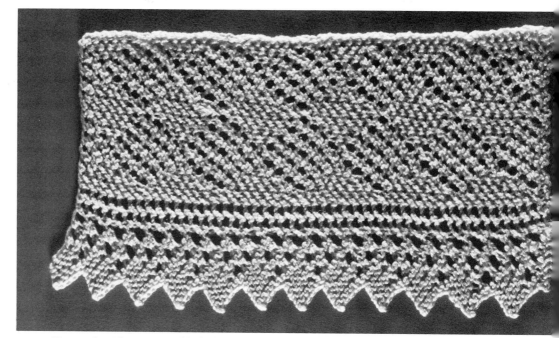

Star Tidy Border (shown two-third size) was knit with size 5 perle cotton on size 0 needles.

A Bit of Italy

I called this popular pattern A Bit of Italy simply because the most recent example I saw of it was in an Italian magazine. I have found directions for this pattern in both nineteenth- and twentieth-century needlework books and decided to include it here because it is so attractive. Knit in a heavier cotton or in wool, the pattern would make a beautiful pillow cover.

This complex, five-needle pattern is for the experienced knitter. The square is begun in the center, and the flower's petals are worked in a two-stitch crossover pattern. The four corners are worked individually after the main part of the pattern is completed, with a series of yarn-overs and decreases used to produce the small leaves. I leave the choice of border for the counterpane up to the knitter (see pp. 144-171).

Special Instructions:
COS *Crossover stitch, as shown in the drawing below, is worked as follows:*
Skip the first stitch, knit through the front loop of the second stitch and slip it over the skipped stitch and off the left needle. Knit the skipped stitch, completing the cross.
Each line of instructions should be repeated 4 times, once on each needle.

Cast on 8 stitches and distribute evenly on 4 needles. Knit with a 5th needle.

Round 1: Knit.
Round 2: Knit.
Round 3: (K1, O)2x.
Round 4: Knit.
Round 5: (K1, O)4x.
Round 6: Knit.
Round 7: (K1, O)8x.
Round 8: Purl.
Round 9: Purl.
Round 10: Purl.
Round 11: (COS)8x.
Round 12: Knit.
Round 13: (K1B, [COS]3x, K1B)2x.
Round 14: Knit.
Round 15: (COS)8x.
Round 16: Knit.
Round 17: (K1B, [COS]3x, K1B, O)2x.
Round 18: Knit.
Round 19: ([COS]4x, O, K1, O)2x.
Round 20: Knit.
Round 21: (K1B, [COS]3x, K1B, O, K3, O)2x.
Round 22: Knit.
Round 23: (RLD, [COS]2x, LRD, O, K5, O)2x.

Crossover Stitch

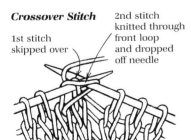

1st stitch skipped over

2nd stitch knitted through front loop and dropped off needle

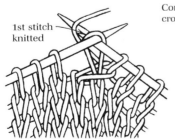

1st stitch knitted

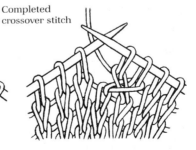

Completed crossover stitch

A Bit of Italy was worked with a doubled strand of Knit-Cro-Sheen on size 2 needles.

Round 24: Knit.

Round 25: (RLD, COS, LRD, O, K7, O)2x.

Round 26: Knit. (Flower finished.)

Round 27: (RLD, LRD, *O, K1, O*, K2, D3, K2, *-*)2x.

Round 28: Knit.

Round 29: (LRD, *O, K3, O*, K1, D3, K1, *-*)2x.

Round 30: Knit.

Round 31: (K1B, *O, LRD, O, K1, O, RLD, O*, D3, *-*)2x.

Round 32: Knit.

Round 33: ([K,P,K,P,K into 1st stitch], *O, LRD, O, K3, O, RLD, O*, K1B, *-*)2x.

Round 34: Knit.

After the last round, reposition the stitches as follows:
K2 from needle 1 onto needle 4, add a new marker. Slip 2 stitches from needle 2 onto needle 1 and continue in this manner with needles 3 and 4.

Round 35: K3, *LRD, O, K4, O, RLD*, D3, *-*, K26.

Round 36: P2, K19, P2, K23.

Round 37: K1, (D3, O, K6, O)2x, K3tog, K24.

Round 38: P2, K17, P2, K23.

Begin working in rows to complete corner shaping.

Row 1: K1, RLD, *O, K2, LRD, K2, O*, D3, *-*, LRD, K1, turn.

Row 2 and all even-numbered rows through Row 14: K2, P until 2 stitches remain, K2, continue to turn at the end of each row.

Row 3: K1, RLD, *O, K1, D3, K1, O*, K3, *-*, LRD, K1.

Row 5: K1, RLD, *O, D3, O*, K5, *-*, LRD, K1.

Row 7: K1, RLD, K1, O, K2, D3, K2, O, K1, LRD, K1.

Row 9: K1, RLD, O, K2, D3, K2, O, LRD, K1.

Row 11: K1, RLD, O, K1, D3, K1, O, LRD, K1.

Row 13: K1, RLD, O, D3, O, LRD, K1.

Row 15: D3, K1, D3.

Row 16: P3tog, fasten off.

Attach thread where the stitches were divided and cast off 22. Slip the last stitch to the left needle and LRD. The stitch now on the right needle is K1 of Row 1. Repeat corner 3 more times.

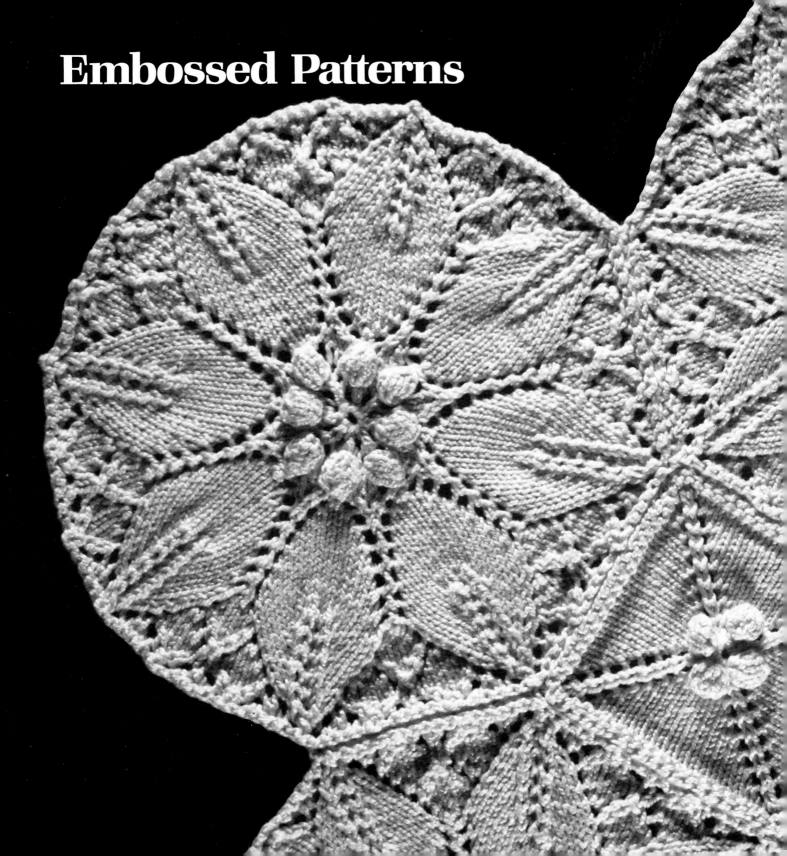

Embossed Patterns

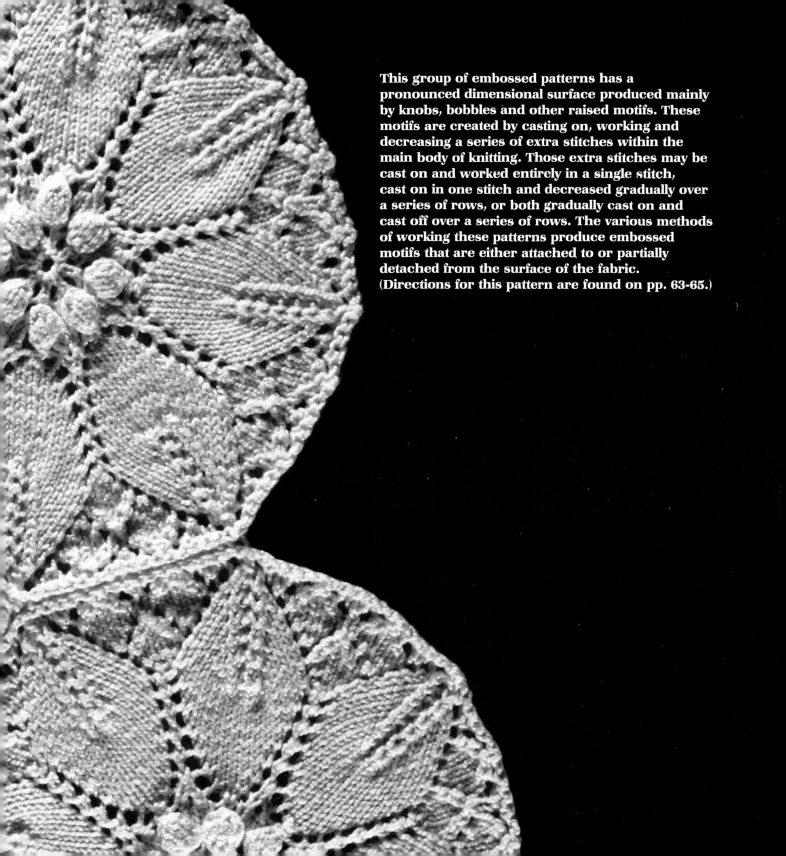

This group of embossed patterns has a pronounced dimensional surface produced mainly by knobs, bobbles and other raised motifs. These motifs are created by casting on, working and decreasing a series of extra stitches within the main body of knitting. Those extra stitches may be cast on and worked entirely in a single stitch, cast on in one stitch and decreased gradually over a series of rows, or both gradually cast on and cast off over a series of rows. The various methods of working these patterns produce embossed motifs that are either attached to or partially detached from the surface of the fabric. (Directions for this pattern are found on pp. 63-65.)

Bath Pattern

The Bath Pattern sample was worked with size 3 perle cotton on size 1 needles.

On a 1984 visit to Bath, England, I found directions for a lovely counterpane pattern in a mid-nineteenth-century issue of The Lady's Newspaper, *published in London. The pattern presented here is my variation on that original pattern. I have seen additional variations on this pattern in counterpanes at Strangers' Hall Museum in Norwich, England, and at Lady Rosse's home in London, now owned by the Victorian Society.*

This is a perfect pattern for the intermediate knitter. Worked on two needles, it offers ample practice in all the basics: the garter stitch, stockinette stitch, reverse stockinette, ribbing and increasing. It also introduces knitters to faggoting and working bobbles (see p. 26 for instructions). And if a knitter wants to experiment with changing a pattern, this one can easily be enlarged overall or have its internal motifs altered or replaced.

The border I have used with this pattern is drawn from the nineteenth-century Weldon's Practical Knitter, *yet any lace edging or fringe (pp. 144-171) would nicely complete the Bath Pattern.*

Cast on 1 stitch.

Row 1: B1.
Row 2: K1, B1.
Row 3: K2, B1.
Rows 4-12: Continue as established, knitting all stitches and working the bar increase at the end of the row (13 stitches at the end of Row 12).
Row 13: K12, B1.
Row 14: P13, B1p.
Row 15: K14, B1.
Row 16: P15, B1p.
Row 17: (K2, P2)4x, B1.
Row 18: (P2, K2)4x, P1, B1.
Row 19: P1, (K2, P2)4x, K1, B1.
Row 20: K1, (P2, K2)4x, P2, B1.
Row 21: (P2, K2)5x, B1.
Row 22: P21, B1p.
Row 23: K22, B1.
Row 24: P23, B1p.
Row 25: K24, B1.
Row 26: K25, B1.
Row 27: K26, B1.

Row 28: K27, B1.
Row 29: K28, B1.
Row 30: K29, B1.
Row 31: K30, B1.
Row 32: P31, B1p.
Row 33: K32, B1.
Row 34: K33, B1.
Row 35: K2, (O, LRD)16x, B1.
Row 36: K35, B1.
Row 37: K36, B1.
Row 38: P37, B1p.
Row 39: K2, (Bobble, K4)7x, Bobble, B1.
Row 40: P39, B1.
Row 41: K40, B1.
Row 42: K41, B1.
Row 43: K2, (O, LRD)20x, B1.
Row 44: K43, B1.
Row 45: K44, B1.
Row 46: P45, B1p.
Row 47: K46, B1.
Row 48: K47, B1.
Row 49: K48, B1.
Row 50: K49, B1.
Row 51: K50, B1.
Row 52: K51, B1.
Row 53: Cast off.

Four units of the Bath Pattern assembled into a square.

Bath Border

Special Instructions:
AP1   *Abbreviated pattern #1 is worked as follows:*
Slp, K3, O, LRD, P1.

Cast on 27 stitches.

Row 1: B1p, P2, K15, P2, K7.
Row 2: AP1, K2, O, P2tog, P10, K1, O, LRD, K4.
Row 3: B1, K17, P3, K7.
Row 4: AP1, K3, O, P2tog, P9, K1, O, LRD, P5.
Row 5: B1p, P4, K13, P4, K7.
Row 6: AP1, K4, O, P2tog, P8, K1, O, LRD, K6.
Row 7: B1, K17, P5, K7.
Row 8: AP1, K5, O, P2tog, P7, K1, O, LRD, P7.
Row 9: B1p, P6, K11, P6, K7.
Row 10: AP1, K6, O, P2tog, P6, K1, O, LRD, K8.
Row 11: B1, K17, P7, K7.
Row 12: AP1, K7, O, P2tog, P5, K1, O, LRD, P9.
Row 13: B1p, P8, K9, P8, K7.
Row 14: AP1, K8, O, P2tog, P4, K1, O, LRD, K10.
Row 15: B1, K17, P9, K7.
Row 16: AP1, K9, O, P2tog, P3, K1, O, LRD, P11.

Row 17: B1p, P10, K7, P10, K7.
Row 18: AP1, K10, O, P2tog, P2, K1, O, LRD, K12.
Row 19: LRD, K16, P11, K7.
Row 20: Repeat Row 16.
Row 21: P2tog, P9, K7, P10, K7.
Row 22: Repeat Row 14.
Row 23: LRD, K16, P9, K7.
Row 24: Repeat Row 12.
Row 25: P2tog, P7, K9, P8, K7.
Row 26: Repeat Row 10.
Row 27: LRD, K16, P7, K7.
Row 28: Repeat Row 8.
Row 29: P2tog, P5, K11, P6, K7.
Row 30: Repeat Row 6.
Row 31: LRD, K16, P5, K7.
Row 32: Repeat Row 4.
Row 33: P2tog, P3, K13, P4, K7.
Row 34: Repeat Row 2.
Row 35: LRD, K16, P3, K7.
Row 36: AP1, K1, O, P2tog, P11, K1, O, LRD, P3.

Repeat rows 1-36 for desired length.

The Bath Border (shown half-size) was worked with the same yarn and needles as the main unit.

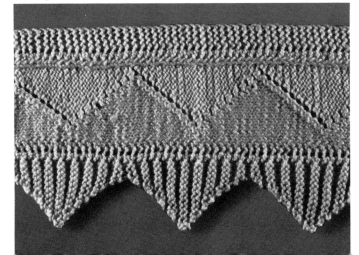

Grandmother Anderson's Pattern

Grandmother Anderson's Pattern (shown half-size) was worked with cotton carpet warp on size 1 needles.

This pattern is from a counterpane belonging to our family friend Mary Elizabeth Allen. It was knit by her grandmother in Canton, Mississippi, around the time of the Civil War. I have also seen examples of counterpanes using this well-known pattern or a variation on it at the Landsmuseum in Zurich, Switzerland, and at Como, a historical restoration near Melbourne, Australia.

Worked on two needles, this intermediate pattern starts with the raised-leaf pattern set on a reverse stockinette ground. Two rows of decorative eyelets introduce the central embossed area of the pattern, which uses the extra cast-on stitches as the foundation for a field of bells. The border repeats the first 40 rows of the main pattern and then can be completed with a tied tassel at the top and bottom points of the edging (see p. 150). You might also want to use the Purse and Garter-Stitch Insert pattern on p. 156 before working the border, as I have seen done in a counterpane similar to this one.

Cast on 2 stitches.

Row 1: O, K2.
Row 2: O, K1, P1, K1.
Row 3: O, (K1, O)2x, K2.
Row 4: O, K2, P3, K2.
Row 5: O, K1, P1, K1, (O, K1)2x, P3.
Row 6: O, K3, P5, K3.
Row 7: O, K1, P2, K2, O, K1, O, K2, P4.
Row 8: O, K4, P7, K4.
Row 9: O, K1, P3, K3, O, K1, O, K3, P5.
Row 10: O, K5, P9, K5.
Row 11: O, K1, P4, K4, O, K1, O, K4, P6.
Row 12: O, K6, P11, K6.
Row 13: O, K1, P5, K5, O, K1, O, K5, P7.
Row 14: O, K7, P13, K7.
Row 15: O, K1, P6, RLD, K9, LRD, P8.
Row 16: O, K8, P11, K8.
Row 17: O, K1, P7, RLD, K7, LRD, P9.
Row 18: O, K9, P9, K9.
Row 19: O, K1, P8, RLD, K5, LRD, P10.
Row 20: O, K10, P7, K10.
Row 21: O, K1, P9, RLD, K3, LRD, P11.
Row 22: O, K11, P5, K11.
Row 23: O, K1, P10, RLD, K1, LRD, P12.
Row 24: O, K12, P3, K12.
Row 25: O, K1, P11, D3, P13.
Row 26: O, K27.
Row 27: O, K1, P27.
Row 28: O, K29.
Row 29: O, K1, P29.
Row 30: O, K1, P30.
Row 31: O, K32.
Row 32: O, K1, P32.
Row 33: O, K1, (O, LRD)16x, K1.
Row 34: O, K1, P34.
Row 35: O, K36.

Row 36: O, K1, P36.
Row 37: O, K1, P37.
Row 38: O, K39.
Row 39: O, K1, P39.
Row 40: O, P41.
Row 41: O, K42.
Row 42: O, P43.
Row 43: O, K1, (O, LRD)21x, K1.
Row 44: O, P45.
Row 45: O, K46.
Row 46: O, P47.
Row 47: O, K1, P2, LCO5, (P4, LCO5)10x, P5.
Row 48: O, K5, P5, (K4, P5)10x, K4.
Row 49: O, K1, P3, *RLD, K1, LRD*, (P4, *-*)10x, P6.
Row 50: O, K6, P3, (K4, P3)10x, K5.
Row 51: O, K1, (P4, D3)11x, P7.
Row 52: O, K6, LRD, (K3, LRD)10x, K6.
Row 53: O, K1, P53.
Row 54: O, K55.
Row 55: O, K1, (P4, LCO5)12x, P7.
Row 56: O, K7, P5, (K4, P5)11x, K6.
Row 57: O, K1, P5, *RLD, K1, LRD*, (P4, *-*)11x, P8.
Row 58: O, K8, P3, (K4, P3)11x, K7.
Row 59: O, K1, P6, D3, (P4, D3)11x, P9.
Row 60: O, K9, LRD, (K3, LRD)11x, K7.
Row 61: O, K1, P61.
Row 62: O, K62.
Row 63: O, K1, P6, LCO5, (P4, LCO5)12x, P9.
Row 64: O, K9, P5, (K4, P5)12x, K8.
Row 65: O, K1, P7, *RLD, K1, LRD*, (P4, *-*)12x, P10.

Row 66: O, K10, P3, (K4, P3)12x, K9.
Row 67: O, K1, P8, D3, (P4, D3)12x, P11.
Row 68: O, K10, LRD, (K3, LRD)12x, K10.
Row 69: O, K1, P69.
Row 70: O, K71.
Row 71: O, K1, P71.
Row 72: O, K1, P72.
Row 73: O, K74.
Row 74: O, K1, (O, P2tog)37x.
Row 75: O, K76.
Row 76: O, K1, P76.
Row 77: O, K78.
Row 78: O, K79.
Row 79: O, K1, P79.
Row 80: O, K78, LRD, K1.
Row 81: O, LRD, K76, LRD, K1.
Row 82: O, P2tog, P75, P2tog, P1.

Row 83: O, LRD, K74, LRD, K1.
Row 84: (O, P2tog)39x.
Row 85: O, LRD, K73, LRD, K1.
Row 86: O, P2tog, P72, P2tog, P1.
Row 87: O, LRD, K71, LRD, K1.
Row 88: O, LRD, K70, LRD, K1.
Row 89: O, P2tog, P13, (*K1, O, K1, O, K1*, P7)4x, *-*, P13, P2tog, P1.
Row 90: O, LRD, K13, (P5, K7)4x, P5, K12, LRD, K1.
Row 91: O, P2tog, P12, (*K2, O, K1, O, K2*, P7)4x, *-*, P12, P2tog, P1.
Row 92: O, LRD, K12, (P7, K7)4x, P7, K11, LRD, K1.
Row 93: O, P2tog, P11, (*K3, O, K1, O, K3*, P7)4x, *-*, P11, P2tog, P1.

Four units of the pattern assembled into a square.

Row 94: O, LRD, K11, (P9, K7)4x, P9, K10, LRD, K1.
Row 95: O, P2tog, P10, (*K4, O, K1, O, K4*, P7)4x, *-*, P10, P2tog, P1.
Row 96: O, LRD, K10, (P11, K7)4x, P11, K9, LRD, K1.
Row 97: O, P2tog, P9, (*K5, O, K1, O, K5*, P7)4x, *-*, P9, P2tog, P1.
Row 98: O, LRD, K9, (P13, K7)4x, P13, K8, LRD, K1.
Row 99: O, P2tog, P8, (*K6, O, K1, O, K6*, P7)4x, *-*, P8, P2tog, P1.
Row 100: O, LRD, K8, (P15, K7)5x, LRD, K1.
Row 101: O, P2tog, P7, (RLD, K11, LRD, P7)5x, P2tog, P1.
Row 102: O, LRD, K7, (P13, K7)4x, P13, K6, LRD, K1.
Row 103: O, P2tog, P6, (*RLD, K9, LRD*, P7)4x, *-*, P6, P2tog, P1.
Row 104: O, LRD, K6, (P11, K7)4x, P11, K5, LRD, K1.
Row 105: O, P2tog, P5, (*RLD, K7, LRD*, P7)4x, *-*, P5, P2tog, P1.
Row 106: O, LRD, K5, (P9, K7)4x, P9, K4, LRD, K1.
Row 107: O, P2tog, P4, (*RLD, K5, LRD*, P7)4x, *-*, P4, P2tog, P1.
Row 108: O, LRD, K4, (P7, K7)4x, P7, K3, LRD, K1.
Row 109: O, P2tog, P3, (*RLD, K3, LRD*, P7)4x, *-*, P3, P2tog, P1.
Row 110: O, LRD, K3, (P5, K7)4x, P5, K2, LRD, K1.
Row 111: O, P2tog, P2, (*RLD, K1, LRD*, P7)4x, *-*, P2, P2tog, P1.
Row 112: O, LRD, K2, (P3, K7)4x, P3, K1, LRD, K1.
Row 113: O, P2tog, P1, (D3, P7)4x, D3, P1, P2tog, P1.

Row 114: O, P2tog, P34, P2tog, P1.
Row 115: O, LRD, K33, LRD, K1.
Row 116: O, P2tog, P32, P2tog, P1.
Row 117: (O, LRD)18x.
Row 118: O, P2tog, P31, P2tog, P1.
Row 119: O, LRD, K30, LRD, K1.
Row 120: O, P2tog, P29, P2tog, P1.
Row 121: O, P2tog, P28, P2tog, P1.
Row 122: O, LRD, K27, LRD, K1.
Row 123: O, P2tog, P26, P2tog, P1.
Row 124: O, P2tog, P25, P2tog, P1.
Row 125: O, LRD, K24, LRD, K1.
Row 126: O, P2tog, P23, P2tog, P1.
Row 127: (O, LRD)13x, K1.
Row 128: O, P2tog, P22, P2tog, P1.
Row 129: O, LRD, K21, LRD, K1.
Row 130: O, P2tog, P20, P2tog, P1.
Row 131: O, P2tog, (P4, LCO5)4x, P3, P2tog, P1.
Row 132: O, LRD, K3, (P5, K4)3x, P5, K3, LRD, K1.
Row 133: O, P2tog, P3, (*RLD, K1, LRD*, P4)3x, *-*, P2, P2tog, P1.
Row 134: O, LRD, K2, (P3, K4)3x, P3, K2, LRD, K1.
Row 135: O, P2tog, P2, (D3, P4)3x, D3, P1, P2tog, P1.
Row 136: O, LRD, K1, (LRD, K3)3x, (LRD)2x, K1.
Row 137: O, P2tog, P3, (LCO5, P4)2x, LCO5, P2, P2tog, P1.

Row 138: O, LRD, K2, (P5, K4)2x, P5, K2, LRD, K1.
Row 139: O, P2tog, P2, (*RLD, K1, LRD*, P4)2x, *-*, P1, P2tog, P1.
Row 140: O, LRD, K1, (P3, K4)2x, P3, K1, LRD, K1.
Row 141: O, P2tog, P1, (D3, P4)2x, D3, P2tog, P1.
Row 142: O, LRD, (LRD, K3)2x, (LRD)2x.
Row 143: O, P2tog, P2, LCO5, P4, LCO5, P1, P2tog, P1.
Row 144: O, LRD, K1, P5, K4, P5, K1, LRD, K1.
Row 145: O, P2tog, P1, *RLD, K1, LRD*, P4, *-*, P2tog, P1.
Row 146: O, LRD, P3, K4, P3, LRD, K1.
Row 147: O, P2tog, D3, P4, D3, P2tog.
Row 148: O, K1, LRD, K3, LRD, K1.
Row 149: O, P2tog, P2, LCO5, P1, P2tog, P1.
Row 150: O, LRD, K1, P5, K1, LRD, K1.
Row 151: O, P2tog, P1, RLD, K1, LRD, P2tog, P1.
Row 152: O, LRD, P3, LRD, K1.
Row 153: O, P2tog, D3, P2tog.
Row 154: (LRD)2x.
Row 155: P2tog, fasten off.

Triangle Border

Cast on 2 stitches.

Work rows 1-39 of the square pattern (41 stitches).

Rows 40 and 42: Knit.
Rows 41 and 43: Purl.

Cast off knitting.

Margaret Murray's Pattern

Margaret Murray's Pattern (shown two-third size) was worked with size 3 perle cotton on size 1 needles.

Melbourne, Australia, boasts a number of Victorian homes called Terrace Houses, which are narrow in width, several stories high and flanked by terraces in front and gardens in back. A resident of one of these wonderful abodes, knitter Margaret Murray, graciously welcomed me into her home during my 1978 Australian sojourn to show me a trio of counterpanes she had made.

One of the spreads was worked in her own variation on an old pattern. To accent the large leaves, I replaced the original reverse stockinette stitch between them with three small leaves. Worked on five needles from the center out, this pattern is for the intermediate knitter.

Special Instructions:
Each line of instruction should be repeated 4 times, once on each needle.

Cast on 8 stitches and distribute evenly on 4 needles. Knit with a 5th needle. Knit 1 round.

Round 1: (O, K1)2x.
Round 2 and all even-numbered rounds: Knit unless otherwise indicated.
Round 3: O, K3, O, K1B.
Round 5: O, K5, O, K1B.
Round 6: (K3, Knob)2x.
Round 7: O, K7, O, K1.
Round 9: (O, RLD, LRD, O, K1)2x.
Round 11: (K1, O, LRD, O, K2)2x.
Round 13: (K2, O, K1B, O, K3)2x.
Round 15: (K3, O, K1B, O, K4)2x.
Round 17: (K4, O, K1B, O, K5)2x.
Round 19: (K5, O, K1B, O, K6)2x.
Round 21: (K6, O, K1B, O, K7)2x.
Round 23: (K7, O, K1B, O, K8)2x.

Round 25: (RLD, K5, O, K3, O, K5, LRD, P1)2x.
Round 27: (RLD, K4, O, K5, O, K4, LRD, P1)2x.
Round 29: (RLD, K3, *O, K1, O*, RLD, K1, LRD, *-*, K3, LRD, P1)2x.
Round 31: (RLD, K2, *O, K3, O*, D3, *-*, K2, LRD, P1)2x.
Round 33: (RLD, K1, O, K11, O, K1, LRD, P1)2x.
Round 35: (RLD, (O, K1, O, RLD, K1, LRD)2x, O, K1, O, LRD, P1)2x.

Reposition stitches as follows:
Slip first stitch of needle 1 onto needle 4.
Move the first stitch from needle 2 to needle 1, the first stitch from needle 3 to needle 2 and the first stitch from needle 4 to needle 3.

Round 37: (O, K3, O, D3)6x.
Round 38: Turn work and cast off by knitting from the back.

Half-Square

Cast on 4 stitches.

Row 1: Knit.
Row 2 and all even-numbered rows: Purl.
Row 3: (O, K1)2x, place marker and repeat.
Row 5: (O, K3, O, K1)2x.

Row 7: (O, K5, O, K1)2x.
Row 9: (O, K7, O, K1)2x.
Row 11: (O, K9, O, K1)2x.
Row 13: (O, K11, O, K1)2x.
Row 15: (O, K13, O, K1)2x.
Row 17: (O, K15, O, K1)2x.
Row 19: (O, K17, O, K1)2x.
Row 20: Purl.

Cast off, purling.

Assembly Diagram

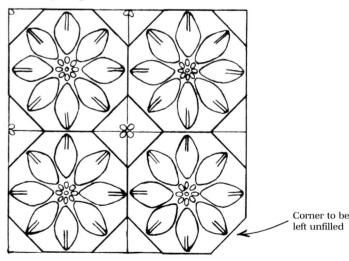

Corner to be left unfilled

The American Flounce Border (shown two-third size) was worked with size 3 perle cotton on size 1 needles.

Filler Square

Special Instructions:
Each line of instruction should be repeated 4 times, once on each needle.

Cast on 8 stitches and distribute them evenly on 4 needles. Knit with a 5th needle.

Rounds l and 2: Knit.
Round 3: Place markers on the needles after the first O. (O, K1)2x.
Round 4: Knit.
Round 5: O, K3, O, K1.
Round 6: K2, Knob, K3.
Round 7: O, K5, O, K1.
Round 8 and all remaining even-numbered rounds: Knit.
Round 9: O, K7, O, K1.
Round 11: O, K9, O, K1.
Round 13: O, K11, O, K1.
Round 15: O, K13, O, K1.
Round 17: O, K15, O, K1.
Round 19: O, K17, O, K1.
Round 21: Turn work and cast off by knitting from the back.

American Flounce Border

Special Instructions:
O2 is the basis for one stitch. Drop one wrap on following row.

Cast on 27 stitches; knit 1 row.

Row 1: Sl, K2, (O, LRD, K3)2x, (O, LRD)2x, O, K10, (turn: Sl, P9; turn: K10)2x, turn: Sl, P9, K10, O, LRD, K3, O, LRD, K1.
Row 2: Sl, K2, O, LRD, K3, O, LRD, K4, (O, LRD)2x, O2, P10, (turn: Sl, K9; turn: P10)2x, turn: Sl, K20, O, LRD, K3, O, LRD, K1.
Row 3: Sl, K2, O, LRD, K3, O, LRD, K5, (O, LRD)2x, O, K10, (turn: Sl, P9; turn: K10)2x, turn: Sl, P9, K12, O, LRD, K3, O, LRD, K1.
Row 4: Sl, K2, O, LRD, K3, O, LRD, K6, (O, LRD)2x, O2, P10, (turn: Sl, K9; turn: P10)2x, turn: Sl, K22, O, LRD, K3, O, LRD, K1.
Row 5: Sl, K2, O, LRD, K3, O, LRD, K7, (O, LRD)2x, O, K10, (turn: Sl, P9; turn: K10)2x, turn: Sl, P9, K14, O, LRD, K3, O, LRD, K1.
Row 6: Sl, K2, O, LRD, K3, O, LRD, K8, (O, LRD)2x, O2, P10, (turn: Sl, K9; turn: P10,)2x, turn: Sl, K24, O, LRD, K3, O, LRD, K1.
Row 7: Sl, K2, O, LRD, K3, O, LRD, K9, (O, LRD)2x, O, K10, (turn: Sl, P9; turn: K10)2x, turn: Sl, P9, K16, O, LRD, K3, O, LRD, K1.
Row 8: Sl, K2, O, LRD, K3, O, LRD, K10, (O, LRD)2x, O2, P10, (turn: Sl, K9; turn: P10)2x, turn: Sl, K26, O, LRD, K3, O, LRD, K1.

Row 9: Sl, K2, O, LRD, K3, O, LRD, K8, LRD, (O, LRD)3x, K9 (turn: Sl, P9; turn: K10)2x, turn: Sl, P9, K16, O, LRD, K3, O, LRD, K1.
Row 10: Sl, K2, O, LRD, K3, O, LRD, K7, (LRD, O)2x, LRD, O2, P2tog, P9, (turn: Sl, K9; turn: P10)2x, turn: Sl, K24, O, LRD, K3, O, LRD, K1.
Row 11: Sl, K2, O, LRD, K3, O, LRD, K6, LRD, (O, LRD)3x, K9, (turn: Sl, P9; turn: K10)2x, turn: Sl, P9, K14, O, LRD, K3, O, LRD, K1.
Row 12: Sl, K2, O, LRD, K3, O, LRD, K5, (LRD, O)2x, LRD, O2, P2tog, P9, (turn: Sl, K9; turn: P10)2x, turn: Sl, K22, O, LRD, K3, O, LRD, K1.
Row 13: Sl, K2, O, LRD, K3, O, LRD, K4, LRD, (O, LRD)3x, K9, (turn: Sl, P9; turn: K10)2x, turn: Sl, P9, K12, O, LRD, K3, O, LRD, K1.
Row 14: Sl, K2, (O, LRD, K3)2x, (LRD,O)2x, LRD, O2, P2tog, P9, (turn: Sl, K9; turn: P10)2x, turn: Sl, K20, O, LRD, K3, O, LRD, K1.
Row 15: Sl, K2, O, LRD, K3, O, LRD, K2, LRD, (O, LRD)3x, K9, (turn: Sl, P9; turn: K10)2x, turn: Sl, P9, K10, O, LRD, K3, O, LRD, K1.
Row 16: Sl, K2, O, LRD, K3, O, LRD, K1, (LRD, O)2x, LRD, O2, P2tog, P9, (turn: Sl, K9; turn: P10)2x, turn: Sl, K18, O, LRD, K3, O, LRD, K1.

Repeat rows 1-16 for desired length. After last repeat, knit 1 row and cast off.

Larnach Castle

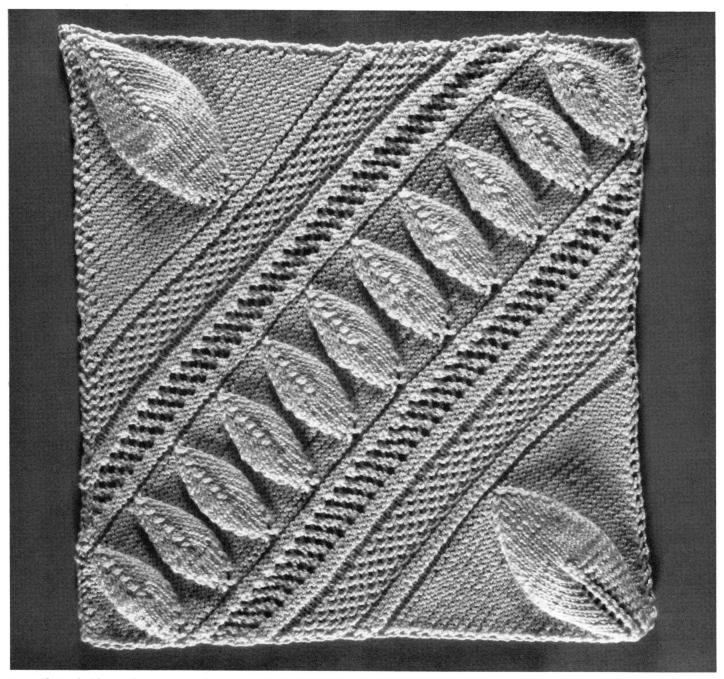

Larnach Castle (shown three-quarter size) was worked with size 5 perle cotton on size 0 needles.

Larnach Castle sits high on a cliff overlooking the city of Dunedin, New Zealand. When I visited Dunedin in 1978 to see an exhibit of counterpanes at the Early Settlers Museum, I took a side trip to this castle, a wonderful neo-Gothic structure with furniture to match. In a light and airy bedroom overlooking the bay, I found a lovely counterpane in this pattern atop a Gothic bed. This is the only spread I have ever seen in this pattern, and I have never found written directions for it in any book or magazine. I was so taken with it that I worked from a photograph of the spread to decipher instructions myself.

This moderately difficult pattern begins and ends with the classic raised-leaf pattern, worked with yarn-overs and paired decreases on a reverse stockinette ground. A band of slip-knit pattern and a second band of lace set off the central "blister" band of leaves. In contrast to the raised leaf that begins the unit, these leaves and that which ends the unit are worked with increases at the edges of the pattern up to the midpoint and with central, rather than paired, decreases.

The insert repeats the slip-knit and lace bands in the main pattern. I suggest finishing off the counterpane with the lace edging used with the Wheat Ears pattern (see pp. 87-89).

Special Instructions:
Slpf   *Slip stitch purlwise, holding yarn to front.*

Cast on 1 stitch.

Row 1: O, K1.
Row 2: O, K2.
Row 3: O, P1, O, K1, O, P1.
Row 4: O, K1, P3, K2.
Row 5: O, P2, (K1, O)2x, K1, P2.
Row 6: O, K2, P5, K3.
Row 7: O, P3, K2, O, K1, O, K2, P3.
Row 8: O, K3, P7, K4.
Row 9: O, P4, K3, O, K1, O, K3, P4.
Row 10: O, K4, P9, K5.
Row 11: O, P5, K4, O, K1, O, K4, P5.
Row 12: O, K5, P11, K6.

Row 13: O, P6, K5, O, K1, O, K5, P6.
Row 14: O, K6, P13, K7.
Row 15: O, P7, K6, O, K1, O, K6, P7.
Row 16: O, K7, P15, K8.
Row 17: O, P8, K7, O, K1, O, K7, P8.
Row 18: O, K8, P17, K9.
Row 19: O, P9, K8, O, K1, O, K8, P9.
Row 20: O, K9, P19, K10.
Row 21: O, P10, K9, O, K1, O, K9, P10.
Row 22: O, K10, P21, K11.
Row 23: O, P11, K10, O, K1, O, K10, P11.
Row 24: O, K11, P23, K12.
Row 25: O, P12, RLD, K19, LRD, P12.

Four units of Larnach Castle assembled into a square.

Row 26: O, K12, P21, K13.
Row 27: O, P13, RLD, K17, LRD, P13.
Row 28: O, K13, P19, K14.
Row 29: O, P14, RLD, K15, LRD, P14.
Row 30: O, K14, P17, K15.
Row 31: O, P15, RLD, K13, LRD, P15.
Row 32: O, K15, P15, K16.
Row 33: O, P16, RLD, K11, LRD, P16.
Row 34: O, K16, P13, K17.
Row 35: O, P17, RLD, K9, LRD, P17.
Row 36: O, K17, P11, K18.
Row 37: O, P18, RLD, K7, LRD, P18.
Row 38: O, K18, P9, K19.
Row 39: O, P19, RLD, K5, LRD, P19.
Row 40: O, K19, P7, K20.
Row 41: O, P20, RLD, K3, LRD, P20.
Row 42: O, K20, P5, K21.
Row 43: O, P21, RLD, K1, LRD, P21.
Row 44: O, K21, P3, K22.
Row 45: O, P22, D3, P22.
Row 46: O, P46.
Row 47: O, K47.
Row 48: O, P48.
Row 49: O, P49.
Row 50: O, K50.
Row 51: O, P51.
Row 52: O, P52.
Row 53: O, K53.
Row 54: O, P54.
Rows 55, 57, 59, 61, 63, 65: O, (P1, Slpf) across row ending P1.
Rows 56, 58, 60, 62, 64, 66: O, P across row.
Row 67: O, K67.
Row 68: O, P68.
Row 69: O, P69.
Row 70: O, K70.

Row 71: O, P71.
Row 72: O, P72.
Rows 73, 75, 77, 79: O, K1, (O, LRD) across row.
Rows 74, 76, 78: O, P across row.
Row 80: O, K80.
Row 81: O, P81.
Row 82: O, K82.
Row 83: O, K83.
Row 84: P84.
Row 85: O, P2, (O, P8)10x, O, P2.
Row 86: O, K2, (P1, K8)10x, P1, K3.
Row 87: O, P3, (O, K1, O, P8)10x, O, K1, O, P3.
Row 88: O, K3, (P3, K8)10x, P3, K4.
Row 89: O, P4, (O, K3, O, P8)10x, O, K3, O, P4.
Row 90: O, K4, (P5, K8)10x, P5, K5.
Row 91: O, P5, (O, K5, O, P8)10x, O, K5, O, P5.
Row 92: O, K5, (P7, K8)10x, P7, K6.
Row 93: O, P6, (O, K7, O, P8)10x, O, K7, O, P6.
Row 94: O, K6, (P9, K8)10x, P9, K7.
Row 95: O, P7, (O, K9, O, P8)10x, O, K9, O, P7.
Row 96: O, K7, (P11, K8)11x.
Row 97: O, P8, (O, K11, O, P8)11x.
Row 98: O, K8, (P13, K8)10x, P13, K9.
Row 99: P1, P2tog, P6, (K5, D3, K5, P8)10x, K5, D3, K5, P9.
Row 100: K1, LRD, K6, (P11, K8)11x.
Row 101: P1, P2tog, P5, (K4, D3, K4, P8)11x.
Row 102: K1, LRD, K5, (P9, K8)10x, P9, K7.
Row 103: P1, P2tog, P4, (K3, D3, K3, P8)10x, K3, D3, K3, P7.

Row 104: K1, LRD, K4, (P7, K8)10x, P7, K6.
Row 105: P1, P2tog, P3, (K2, D3, K2, P8)10x, K2, D3, K2, P6.
Row 106: K1, LRD, K3, (P5, K8)10x, P5, K5.
Row 107: P1, P2tog, P2, (K1, D3, K1, P8)10x, K1, D3, K1, P5.
Row 108: K1, LRD, K2, (P3, K8)10x, P3, K4.
Row 109: P1, P2tog, P1, (D3, P8)10x, D3, P4.
Row 110: P1, P2tog, P1, (P2tog, P7)10x, P2tog, P2.
Row 111: K1, LRD, K83.
Row 112: K1, LRD, K82.
Row 113: P1, P2tog, P81.
Row 114: K1, LRD, K80.
Rows 115, 117, 119, 121: K1, LRD, (O, LRD) across row. K last stitch.
Row 116, 118, 120: P1, P2tog, P across row.
Row 122: K1, LRD, K72.
Row 123: P1, P2tog, P71.
Row 124: K1, LRD, K70.
Row 125: K1, LRD, K69.
Row 126: P1, P2tog, P68.
Row 127: K1, LRD, K67.
Row 128: P1, P2tog, P66.
Row 129, 131, 133, 135, 137, 139: P1, P2tog, (Slpf, P1) across row. P last stitch.
Row 130, 132, 134, 136, 138, 140: P1, P2tog, P across row.
Row 141: K1, LRD, K53.
Row 142: K1, LRD, K52.
Row 143: P1, P2tog, P51.
Row 144: K1, LRD, K50.

Row 145: K1, LRD, K49.
Row 146: P1, P2tog, P48.
Row 147: P1, P2tog, P22, O, P25.
Row 148: K1, LRD, K22, P1, K24.
Row 149: P1, P2tog, P21, O, K1, O, P24.
Row 150: K1, LRD, K21, P3, K23.
Row 151: P1, P2tog, P20, O, K3, O, P23.
Row 152: K1, LRD, K20, P5, K22.
Row 153: P1, P2tog, P19, O, K5, O, P22.
Row 154: K1, LRD, K19, P7, K21.
Row 155: P1, P2tog, P18, O, K7, O, P21.
Row 156: K1, LRD, K18, P9, K20.
Row 157: P1, P2tog, P17, O, K9, O, P20.
Row 158: K1, LRD, K17, P11, K19.
Row 159: P1, P2tog, P16, O, K11, O, P19.
Row 160: K1, LRD, K16, P13, K18.
Row 161: P1, P2tog, P15, O, K13, O, P18.
Row 162: K1, LRD, K15, P15, K17.
Row 163: P1, P2tog, P14, O, K15, O, P17.
Row 164: K1, LRD, K14, P17, K16.
Row 165: P1, P2tog, P13, O, K17, O, P16.
Row 166: K1, LRD, K13, P19, K15.
Row 167: P1, P2tog, P12, O, K19, O, P15.
Row 168: K1, LRD, K12, P21, K14.
Row 169: P1, P2tog, P11, O, K21, O, P14.

Row 170: K1, LRD, K11, P23, K13.
Row 171: P1, P2tog, P10, K10, D3, K10, P13.
Row 172: K1, LRD, K10, P21, K12.
Row 173: P1, P2tog, P9, K9, D3, K9, P12.
Row 174: K1, LRD, K9, P19, K11.
Row 175: P1, P2tog, P8, K8, D3, K8, P11.
Row 176: K1, LRD, K8, P17, K10.
Row 177: P1, P2tog, P7, K7, D3, K7, P10.
Row 178: K1, LRD, K7, P15, K9.
Row 179: P1, P2tog, P6, K6, D3, K6, P9.
Row 180: K1, LRD, K6, P13, K8.

Row 181: P1, P2tog, P5, K5, D3, K5, P8.
Row 182: K1, LRD, K5, P11, K7.
Row 183: P1, P2tog, P4, K4, D3, K4, P7.
Row 184: K1, LRD, K4, P9, K6.
Row 185: P1, P2tog, P3, K3, D3, K3, P6.
Row 186: K1, LRD, K3, P7, K5.
Row 187: P1, P2tog, P2, K2, D3, K2, P5.
Row 188: K1, LRD, K2, P5, K4.
Row 189: P1, P2tog, P1, K1, D3, K1, P4.
Row 190: K1, LRD, K1, P3, K3.
Row 191: P1, P2tog, D3, P3.
Row 192: K1, (LRD)2x, K1.
Row 193: P1, P2tog, P1.
Row 194: D3, fasten off.

Larnach Castle Insert

Special Instructions:
AP1 *Abbreviated Pattern #1 is worked as follows:*
K2, (O, LRD)2x, K1.
Slpf *Slip stitch purlwise, holding yarn to front.*

Cast on 60 stitches..

Rows 1 and 2: K2, AP1, K42, AP1, K2.
Row 3: K2, AP1, P42, AP1, K2.
Row 4: Repeat Row 1.
Row 5: K2, AP1, (O, LRD)21x, AP1, K2.
Row 6: Repeat Row 3.
Row 7: K2, AP1, K1, (O, LRD)20x, K1, AP1, K2.
Row 8: Repeat Row 3.
Row 9: Repeat Row 5.
Row 10: Repeat Row 3.
Row 11: Repeat Row 7.
Row 12: Repeat Row 1.
Row 13: Repeat Row 3.
Row 14: Repeat Row 1.
Row 15: Repeat Row 1.
Row 16: Repeat Row 3.
Row 17: Repeat Row 1.
Row 18: Repeat Row 3.
Row 19: K2, AP1, (Slpf, P1)21x, AP1, K2.
Row 20: Repeat Row 3.
Row 21: K2, AP1, (P1, Slpf)21x, AP1, K2.
Row 22: Repeat Row 3.
Row 23: Repeat Row 19.

Row 24: Repeat Row 3.
Row 25: Repeat Row 21.
Row 26: Repeat Row 3.
Row 27: Repeat Row 19.
Row 28: Repeat Row 3.
Row 29: Repeat Row 21.
Row 30: Repeat Row 3.

Repeat rows 1-30 for desired length.

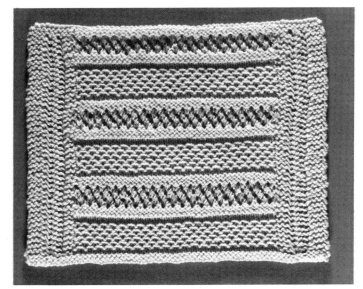

The Larnach Castle Insert (shown half-size) was knit with size 5 perle cotton on size 0 needles.

Leaves and Lines

I have found counterpanes in this pattern at the D.A.R. Museum in Washington, D.C., and, in an enlarged version, at the Gewebenmuseum in Basel, Switzerland. Neither museum, however, had any information on the pieces. I have also seen, in the October, 1981, issue of Architectural Digest, a variation on this pattern in a bedspread at The Menagerie, a grand 1754 home in Northhampton, England. I have come across directions for the enlarged version of this pattern in both French and German nineteenth-century needlework publications, and I have incorporated some corrections and changes in the instructions to present them here.

Worked on two needles, this pattern is good for the advanced beginner. It incorporates the raised-leaf motif shaped with paired decreases, with bands of faggoting and reverse stockinette stitch. The pattern can be assembled to produce diagonal lines of the raised motif, as it was in the original D.A.R. example (see the diagram on the facing page), or the units could be joined, as they usually are, to produce a central square of raised leaves. I leave the choice of borders (pp.144-171) up to the knitter.

Special Instructions:
M1 *Pick up running thread from front to back and knit into front, being careful not to close loop.*

Cast on 3 stitches.

Row 1: K3.
Row 2: K1, (M1, K1)2x.
Row 3: K5.
Row 4: K1, M1, (K1, O)2x, K1, M1, K1.
Row 5: K3, P3, K3.
Row 6: K1, M1, K2, O, K3, O, K2, M1, K1.
Row 7: K4, P5, K4.
Row 8: K1, M1, K3, O, K5, O, K3, M1, K1.
Row 9: K5, P7, K5.
Row 10: K1, M1, K4, O, K7, O, K4, M1, K1.
Row 11: K6, P9, K6.
Row 12: K1, M1, K5, RLD, K5, LRD, K5, M1, K1.

Row 13: K7, P7, K7.
Row 14: K1, M1, K6, RLD, K3, LRD, K6, M1, K1.
Row 15: K8, P5, K8.
Row 16: K1, M1, K7, RLD, K1, LRD, K7, M1, K1.
Row 17: K9, P3, K9.
Row 18: K1, M1, K8, D3, K8, M1, K1.
Row 19: K21.
Row 20: K1, M1, K4, *O, K1, O*, K9, *-*, K4, M1, K1.
Row 21: K6, P3, K9, P3, K6.
Row 22: K1, M1, K5, *O, K3, O*, K9, *-*, K5, M1, K1.
Row 23: K7, P5, K9, P5, K7.
Row 24: K1, M1, K6, *O, K5, O*, K9, *-*, K6, M1, K1.

Row 25: K8, P7, K9, P7, K8.
Row 26: K1, M1, K7, *O, K7, O*, K9, *-*, K7, M1, K1.
Row 27: (K9, P9)2x, K9.
Row 28: K1, M1, K8, *RLD, K5, LRD*, K9, *-*, K8, M1, K1.
Row 29: K10, P7, K9, P7, K10.
Row 30: K1, M1, (K9, RLD, K3, LRD)2x, K9, M1, K1.
Row 31: K11, P5, K9, P5, K11.
Row 32: K1, M1, K10, *RLD, K1, LRD*, K9, *-*, K10, M1, K1.
Row 33: K12, P3, K9, P3, K12.
Row 34: K1, M1, K11, D3, K9, D3, K11, M1, K1.
Row 35: K37.
Row 36: K1, M1, K7, (*O, K1, O*, K9)2x, *-*, K7, M1, K1.
Row 37: (K9, P3)3x, K9.
Row 38: K1, M1, K8, (*O, K3, O*, K9)2x, *-*, K8, M1, K1.

Row 39: K10, (P5, K9)2x, P5, K10.
Row 40: K1, M1, K9, (*O, K5, O*, K9)2x, *-*, K9, M1, K1.
Row 41: K11, (P7, K9)2x, P7, K11.
Row 42: K1, M1, K10, (*O, K7, O*, K9)2x, *-*, K10, M1, K1.
Row 43: K12, (P9, K9)2x, P9, K12.
Row 44: K1, M1, K11, (*RLD, K5, LRD*, K9)2x, *-*, K11, M1, K1.
Row 45: K13, (P7, K9)2x, P7, K13.
Row 46: K1, M1, K12, (*RLD, K3, LRD*, K9)2x, *-*, K12, M1, K1.
Row 47: K14, (P5, K9)2x, P5, K14.

Row 48: K1, M1, K13, (*RLD, K1, LRD*, K9)2x, *-*, K13, M1, K1.

Row 49: K15, (P3, K9)2x, P3, K15.

Row 50: K1, M1, K14, (D3, K9)2x, D3, K14, M1, K1.

Row 51: K53.

Row 52: RLD, K49, LRD.

Row 53: P51.

Row 54: RLD, K47, LRD.

Row 55: P49.

Row 56: RLD, K1, (O, LRD)22x, LRD.

Row 57: K47.

Row 58: RLD, P43, LRD.

Row 59: K45.

Row 60: RLD, P41, LRD.

Row 61: K43.

Row 62: RLD, K39, LRD.

Row 63: P41.

Row 64: RLD, K37, LRD.

Row 65: P39.

Row 66: RLD, K1, (O, LRD)17x, LRD.

Row 67: K37.

Row 68: RLD, P33, LRD.

Row 69: K35.

Row 70: RLD, P31, LRD.

Row 71: K33.

Row 72: RLD, K29, LRD.

Row 73: P31.

Row 74: RLD, K27, LRD.

Row 75: P29.

Row 76: RLD, K1, (O, LRD)12x, LRD.

Row 77: K27.

Row 78: RLD, P23, LRD.

Row 79: K25.

Row 80: RLD, P21, LRD.

Row 81: K23.

Row 82: RLD, K19, LRD.

Row 83: P21.

Row 84: RLD, K17, LRD.

Row 85: P19.

Row 86: RLD, K1, (O, LRD)7x, LRD.

Row 87: K17.

Row 88: RLD, P13, LRD.

Row 89: K15.

Row 90: RLD, P11, LRD.

Row 91: K13.

Row 92: RLD, K9, LRD.

Row 93: P11.

Row 94: RLD, K7, LRD.

Row 95: P9.

Row 96: RLD, K1, (O, LRD)2x, LRD.

Row 97: K7.

Row 98: RLD, P3, LRD.

Row 99: K5.

Row 100: RLD, P1, LRD.

Row 101: K3.

Row 102: D3, fasten off.

Leaves and Lines was worked with Antique Bedspread Cotton on size 0 needles.

Assembly Methods

Assembly of Leaves and Lines Counterpane

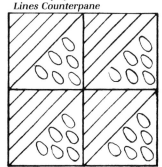

Alternate Assembly Method

Corinthian Squares

In my several trips to Australia and New Zealand, I came across eight examples of counterpanes worked in the Corinthian pattern and later found directions for this pattern in the nineteenth-century Weldon's Practical Knitter. *It is not difficult to understand the appeal of this elegant pattern, with its varied, three-dimensional surface. If four units are used for a pillow cover, they can be assembled as shown in the photo on p. 74, or with the opposite ends positioned in the center. Both methods of assembly would, of course, be seen in a full counterpane.*

Though certainly not for the beginning knitter, this two-needle pattern looks more complicated than it really is. The square begins on a corner, with knobs worked on a garter-stitch background. The other patterns making up the textured surface include the wheat ears motif, produced with yarn-overs, increases and central decreases; faggoting; and diamonds, worked with yarn-overs, increases and paired decreases. The border is the one used with the original counterpanes I saw and incorporates the three basic elements of the main pattern. I suggest completing the border with the one used for the Wheat Ears pattern (see pp. 87-89) or with a lace edging (pp.144-171).

Cast on 2 stitches.

Row 1: K2.
Row 2: Sl, M1L, K1.
Row 3: Sl, K1, O, K1.
Row 4: Sl, K3, (knit O closed).
Row 5: Sl, K1, O, K2.
Row 6: Sl, K4, (knit O closed).
Row 7: Sl, (K1, O)2x, K2.
Row 8: Sl, K6, (knit O's closed).
Row 9: Sl, K1, O, K3, O, K2.
Row 10: Sl, K8, (knit O's closed).
Row 11: Sl, K1, O, K5, O, K2.
Row 12: Sl, K10, (knit O's closed).
Row 13: Sl, K1, O, K7, O, K2.
Row 14: Sl, K12, (knit O's closed).

Row 15: Sl, K1, O, K9, O, K2.
Row 16: Sl, K14, (knit O's closed).
Row 17: Sl, K1, O, K5, Knob, K5, O, K2.
Row 18: Sl, K16, (O's remain open from this point on).
Row 19: Sl, K1, O, K13, O, K2.
Row 20: Sl, K18.
Row 21: Sl, K1, O, K5, Knob, K3, Knob, K5, O, K2.
Row 22: Sl, K20.
Row 23: Sl, K1, O, K17, O, K2.
Row 24: Sl, K22.
Row 25: Sl, K1, O, K5, (Knob, K3)2x, Knob, K5, O, K2.
Row 26: Sl, K24.
Row 27: Sl, K1, O, K21, O, K2.
Row 28: Sl, K26.

Row 29: Sl, K1, O, K9, Knob, K3, Knob, K9, O, K2.
Row 30: Sl, K28.
Row 31: Sl, K1, O, K25, O, K2.
Row 32: Sl, K30.
Row 33: Sl, K1, O, K13, Knob, K13, O, K2.
Row 34: Sl, K32.
Row 35: Sl, K1, O, K29, O, K2.
Row 36: Sl, K34.
Row 37: Sl, K1, O, K31, O, K2.
Row 38: Sl, K1, P33, K2.
Row 39: Sl, K1, O, K33, O, K2.
Row 40: Sl, K38.
Row 41: Sl, K1, O, P35, O, K2.
Row 42: Sl, K40.
Row 43: Sl, K1, O, K37, O, K2.
Row 44: Sl, K1, P39, K2.

Row 45: Sl, K1, O, K39, O, K2.
Row 46: Sl, K1, P41, K2.
Row 47: Sl, K1, O, P2, (O, K1, O, P5)6x, O, K1, O, P2, O, K2.
Row 48: Sl, K4, (P3, K5)6x, P3, K5.
Row 49: Sl, K1, O, P3, (O, K3, O, P5)6x, O, K3, O, P3, O, K2.
Row 50: Sl, (K5, P5)7x, K6.
Row 51: Sl, K1, O, P4, (O, K1, D3, K1, O, P5)6x, O, K1, D3, K1, O, P4, O, K2.
Row 52: Sl, K6, (P5, K5)6x, P5, K7.
Row 53: Sl, K1, O, P5, (O, K1, D3, K1, O, P5)7x, O, K2.
Row 54: Sl, K7, (P5, K5)6x, P5, K8.
Row 55: Sl, K1, O, P6, (O, K1, D3, K1, O, P5)6x, O, K1, D3, K1, O, P6, O, K2.

The Corinthian Squares sample was worked with Antique Bedspread Cotton on size 0 needles.

Row 56: Sl, K8, (P5, K5)6x, P5, K9.

Row 57: Sl, K1, O, P7, (O, K1, D3, K1, O, P5)6x, O, K1, D3, K1, O, P7, O, K2.

Row 58: Sl, K9, (P5, K5)6x, P5, K10.

Row 59: Sl, K1, O, P8, (K1, D3, K1, P5)6x, K1, D3, K1, P8, O, K2.

Row 60: Sl, K10, (P3, K5)6x, P3, K11.

Row 61: Sl, K1, O, P9, (D3, P5)6x, D3, P9, O, K2.

Row 62: Sl, K1, P57, K2.

Row 63: Sl, K1, O, K57, O, K2.

Row 64: Sl, K1, P59, K2.

Row 65: Sl, K1, O, K59, O, K2.

Row 66: Sl, K64.

Row 67: Sl, K1, O, P61, O, K2.

Row 68: Sl, K66.

Row 69: Sl, K1, O, K63, O, K2.

Row 70: Sl, K1, P65, K2.

Row 71: Sl, K1, O, K2, (O, LRD)31x, K1, O, K2.

Row 72: Sl, K1, P67, K2.

Row 73: Sl, K1, O, K67, O, K2.

Row 74: Sl, K72.

Row 75: Sl, K1, O, P69, O, K2.

Row 76: Sl, K74.

Row 77: Sl, K1, O, K71, O, K2.

Row 78: Sl, K1, P73, K2.

Row 79: Sl, K1, O, K73, O, K2.

Row 80: Sl, K1, P75, K2.

Row 81: Sl, K1, O, LRD, (Knob, K4)14x, Knob, LRD, O, K2.

Row 82: Sl, K1, P75, K2.

Row 83: Sl, *RLD, O, LRD*, K69, *-*, K1.

Row 84: Sl, K1, P73, K2.

Row 85: Sl, *RLD, O, LRD*, K67, *-*, K1.

Row 86: Sl, K74.

Row 87: Sl, RLD, O, P2tog, P65, P2tog, O, LRD, K1.

Row 88: Sl, K72.

Row 89: Sl, *RLD, O, LRD*, K63, *-*, K1.

Row 90: Sl, K1, P67, K2.

Row 91: Sl, RLD, (O, LRD)31x, O, D3, O, LRD, K1.

Row 92: Sl, K1, P65, K2.

Row 93: Sl, *RLD, O, LRD*, K59, *-*, K1.

Row 94: Sl, K66.

Row 95: Sl, RLD, O, P2tog, P57, P2tog, O, LRD, K1.

Row 96: Sl, K64.

Row 97: Sl, *RLD, O, LRD*, K55, *-*, K1.

Row 98: Sl, K1, P59, K2.

Row 99: Sl, *RLD, O, LRD*, K53, *-*, K1.

Row 100: Sl, K1, P57, K2.

Row 101: Sl, *RLD, O, LRD*, K2, LRD, (O, K1, O, RLD, K1, LRD)7x, O, K1, O, RLD, K2, *-*, K1.

Row 102: Sl, K1, P55, K2.

Row 103: Sl, RLD, O, (LRD)2x, (O, K3, O, D3)7x, O, K3, O, (RLD)2x, O, LRD, K1.

Row 104: Sl, K1, P53, K2.

Row 105: Sl, *RLD, O, LRD*, (O, RLD, K1, LRD, O, K1)7x, O, RLD, K1, LRD, O, *-*, K1.

Row 106: Sl, K1, P51, K2.

Row 107: Sl, *RLD, O, LRD*, (O, D3, O, K3)7x, O, D3, O, *-*, K1.

Row 108: Sl, K1, P49, K2.

Row 109: Sl, *RLD, O, LRD, K1*, (O, RLD, K1, LRD, O, K1)7x, *-*.

Row 110: Sl, K1, P47, K2.

Row 111: Sl, *RLD, O, LRD, K1*, (O, D3, O, K3)6x, O, D3, O, K1, *-*.

Row 112: Sl, K1, P45, K2.

Row 113: Sl, *RLD, O, LRD*, K2, (O, RLD, K1, LRD, O, K1)6x, K1, *-*, K1.

Row 114: Sl, K1, P43, K2.

Row 115: Sl, *RLD, O, LRD*, K2, (O, D3, O, K3)5x, O, D3, O, K2, *-*, K1.

Row 116: Sl, K1, P41, K2.

Row 117: Sl, *RLD, O, LRD*, K35, *-*, K1.

Row 118: Sl, K1, P39, K2.

Row 119: Sl, *RLD, O, LRD*, K33, *-*, K1.

Row 120: Sl, K40.

Row 121: Sl, *RLD, O, P2tog, P31, P2tog, O, LRD, K1.

Row 122: Sl, K38.

Row 123: Sl, *RLD, O, LRD*, K29, *-*, K1.

Row 124: Sl, K1, P33, K2.

Row 125: Sl, *RLD, O, LRD*, K27, *-*, K1.

Row 126: Sl, K34.

Row 127: Sl, *RLD, O, LRD*, K25, *-*, K1.

Row 128: Sl, K32.

Row 129: Sl, *RLD, O, LRD*, K11, Knob, K11, *-*, K1.

Row 130: Sl, K30.

Row 131: Sl, *RLD, O, LRD*, K21, *-*, K1.

Row 132: Sl, K28.

Row 133: Sl, *RLD, O, LRD*, K7, Knob, K3, Knob, K7, *-*, K1.

Four units of the Corinthian Squares pattern assembled into a square.

Row 134: Sl, K26.
Row 135: Sl, *RLD, O, LRD*, K17, *-*, K1.
Row 136: Sl, K24.
Row 137: Sl, *RLD, O, LRD*, (K3, Knob)3x, K3, *-*, K1.
Row 138: Sl, K22.
Row 139: Sl, *RLD, O, LRD*, K13, *-*, K1.
Row 140: Sl, K20.
Row 141: Sl, *RLD, O, LRD*, (K3, Knob)2x, K3, *-*, K1.
Row 142: Sl, K18.
Row 143: Sl, *RLD, O, LRD*, K9, *-*, K1.
Row 144: Sl, K16.
Row 145: Sl, *RLD, O, LRD*, K3, Knob, K3, *-*, K1.
Row 146: Sl, K14.
Row 147: Sl, *RLD, O, LRD*, K5, *-*, K1.
Row 148: Sl, K12.
Row 149: Sl, *RLD, O, LRD*, K3, *-*, K1.
Row 150: Sl, K10.
Row 151: Sl, (RLD, O, LRD, K1)2x.
Row 152: Sl, K8.
Row 153: Sl, RLD, O, D3, O, LRD, K1.
Row 154: Sl, K6.
Row 155: Sl, RLD, O, D3, K1.
Row 156: Sl, K4.
Row 157: Sl, D3, K1.
Row 158: Sl, K2.
Row 159: D3, fasten off.

Corinthian Border

Special Instructions:
This edge uses three patterns—the knob, diamond and wheat ear—separated by an insert pattern. The edge begins with the insert pattern, and the three patterns can alternate in any order. The sequence should be repeated as established until the desired length is produced. The border can then be finished with the insert pattern and, if you like, a lace edging from pp. 144-171.

Cast on 47 stitches. Follow the row pattern on the center 31 stitches, keeping the first 8 stitches and the last 8 stitches in garter stitch throughout.

INSERT PATTERN
Row 1: Knit.
Row 2: Purl.
Rows 3 and 4: Knit.
Row 5: Purl.
Rows 6 and 7: Knit.
Row 8: Purl.

Row 9: K1, (O, LRD)15x.
Row 10: Purl.
Rows 11 and 12: Knit.
Row 13: Purl.
Rows 14 and 15: Knit.
Row 16: Purl.

KNOB PATTERN
Row 1: Knit.
Row 2: Purl 29, P2tog.
Row 3: K2, (Knob, K4)5x, Knob, K2.
Row 4: Purl 30, LCO.

The Corinthian Border (shown two-third size) was knit with Antique Bedspread Cotton on size 0 needles.

Repeat rows 1-16 of the Insert Pattern following the Knob Pattern.

DIAMOND PATTERN
Row 1: (K1, O, RLD, K1, LRD, O)5x, K1.
Row 2: Purl.
Row 3: K2, (O, D3, O, K3)4x, O, D3, O, K2.
Row 4: Purl.
Row 5: K1, LRD, (O, K1, O, RLD, K1, LRD)4x, O, K1, O, RLD, K1.
Row 6: Purl.
Row 7: LRD, (O, K3, O, D3)4x, O, K3, O, RLD.
Row 8: Purl.

Repeat rows 1-16 of the Insert Pattern following the Diamond Pattern.

WHEAT EAR PATTERN
Row 1: (O, K1, O, P5)5x, O, K1, O.
Row 2: (P3, K5)5x, P3.
Row 3: (O, K3, O, P5)5x, O, K3, O.
Rows 4, 6, 8, 10, 12, 14: (P5, K5)5x, P5.
Rows 5, 7, 9, 11, 13: (O, K1, D3, K1, O, P5)5x, O, K1, D3, K1, O.
Row 15: (K1, D3, K1, P5)5x, D3, K1.
Row 16: (P3, K5)5x, P3.
Row 17: (D3, P5)5x, D3.
Row 18: Purl.

Repeat rows 3-16 of the Insert Pattern following the Wheat Ear Pattern.

Bisceglia Pattern

My good friend Jean Bisceglia in California has a trove of seven counterpanes knitted by her mother-in-law, Amalia, for her six children and first grandaughter. They are all beautiful, but the pattern in this one particularly intrigued me. Since I could not find written directions for it in any of my research, I set about deciphering it myself. For a while it had me stumped (see p. 16), but in the end patience and a lot of knitting and ripping prevailed. Although it is definitely not for the beginner, this two-needle pattern looks far more difficult than it actually is.

The fields of embossed bells on the reverse stockinette ground are formed by casting on and working extra stitches, which are then gradually decreased. The central band is made up of rows of eyelets separated by blocks of reverse stockinette stitch. In place of the original, elaborately crocheted border, I substituted an attractive knitted edging, which I found in the twentieth-century needlework magazine Needlecraft (see the bibliography, pp. 176-177).

Special Instructions:

AP1 *Abbreviated Pattern #1 is worked on the center 60 stitches of rows 75, 77, 79, 81, 83 and 85 as follows:*
[(O, LRD)6X, P12]2X, (O, LRD)6X.

AP2 *Abbreviated Pattern #2 is worked on the center 60 stitches of rows 76, 78, 80, 82, 84 and 86 as follows:*
(P12, K12)2X, P12.

Cast on 1 stitch.

Row 1: B1.
Row 2: K2.
Row 3: Slp, LCO, P1.
Row 4: Sl, K2.
Row 5: Slp, (LCO, P1)2x.
Row 6: Sl, K4.
Row 7: Slp, O, P3, O, P1.
Row 8: Sl, K6.
Row 9: Slp, O, P2, LCO6, P2tog, P1, O, P1.
Row 10: Sl, K3, P6, K4.
Row 11: Slp, O, P3, RLD, K2, LRD, P3, O, P1.
Row 12: Sl, K4, P4, K5.
Row 13: Slp, O, P4, RLD, LRD, P4, O, P1.
Row 14: Sl, K5, P2, K6.
Row 15: Slp, O, P5, RLD, P5, O, P1.
Row 16: Sl, K14.
Row 17: Slp, O, P3, LCO6, P2tog, P4, LCO6, P2tog, P2, O, P1.
Row 18: Sl, K4, (P6, K5)2x.
Row 19: Slp, O, P4, *RLD, K2, LRD*, P5, *-*, P4, O, P1.
Row 20: Sl, (K5, P4)2x, K6.

Row 21: Slp, O, P5, (RLD, LRD, P5)2x, O, P1.
Row 22: Sl, K6, P2, K5, P2, K7.
Row 23: Slp, O, P6, RLD, P5, LRD, P6, O, P1.
Row 24: Sl, K22.
Row 25: Slp, O, (P4, LCO6, P2tog)3x, P3, O, P1.
Row 26: Sl, (K5, P6)3x, K6.
Row 27: Slp, O, P5, (RLD, K2, LRD, P5)3x, O, P1.
Row 28: Sl, K6, (P4, K5)2x, P4, K7.
Row 29: Slp, O, P6, (RLD, LRD, P5)2x, RLD, LRD, P6, O, P1.
Row 30: Sl, K7, (P2, K5)2x, P2, K8.
Row 31: Slp, O, P7, (RLD, P5)2x, RLD, P7, O, P1.
Row 32: Sl, K30.
Row 33: Slp, O, P5, (LCO6, P2tog, P4)4x, O, P1.
Row 34: Sl, K6, (P6, K5)3x, P6, K7.

Row 35: Slp, O, P6, (RLD, K2, LRD, P5)3x, RLD, K2, LRD, P6, O, P1.
Row 36: Sl, K7, (P4, K5)3x, P4, K8.
Row 37: Slp, O, P7, (RLD, LRD, P5)3x, RLD, LRD, P7, O, P1.
Row 38: Sl, K8, (P2, K5)3x, P2, K9.
Row 39: Slp, O, P8, (RLD, P5)3x, RLD, P8, O, P1.
Row 40: Sl, K38.
Row 41: Slp, O, P6, (LCO6, P2tog, P4)4x, LCO6, P2tog, P5, O, P1.
Row 42: Sl, K7, (P6, K5)4x, P6, K8.
Row 43: Slp, O, P7, (RLD, K2, LRD, P5)4x, RLD, K2, LRD, P7, O, P1.
Row 44: Sl, K8, (P4, K5)4x, P4, K9.
Row 45: Slp, O, P8, (RLD, LRD, P5)4x, RLD, LRD, P8, O, P1.

The Bisceglia Pattern sample (shown three-quarter size) was knit with size 3 perle cotton on size 1 needles.

Row 46: Sl, K9, (P2, K5)4x, P2, K10.
Row 47: Slp, O, P9, (RLD, P5)4x, RLD, P9, O, P1.
Row 48: Sl, K46.
Row 49: Slp, O, P7, (LCO6, P2tog, P4)5x, LCO6, P2tog, P6, O, P1.
Row 50: Sl, K8, (P6, K5)5x, P6, K9.
Row 51: Slp, O, P8, (RLD, K2, LRD, P5)5x, RLD, K2, LRD, P8, O, P1.
Row 52: Sl, K9, (P4, K5)5x, P4, K10.
Row 53: Slp, O, P9, (RLD, LRD, P5)5x, RLD, LRD, P9, O, P1.
Row 54: Sl, K10, (P2, K5)5x, P2, K11.
Row 55: Slp, O, P10, (RLD, P5)5x, RLD, P10, O, P1.
Row 56: Sl, P54.
Row 57: Slp, O, K53, O, K1.
Row 58: Sl, (P2tog, O)27x, P2.
Row 59: Slp, O, K55, O, K1.
Row 60: Sl, P58.
Row 61: Slp, O, P57, O, P1.
Row 62: Sl, K60.
Row 63: Slp, O, P59, O, P1.
Row 64: Sl, P62.
Row 65: Slp, O, K61, O, K1.
Row 66: Sl, P64.
Row 67: Slp, O, P63, O, P1.
Row 68: Sl, K66.
Row 69: Slp, O, P65, O, P1.
Row 70: Sl, P68.
Row 71: Slp, O, K67, O, K1.
Row 72: Sl, (P2tog, O)34x, P2.
Row 73: Slp, K69, O, K1.
Row 74: Sl, P71.
Row 75: Divide stitches as follows, using markers: 6/12/12/12/12/12/6
Slp, O, P5, AP1, P5, O, P1.
Row 76: Sl, K6, AP2, K7.

Row 77: Slp, O, P6, AP1, P6, O, P1.
Row 78: Sl, K7, AP2, K8.
Row 79: Slp, O, P7, AP1, P7, O, P1.
Row 80: Sl, K8, AP2, K9.
Row 81: P2tog, P7, AP1, P7, P2tog.
Row 82: Sl, K7, AP2, K8.
Row 83: P2tog, P6, AP1, P6, P2tog.
Row 84: Sl, K6, AP2, K7.
Row 85: P2tog, P5, AP1, P5, P2tog.
Row 86: Sl, K5, AP2, K6.
Row 87: LRD, K68, RLD, remove markers.
Row 88: Sl, (P2tog, O)34x, P1.
Row 89: LRD, K66, RLD.
Row 90: Sl, P67.
Row 91: P2tog, P64, P2tog.
Row 92: Sl, K65.
Row 93: P2tog, P62, P2tog.
Row 94: Sl, P63.
Row 95: LRD, K60, RLD.
Row 96: Sl, P61.
Row 97: P2tog, P58, P2tog.
Row 98: Sl, K59.
Row 99: P2tog, P56, P2tog.
Row 100: Sl, P57.
Row 101: LRD, K54, RLD.
Row 102: Sl, (O, P2tog)27x, O, P1.
Row 103: LRD, K53, RLD.
Row 104: Sl, P54.
Row 105: P2tog, P10, (LCO6, P2tog, P4)5x, LCO6, P2tog, P9, P2tog.
Row 106: Sl, K10, (P6, K5)5x, P6, K11.
Row 107: P2tog, P9, (RLD, K2, LRD, P5)5x, RLD, K2, LRD, P9, P2tog.
Row 108: Sl, K9, (P4, K5)5x, P4, K10.
Row 109: P2tog, P8, (RLD, LRD, P5)5x, RLD, LRD, P8, P2tog.

Row 110: Sl, K8, (P2, K5)5x, P2, K9.
Row 111: P2tog, P7, (RLD, P5)5x, RLD, P7, P2tog.
Row 112: Sl, K46.
Row 113: P2tog, P9, (LCO6, P2tog, P4)4x, LCO6, P2tog, P8, P2tog.
Row 114: Sl, K9, (P6, K5)4x, P6, K10.
Row 115: P2tog, P8, (RLD, K2, LRD, P5)4x, RLD, K2, LRD, P8, P2tog.
Row 116: Sl, K8, (P4, K5)4x, P4, K9.
Row 117: P2tog, P7, (RLD, LRD, P5)4x, RLD, LRD, P7, P2tog.
Row 118: Sl, K7, (P2, K5)4x, P2, K8.
Row 119: P2tog, P6, (RLD, P5)4x, RLD, P6, P2tog.

Row 120: Sl, K38.
Row 121: P2tog, P8, (LCO6, P2tog, P4)3x, LCO6, P2tog, P7, P2tog.
Row 122: Sl, K8, (P6, K5)3x, P6, K9.
Row 123: P2tog, P7, (RLD, K2, LRD, P5)3x, RLD, K2, LRD, P7, P2tog.
Row 124: Sl, K7, (P4, K5)3x, P4, K8.
Row 125: P2tog, P6, (RLD, LRD, P5)3x, RLD, LRD, P6, P2tog.
Row 126: Sl, K6, (P2, K5)3x, P2, K7.
Row 127: P2tog, P5, (RLD, P5)3x, RLD, P5, P2tog.
Row 128: Sl, K30.
Row 129: P2tog, P7, (LCO6, P2tog, P4)2x, LCO6, P2tog, P6, P2tog.

Four units of the Bisceglia Pattern assembled into a square.

Row 130: Sl, K7, (P6, K5)2x, P6, K8.

Row 131: P2tog, P6, (RLD, K2, LRD, P5)2x, RLD, K2, LRD, P6, P2tog.

Row 132: Sl, K6, (P4, K5)2x, P4, K7.

Row 133: P2tog, P5, (RLD, LRD, P5)3x, P2tog.

Row 134: Sl, K5, (P2, K5)2x, P2, K6.

Row 135: P2tog, P4, (RLD, P5)2x, RLD, P4, P2tog.

Row 136: Sl, K22.

Row 137: P2tog, P6, LCO6, P2tog, P4, LCO6, P2tog, P5, P2tog.

Row 138: Sl, K1, (K5, P6)2x, K7.

Row 139: P2tog, P5, (RLD, K2, LRD, P5)2x, P2tog.

Row 140: Sl, (K5, P4)2x, K6.

Row 141: P2tog, P4, RLD, LRD, P5, RLD, LRD, P4, P2tog.

Row 142: Sl, K4, (P2, K5)2x.

Row 143: P2tog, P3, RLD, P5, RLD, P3, P2tog.

Row 144: Sl, K14.

Row 145: P2tog, P5, LCO6, P2tog, P4, P2tog.

Row 146: Sl, K5, P6, K6.

Row 147: P2tog, P4, RLD, K2, LRD, P4, P2tog.

Row 148: Sl, K4, P4, K5.

Row 149: P2tog, P3, RLD, LRD, P3, P2tog.

Row 150: Sl, K3, P2, K4.

Row 151: P2tog, P2, RLD, P2, P2tog.

Row 152: Sl, K6.

Row 153: P2tog, P3, P2tog.

Row 154: Sl, K4.

Row 155: P2tog, P1, P2tog.

Row 156: D3, fasten off.

Bisceglia Border

Cast on 21 stitches and knit 1 row.

Row 1 (front side): Slp, O, LRD, K7, (O, LRD)3x, O, K2, O2, LRD, K1.

Row 2: K3, P1, K17, O, LRD.

Row 3: Slp, O, LRD, K8, (O, LRD)3x, O, K6.

Row 4: K22, O, LRD.

Row 5: Slp, O, LRD, K9, (O, LRD)3x, O, K2, O2, LRD, O2, K2.

Row 6: K3, P1, K2, P1, K19, O, LRD.

Row 7: Slp, O, LRD, K10, (O, LRD)3x, O, K9.

Row 8: K27, O, LRD.

Row 9: Slp, O, LRD, K11, (O, LRD)3x, O, K2, (O2, LRD)3x, K1.

Row 10: K3, P1, (K2, P1)2x, K21, O, LRD.

Row 11: Slp, O, LRD, K12, (O, LRD)3x, O, K12.

Row 12: Cast off 7, K24, O, LRD.

Row 13: Slp, O, LRD, K13, (O, LRD)3x, O, K2, O2, LRD, K1.

Row 14: K3, P1, K23, O, LRD.

Row 15: Slp, O, LRD, K14, (O, LRD)3x, O, K6.

Row 16: K28, O, LRD.

Row 17: Slp, O, LRD, K15, (O, LRD)3x, O, K2, O2, LRD, O2, K2.

Row 18: K3, P1, K2, P1, K25, O, LRD.

Row 19: Slp, O, LRD, K31.

Row 20: K8, LRD, (O, LRD)4x, K14, O, LRD.

Row 21: Slp, O, LRD, K23, (O2, LRD)3x, K1.

Row 22: K3, P1, (K2, P1)2x, K1, LRD, (O, LRD)4x, K13, O, LRD.

Row 23: Slp, O, LRD, K32.

Row 24: Cast off 7, K3, LRD, (O, LRD)4x, K12, O, LRD.

Row 25: Slp, O, LRD, K21, O2, LRD, K1.

Row 26: K3, P1, K1, LRD, (O, LRD)4x, K11, O, LRD.

Row 27: Slp, O, LRD, K24.

Row 28: K5, LRD, (O, LRD)4x, K10, O, LRD.

Row 29: Slp, O, LRD, K19, O2, LRD, O2, K2.

Row 30: K3, P1, K2, P1, K1, LRD, (O, LRD)4x, K9, O, LRD.

Row 31: Slp, O, LRD, K25.

Row 32: K8, LRD, (O, LRD)4x, K8, O, LRD.

Row 33: Slp, O, LRD, K17, (O2, LRD)3x, K1.

Row 34: K3, P1, (K2, P1)2x, K1, LRD, (O, LRD)4x, K7, O, LRD.

Row 35: Slp, O, LRD, K26.

Row 36: Cast off 7, K3, LRD, K14, O, LRD.

Repeat rows 1-36 for desired length. Cast off remaining stitches.

The Bisceglia Border (shown half-size) was worked with size 3 perle cotton on size 1 needles.

Brompton Square

Brompton Square (shown three-quarter size) was knit on size 5 perle cotton on size 0 needles.

When visiting New Zealand in 1978, I was put in touch with a number of local knitters. One new friend in Christchurch, New Zealand, was a lovely lady named Jean Double, who showed me a counterpane knitted by her grandmother in the Brompton Square pattern. I have never seen another counterpane worked in this pattern, though I did later find directions for it in the nineteenth-century Weldon's Practical Knitter.

A good pattern for an intermediate knitter, the Brompton Square has as its most interesting feature a field of bells worked on a reverse stockinette ground. Unlike most bell patterns, this one is formed with paired decreases on the outer edge that slant down rather than up toward the center of the bell. I suggest using the Scalloped Edging (see p. 164) or the Frisby Edging (see p. 155) to complete the counterpane.

Cast on 1 stitch.

Row 1: KP1.
Row 2: O, P2.
Row 3: O, K3.
Row 4: O, K4.
Row 5: O, P5.
Row 6: O, K6.
Row 7: O, K7.
Row 8: O, P8.
Row 9: O, K9.
Row 10: O, K10.
Row 11: O, P11.
Row 12: O, K12.
Row 13: O, K13.
Row 14: O, P14.
Row 15: O, K1, (O, LRD)7x.
Row 16: O, P16.
Row 17: O, K17.
Row 18: O, K18.
Row 19: O, P19.
Row 20: O, K20.
Row 21: O, K21.
Row 22: O, P22.
Row 23: O, K23.
Row 24: O, K24.
Row 25: O, P25.
Row 26: O, K26.
Row 27: O, K27.
Row 28: O, P28.
Row 29: O, K1, (O, LRD)14x.
Row 30: O, P30.
Row 31: O, K31.
Row 32: O, K32.
Row 33: O, P33.
Row 34: O, K34.
Row 35: O, K35.
Row 36: O, P36.
Row 37: O, K37.
Row 38: O, K38.
Row 39: O, P39.
Row 40: O, K40.
Row 41: O, K41.
Row 42: O, P42.
Row 43: O, K1, (O, LRD)21x.
Row 44: O, P44.
Row 45: O, K45.

Row 46: O, K46.
Row 47: O, P47.
Row 48: O, K48.
Row 49: O, K49.
Row 50: O, P50.
Row 51: O, K51.
Row 52: O, K52.
Row 53: O, P1, P2tog, (LCO6, P4, P2tog)8x, LCO6, P2.
Row 54: O, K2, (P6, K5)8x, P6, K3.
Row 55: O, K1, P2, (*LRD, K2, RLD*, P5)8x, *-*, P3.
Row 56: O, K3, (P4, K5)8x, P4, K4.
Row 57: O, K1, P3, (LRD, RLD, P5)8x, LRD, RLD, P4.
Row 58: O, K4, (P2, K5)8x.
Row 59: O,P5, (LRD, P5)9x.
Row 60: O, K5, (P1, K5)9x, K1.

Row 61: O, P2, P2tog, (LCO6, P4, P2tog)9x, LCO6, P3.
Row 62: O, K3, (P6, K5)9x, P6, K4.
Row 63: O, P4, (*LRD, K2, RLD*, P5)9x, *-*, P4.
Row 64: O, K4, (P4, K5)10x.
Row 65: O, P5, (LRD, RLD, P5)10x.
Row 66: O, (K5, P2)10x, K6.
Row 67: O, P6, (LRD, P5)9x, LRD, P6.
Row 68: O, K6, (P1, K5)9x, P1, K7.
Row 69: O, P3, P2tog, (LCO6, P4, P2tog)10x, LCO6, P4.
Row 70: O, K4, (P6, K5)10x.
Row 71: O, P5, (LRD, K2, RLD, P5)11x.

Row 72: O, (K5, P4)11x, K6.
Row 73: O, P6, (LRD, RLD, P5)10x, LRD, RLD, P6.
Row 74: O, K6, (P2, K5)10x, P2, K7.
Row 75: O, P7, (LRD, P5)10x, LRD, P7.
Row 76: O, K7, (P1, K5)10x, P1, K8.
Row 77: O, K77.
Row 78: O, P78.
Row 79: O, K1, (O, LRD)39x.
Row 80: O, P80.
Row 81: O, K81.
Row 82: O, K82.
Row 83: O, P83.
Row 84: O, K84.

Cast off.

Four units of the Brompton Square pattern assembled into a square.

Bassett Pattern, Plain and Fancy

The Bassett Pattern samples (shown half-size) were worked with Antique Bedspread Cotton on size 0 needles.

These patterns are from a counterpane in the collection of The Brooklyn Museum. The original spread was made of plain lace units banded across the top by a single row of fancy raised-leaf squares. I have never seen another counterpane using this pattern, nor have I found directions for it. Thus I wrote my own instructions, which involved some experimentation to decipher the pattern's unusual faggoting stitch (see p. 16).

I find the leaf motif so compelling when completed that I suggest using it in a four-unit configuration. The plain pattern is much enhanced by the leaf pattern and should, I think, be used with it throughout the counterpane. The patterns can be combined in a variety of ways—in alternating horizontal, vertical or diagonal bands, for example, in alternating concentric squares, or in some more whimsical fashion.

The border pattern makes use of the banding in the main pattern units. A simple crocheted edge (p. 86) can be used to complete the border.

Plain Pattern

Cast on 1 stitch.

Row 1: O, K1.
Row 2: O, K2.
Row 3: O, K3.
Rows 4-19: Continue to work in established pattern as follows: O, K to end. At the completion of Row 19 there will be 20 stitches.
Row 20: O, K1, (O, LRD)9x, K1.

Note that throughout this pattern the (O, LRD)'s are worked on the back side of the piece.

Row 21 and all odd-numbered rows through Row 71: O, K to end.
Row 22: O, K1, (O, LRD) 10x, K1.
Row 24: O, K24.
Row 26: O, K12, O, LRD, K12.
Row 28: O, K12, (O, LRD)2x, K12.
Row 30: O, K12, (O, LRD)3x, K12.
Row 32: O, K12, (O, LRD)4x, K12.
Row 34 and all even-numbered rows through Row 66: O, K12, (O, LRD) 1 time more than on the previous even-numbered row, K12. On Row 66 (O, LRD) will be worked 21x.
Row 68: O, K2, (O, LRD)32x, K2.
Row 70: O, P70.
Row 72: O, K72.
Row 73: O, P73.
Row 74: O, K74.
Row 75: O, P75.
Row 76: LRD, K74.
Row 77: P2tog, P73.

Row 78: LRD, K72.
Row 79: LRD, K71.
Row 80: P2tog, P70.
Row 81: LRD, K69.
Row 82: LRD, K1 (O, LRD)33x, K1.
Row 83: LRD, K67.
Row 84: LRD, K1, (O, LRD)32x, K1.
Row 85: LRD, K65.
Row 86: P2tog, P64.
Row 87: LRD, K63.
Row 88: LRD, K62.
Row 89: P2tog, P61.
Row 90: LRD, K60.
Row 91: P2tog, P59.
Row 92: LRD, K58.
Row 93: P2tog, P57.
Row 94: LRD, K56.
Row 95: LRD, K55.
Row 96: P2tog, P54.
Row 97: LRD, K53.
Row 98: LRD, K1, (O, LRD)25x, K1.
Row 99: LRD, K51.
Row 100: P2tog, P50.
Row 101: LRD, K49.
Row 102: LRD, K48.
Row 103: P2tog, P47.

Row 104: LRD, K46.
Row 105: P2tog, P45.
Row 106: LRD, K44.
Row 107: P2tog, P43.
Row 108: LRD, K42.
Row 109: P2tog, P41.
Row 110: P2tog, P40.
Row 111: LRD, K39.
Row 112: LRD, K1, (O, LRD)18x, K1.
Row 113: LRD, K37.
Row 114: P2tog, P36.
Row 115: LRD, K35.
Row 116: LRD, K34.
Row 117: P2tog, P33.
Row 118: LRD, K32.
Row 119: P2tog, P31.
Row 120: LRD, K30.
Row 121: P2tog, P29.
Row 122: LRD, K28.
Row 123 and all odd-numbered rows through Row 145: LRD, K all remaining stitches.
Row 124: P2tog, P26.
Row 126: LRD, K1, (O, LRD)11x, K1.
Row 128: LRD, K1, (O, LRD)10x, K1.

Row 130: LRD, K1, (O, LRD)9x, K1.
Row 132 and all even-numbered rows through Row 144: LRD, K1, (O, LRD) 1 time less than on the previous even-numbered row.
Row 146: LRD, K1, O, LRD, K1.
Row 147: LRD, K3.
Row 148: LRD, K2.
Row 149: D3, fasten off.

Fancy Pattern

Cast on 1 stitch.

Row 1: O, K1.
Row 2: O, K2.
Row 3: (O, K1)3x.
Row 4: O, K1, P3, K2.
Row 5: O, K2, O, K3, O, K2.
Row 6: O, K2, P5, K3.
Row 7: O, K3, O, K5, O, K3.
Row 8: O, K3, P7, K4.
Row 9: O, K4, O, K7, O, K4.
Row 10: O, K4, P9, K5.

Left: four plain units assembled into a square. Right: four fancy units assembled into a square.

Row 11: O, K5, O, K9, O, K5.

Row 12: O, K5, P11, K6.

Row 13: O, K6, O, K11, O, K6.

Row 14: O, K6, P13, K7.

Row 15: O, K7, O, K13, O, K7.

Row 16: O, K7, P15, K8.

Row 17: O, K31.

Row 18: O, K8, P15, K9.

Row 19 and all odd-numbered rows through Row 29: O, K remaining stitches.

Row 20: O, K9, P15, K10.

Row 22: O, K10, P15, K11.

Row 24: O, K11, P15, K12.

Row 26: O, K12, P15, K13 .

Row 28: O, K13, P15, K14.

Row 30: O, K14, P15, K15.

Row 31: O, K15, RLD, K28.

Row 32: O, K15, P2tog, P12, K16.

Row 33: O, K16, RLD, K27.

Row 34: O, K16, P2tog, P10, K17.

Row 35: O, K17, RLD, K26.

Row 36: O, K17, P2tog, P8, K18.

Row 37: O, K18, RLD, K25.

Row 38: O, K18, P2tog, P6, K19.

Row 39: O, K19, RLD, K24.

Row 40: O, K19, P2tog, P4, K20.

Row 41: O, K20, RLD, K23.

Row 42: O, K20, P2tog, P2, K21.

Row 43: O, K21, RLD, K22.

Row 44: O, K21, (O, LRD)2x, K20.

Row 45: O, K46.

Row 46: O, K21, (O, LRD)3x, K20.

Row 47 and all odd-numbered rows through Row 67: O, K remaining stitches.

Row 48: O, K21, (O, LRD)4x, K20.

Row 50: O, K21, (O, LRD)5x, K20.

Row 52 and all even-numbered rows through Row 60: O, K21, (O, LRD) 1 time more than on the previous even-numbered row, K20. On Row 60, (O, LRD) will be worked 10x.

Row 62: O, K1, (O, LRD)31x.

Row 64: O, K1, (O, LRD)32x.

Row 66: O, K1, (O, LRD)33x.

Row 68: O, P69.

Row 69: O, K70.

Row 70: O, K71.

Row 71: O, P72.

Row 72: O, K73.

Row 73: O, P74.

Row 74: O, K75.

Row 75: O, K76.

Row 76: O, P77.

Row 77: O, K78.

Row 78: O, K1, (O, LRD)39x.

Row 79: RLD, K78.

Row 80: RLD, (O, LRD)38x, K1.

Row 81: RLD, K76.

Row 82: P2tog, P75.

Row 83: RLD, K74.

Row 84: RLD, K73.

Row 85: P2tog, P72.

Row 86: RLD, K71.

Row 87: RLD, (O, LRD)35x.

Row 88: RLD, K69.

Row 89: P2tog, P68.

Row 90: RLD, K67.

Row 91: RLD, K66.

Row 92: P2tog, P65.

Row 93: RLD, K64.

Row 94: RLD, (O, LRD)31x, K1.

Row 95: RLD, K62.

Row 96: RLD, (O, LRD)30x, K1.

Row 97: RLD, K60.

Row 98: RLD, (O, LRD)29x, K1.

Row 99: RLD, K58.

Row 100: P2tog, P57.

Row 101: RLD, K56.

Row 102: RLD, K55.

Row 103: P2tog, P54.

Row 104: RLD, K53.

Row 105: RLD, (O, LRD)26x.

Row 106: RLD, K51.

Row 107: P2tog, P50.

Row 108: RLD, K49.

Row 109: RLD, K48.

Row 110: P2tog, P47.

Row 111: RLD, K46.

Row 112: RLD, (O, LRD)22x, K1.

Row 113: RLD, K44.

Row 114: RLD, (O, LRD)21x, K1.

Row 115: RLD, K42.

Row 116: P2tog, P41.

Row 117: RLD, K40.

Row 118: RLD, K39.

Row 119: P2tog, P38.

Row 120: RLD, K37.

Row 121: RLD, K36.

Row 122: P2tog, P35.

Row 123: RLD, K34.

Row 124: RLD, (O, LRD)16x, K1.

Row 125: RLD, K32.

Row 126: RLD, (O, LRD)15x, K1.

Row 127: RLD, K30.

Row 128: RLD, (O, LRD)14x, K1.

Row 129: RLD, K28.

Row 130: P2tog, P27.

Row 131: RLD, K26.

Row 132: RLD, K25.

Row 133: P2tog, P24.

Row 134: RLD, K23.

Row 135: RLD, K22.

Row 136: P2tog, P21.

Row 137: RLD, K20.

Row 138: RLD, (O, LRD)9x, K1.

Row 139 and all odd-numbered rows through Row 153: RLD, K remaining stitches.

Row 140: RLD, (O, LRD)8x, K1.

Row 142: RLD, (O, LRD)7x, K1.

Row 144 and all even-numbered rows through Row 152: RLD, (O, LRD) 1 time less than on the previous even-numbered row, K1.

Row 154: RLD, O, LRD, K1.

Row 155: RLD, K2.

Row 156: D3, fasten off.

Bassett Border

Special Instructions:

Because this border has mitered corners, it must fit the counterpane exactly. To make the border easier to work with and fit more accurately, it is divided into four right-angle segments, which are seamed at the corners and in the middle of the straight sections. A left and a right miter, each followed by a length of the straight section, make up the four right-angle segments. For information on joining the segments, see p. 14.

LEFT MITER

Cast on 2 stitches.

Row 1: O, P2.
Row 2: K3.
Row 3: O, P3.
Row 4: K4.
Row 5: O, P4.
Row 6: K5.
Row 7: O, P5.
Row 8: P6.
Row 9: O, K6.
Row 10: P7.
Row 11: O, K7.
Row 12: P8.
Row 13: O, K8.
Row 14: P9.
Row 15: O, P9.
Row 16: K10.
Row 17: O, P10.
Row 18: K11.
Row 19: O, P11.
Row 20: K12.
Row 21: O, P12.
Row 22: P13.
Row 23: O, K13.
Row 24: K1, (O,LRD)6x, K1.
Row 25: O, K14.
Row 26: K2, (O, LRD)6x, K1.
Row 27: O, K15.
Row 28: P16.
Row 29: O, K16.
Row 30: K17.
Row 31: O, P17.
Row 32: K18.
Row 33: O, P18.
Row 34: K19.
Row 35: O, P19.
Row 36: K20.
Row 37: O, K20.
Row 38: P21.
Row 39: O, K21.
Row 40: P22.
Row 41: O, K22.
Row 42: K23.
Row 43: O, P23.
Row 44: K24.
Row 45: O, P24.
Row 46: K25.
Row 47: O, P25.
Row 48: K26.
Row 49: O, K26.
Row 50: P27.
Row 51: O, K27.
Row 52: K1, (O, LRD)13x, K1.
Row 53: O, K28.
Row 54: K2, (O, LRD)13x, K1.
Row 55: O, K29.
Row 56: P30.
Row 57: O, K30.
Row 58: K31.
Row 59: O, P31.
Row 60: K32.
Row 61: O, P32.
Row 62: K33.
Row 63: O, P33.
Row 64: K34.
Row 65: O, K34.
Row 66: P35.
Row 67: O, K35.
Row 68: P36.
Row 69: O, K36.
Row 70: K37.
Row 71: O, P37.
Row 72: K38.
Row 73: O, P38.
Row 74: K39.
Row 75: O, P39.
Row 76: K40.
Row 77: O, K40.
Row 78: P41.

A mitered and seamed corner of the border (shown half-size), knit with Antique Bedspread Cotton on size 0 needles (seam in middle of straight sections not shown in photo). The crocheted edging was worked with a B/1 (2mm) crochet hook.

Row 79: O, K41.
Row 80: K1, (O, LRD)20x, K1.
Row 81: O, K42.
Row 82: K2, (O, LRD)20x, K1.
Row 83: O, K43.
Row 84: P44.
Row 85: O, K44.
Row 86: K45.
Row 87: O, P45.
Row 88: K46.
Row 89: O, P46.
Row 90: K47.
Row 91: O, P47.
Row 92: K48.

Do not cast off.

These 92 rows finish the left miter. Complete this segment with a length of the the straight section.

RIGHT MITER

Cast on 2 stitches.

Row 1: P1, B1.
Row 2: K3.
Row 3: P2, B1.
Row 4: K4.
Row 5: P3, B1.
Row 6: K5.
Row 7: P4, B1.
Row 8: P6.
Row 9: K5, B1.
Row 10: P7.
Row 11: K6, B1.
Row 12: P8.
Row 13: K7, B1.
Row 14: P9.
Row 15: P8, B1.
Row 16: K10.
Row 17: P9, B1.
Row 18: K11.
Row 19: P10, B1.
Row 20: K12.
Row 21: P11, B1.
Row 22: P13.

Row 23: K12, B1.
Row 24: K1, (O, LRD)6x, K1.
Row 25: K13, B1.
Row 26: K1, (O, LRD)6x, K2.
Row 27: K14, B1.
Row 28: P16.
Row 29: K15, B1.
Row 30: K17.
Row 31: P16, B1.
Row 32: K18.
Row 33: P17, B1.
Row 34: K19.
Row 35: P18, B1.
Row 36: K20.
Row 37: P19, B1.
Row 38: P21.
Row 39: K20, B1.
Row 40: P22.
Row 41: K21, B1.
Row 42: K23.
Row 43: P22, B1.
Row 44: K24.
Row 45: P23, B1.
Row 46: K25.
Row 47: P24, B1.
Row 48: K26.
Row 49: K25, B1.
Row 50: P27.
Row 51: K26, B1.
Row 52: K1, (O, LRD)13x, K1.
Row 53: K27, B1.
Row 54: K1, (O, LRD)13x, K2.
Row 55: K28, B1.
Row 56: P30.
Row 57: K29, B1.
Row 58: K31.
Row 59: P30, B1.
Row 60: K32.
Row 61: P31, B1.
Row 62: K33.
Row 63: P32, B1.
Row 64: K34.
Row 65: K33, B1.
Row 66: P35.
Row 67: K34, B1.
Row 68: P36.
Row 69: K35, B1.

Row 70: K37.
Row 71: P36, B1.
Row 72: K38.
Row 73: P37, B1.
Row 74: K39.
Row 75: P38, B1.
Row 76: K40.
Row 77: K39, B1.
Row 78: P41.
Row 79: K40, B1.
Row 80: K1, (O, LRD)20x, K1.
Row 81: K41, B1.
Row 82: K1, (O, LRD)20x, K2.
Row 83: K42, B1.

Row 84: K44.
Row 85: K43, B1.
Row 86: K45.
Row 87: P44, B1.
Row 88: K46.
Row 89: P45, B1.
Row 90: K47.
Row 91: P46, B1.
Row 92: K48.

Do not cast off.

These 92 rows finish the right miter of the border. Complete this segment with a length of the straight section.

Bassett Border, Straight Section

Special Instructions:
Work this pattern for the straight section of the border following the left and right miters. Knit the section to half the length of the counterpane side in question. The section will eventually be seamed to the corresponding leg on the adjacent right-angle segment.

There are 48 stitches on the needle.

Row 1: K48.
Row 2: P48.
Row 3: Knit.
Row 4: Purl.
Row 5: Knit.
Rows 6-10: Repeat rows 1-5.
Row 11: Purl.
Rows 12 and 13: Knit.
Row 14: Purl.
Row 15: Knit.
Row 16: K1, (O, LRD)23x, K1.
Row 17: Knit.
Row 18: K2, (O, LRD)23x.
Row 19: Knit.
Row 20: Purl.

Row 21: Knit.
Rows 22-26: Repeat rows 1-5.
Row 27: Purl.
Row 28: Knit.

Repeat rows 1-28 for desired length; cast off.

Crocheted Edging

Work 1 single crochet in each of first 2 stitches at beginning edge. *In next stitch, work 4 double crochet stitches, then work 1 single crochet in each of the next 3 stitches.* Repeat from * along entire edge.

Wheat Ears

I have never seen a counterpane knitted in this handsome pattern, which I found in the nineteenth-century Weldon's Practical Knitter. *This two-needle pattern is not very difficult, using yarn-overs and triple decreases for the wheat ears and a slip-knit pattern for the surrounding bands.*

The insert and lace edging patterns are from the nineteenth-century Weldon's Practical Shilling Guide to Fancy Work. *If worked in a heavier weight of cotton or in wool, the Wheat Ears pattern would make a perfect pillow cover. This might also be a good pattern to work in one or more colors.*

The Wheat Ears samples (shown half-size) were knit with Wondersheen Cotton on size 0 needles.

Special Instructions:
Slpf   *Slip stitch purlwise, holding yarn to front.*

Cast on 2 stitches.

Row 1: B1, K1.
Row 2: P3.
Row 3: B1, (O, K1)2x.
Row 4: B1, P3, K2.
Row 5: B1, P1, O, K3, O, P2.
Row 6: B1, K1, P5, K3.
Row 7: B1, P2, O, K1, D3, K1, O, P3.
Row 8: B1, K2, P5, K4.
Row 9: B1, P3, O, K1, D3, K1, O, P4.
Row 10: B1, K3, P5, K5.
Row 11: B1, P4, O, K1, D3, K1, O, P5.
Row 12: B1, K4, P5, K6.
Row 13: B1, P5, O, K1, D3, K1, O, P6.
Row 14: B1, K5, P5, K7.
Row 15: B1, P6, O, K1, D3, K1, O, P7.
Row 16: B1, K6, P5, K8.
Row 17: B1, P7, O, K1, D3, K1, O, P8.
Row 18: B1, K7, P5, K9.
Row 19: B1, P8, O, K1, D3, K1, O, P9.
Row 20: B1, K8, P5, K10.
Row 21: B1, P9, K1, D3, K1, P10.
Row 22: B1, K9, P3, K11.
Row 23: B1, P10, D3, P11.
Row 24: B1, P23.
Row 25: K1, O, K24.
Row 26: P1, O, P25.
Row 27: P1, O, P26.
Row 28: K1, O, K27.
Row 29: P1, O, P28.
Row 30: P1, O, P29.
Row 31: K1, O, K30.
Row 32: B1, P31.
Row 33: B1, (Slpf, P1)16x.
Row 34: KP1, P33.
Row 35: B1, (Slpf, P1)17x.

Row 36: KP1, P35.
Row 37: B1, (Slpf, P1)18x.
Row 38: KP1, P37.
Row 39: B1, (Slpf, P1)19x.
Row 40: KP1, P39.
Row 41: B1, (Slpf, P1)20x.
Row 42: KP1, P41.
Row 43: B1, (Slpf, P1)21x.
Row 44: KP1, P43.
Row 45: KP1, K44.
Row 46: KP1, P45.
Row 47: KP1, P46.
Row 48: KP1, P47.
Row 49: KP1, P48.
Row 50: KP1, P49.
Row 51: KP1, K50.
Row 52: KP1, P51.
Row 53: KP1, P1, (O, K1, O, P5)8x, O, K1, O, P2.
Row 54: KP1, K1, (P3, K5)8x, P3, K3.
Row 55: KP1, P2, (O, K3, O, P5)8x, O, K3, O, P3.
Row 56: KP1, K2, (P5, K5)8x, P5, K4.
Row 57: KP1, P3, (O, K1, D3, K1, O, P5)8x, O, K1, D3, K1, O, P4.
Row 58: KP1, K3, (P5, K5)9x.
Row 59: KP1, P4, (O, K1, D3, K1, O, P5)8x, O, K1, D3, K1, O, P5.
Row 60: KP1, K4, (P5, K5)8x, P5, K6.
Row 61: KP1, P5, (O, K1, D3, K1, O, P5)8x, O, K1, D3, K1, O, P6.
Row 62: KP1, K5, (P5, K5)8x, P5, K7.
Row 63: KP1, P6, (O, K1, D3, K1, O, P5)8x, O, K1, D3, K1, O, P7.
Row 64: KP1, K6, (P5, K5)8x, P5, K8.

Row 65: KP1, P7, (O, K1, D3, K1, O, P5)8x, O, K1, D3, K1, O, P8.
Row 66: KP1, K7, (P5, K5)8x, P5, K9.
Row 67: KP1, P8, (O, K1, D3, K1, O, P5)8x, O, K1, D3, K1, O, P9.
Row 68: KP1, K8, (P5, K5)8x, P5, K10.
Row 69: KP1, P9, (K1, D3, K1, P5)8x, K1, D3, K1, P10.
Row 70: KP1, K9, (P3, K5)8x, P3, K11.
Row 71: KP1, P10, (D3, P5)8x, D3, P11.
Row 72: KP1, P71.
Row 73: KP1, K72.
Row 74: KP1, P73.
Row 75: KP1, P74.
Row 76: KP1, K75.
Row 77: KP1, P76.
Row 78: KP1, P77.
Row 79: KP1, K78.
Row 80: KP1, P79.
Row 81: KP1, (Slpf, P1)40x.
Row 82: KP1, P81.
Row 83: KP1, (Slpf, P1)41x.
Row 84: KP1, P83.
Row 85: KP1, (Slpf, P1)42x.
Row 86: KP1, P85.
Row 87: KP1, (Slpf, P1)43x.
Row 88: KP1, P87.
Row 89: KP1, (Slpf, P1)44x.
Row 90: KP1, P89.
Row 91: KP1, (Slpf, P1)45x.
Row 92: KP1, P91.
Row 93: P2tog, P1, (Slpf, P1)45x.
Row 94: P2tog, P90.
Row 95: P2tog, P1, (Slpf, P1)44x.
Row 96: P2tog, P88.
Row 97: P2tog, P1, (Slpf, P1)43x.
Row 98: P2tog, P86.
Row 99: P2tog, P1, (Slpf, P1)42x.
Row 100: P2tog, P84.

Row 101: P2tog, P1, (Slpf, P1)41x.
Row 102: P2tog, P82.
Row 103: P2tog, P1, (Slpf, P1)40x.
Row 104: P2tog, P80.
Row 105: LRD, K79.
Row 106: P2tog, P78.
Row 107: P2tog, P77.
Row 108: LRD, K76.
Row 109: P2tog, P75.
Row 110: P2tog, P74.
Row 111: LRD, K73.
Row 112: P2tog, P72.
Row 113: P2tog, P10, (O, K1, O, P5)8x, O, K1, O, P12.
Row 114: LRD, K10, (P3, K5)8x, P3, K11.
Row 115: P2tog, P9, (O, K3, O, P5)8x, O, K3, O, P11.
Row 116: LRD, K9, (P5, K5)8x, P5, K10.
Row 117: P2tog, P8, (O, K1, D3, K1, O, P5)8x, O, K1, D3, K1, O, P10.
Row 118: LRD, K8, (P5, K5)8x, P5, K9.
Row 119: P2tog, P7, (O, K1, D3, K1, O, P5)8x, O, K1, D3, K1, O, P9.
Row 120: LRD, K7, (P5, K5)8x, P5, K8.
Row 121: P2tog, P6, (O, K1, D3, K1, O, P5)8x, O, K1, D3, K1, O, P8.
Row 122: LRD, K6, (P5, K5)8x, P5, K7.
Row 123: P2tog, P5, (O, K1, D3, K1, O, P5)8x, O, K1, D3, K1, O, P7.
Row 124: LRD, K5, (P5, K5)8x, P5, K6.
Row 125: P2tog, P4, (O, K1, D3, K1, O, P5)8x, O, K1, D3, K1, O, P6.
Row 126: LRD, K4, (P5, K5)9x.
Row 127: P2tog, P3, (O, K1, D3, K1, O, P5)9x.

Row 128: LRD, K3, (P5, K5)8x, P5, K4.
Row 129: P2tog, P2, (K1, D3, K1, P5)8x, K1, D3, K1, P4.
Row 130: LRD, K2, (P3, K5)8x, P3, K3.
Row 131: P2tog, P1, (D3, P5)8x, D3, P3.
Row 132: P2tog, P52.
Row 133: LRD, K51.
Row 134: P2tog, P50.
Row 135: P2tog, P49.
Row 136: LRD, K48.
Row 137: P2tog, P47.
Row 138: P2tog, P46.
Row 139: LRD, K45.
Row 140: P2tog, P44.
Row 141: P2tog, P1, (Slpf, P1)21x.
Row 142: P2tog, P42.
Row 143: P2tog, P1, (Slpf, P1)20x.
Row 144: P2tog, P40.
Row 145: P2tog, P1, (Slpf, P1)19x.
Row 146: P2tog, P38.
Row 147: P2tog, P1, (Slpf, P1)18x.
Row 148: P2tog, P36.
Row 149: P2tog, P1, (Slpf, P1)17x.
Row 150: P2tog, P34.
Row 151: P2tog, P1, (Slpf, P1)16x.
Row 152: P2tog, P32.
Row 153: LRD, K31.
Row 154: P2tog, P30.
Row 155: P2tog, P29.
Row 156: LRD, K28.
Row 157: P2tog, P27.
Row 158: P2tog, P26.
Row 159: LRD, K25.
Row 160: P2tog, P24.
Row 161: P2tog, P10, O, K1, O, P12.
Row 162: LRD, K10, P3, K11.
Row 163: P2tog, P9, O, K3, O, P11.

Row 164: LRD, K9, P5, K10.
Row 165: P2tog, P8, O, K1, D3, K1, O, P10.
Row 166: LRD, K8, P5, K9.
Row 167: P2tog, P7, O, K1, D3, K1, O, P9.
Row 168: LRD, K7, P5, K8.
Row 169: P2tog, P6, O, K1, D3, K1, O, P8.
Row 170: LRD, K6, P5, K7.
Row 171: P2tog, P5, O, K1, D3, K1, O, P7.
Row 172: LRD, K5, P5, K6.
Row 173: P2tog, P4, O, K1, D3, K1, O, P6.
Row 174: LRD, K4, P5, K5.
Row 175: P2tog, P3, O, K1, D3, K1, O, P5.
Row 176: LRD, K3, P5, K4.
Row 177: P2tog, P2, K1, D3, K1, P4.
Row 178: LRD, K2, P3, K3.
Row 179: P2tog, P1, D3, P3.
Row 180: LRD, K4.
Row 181: P2tog, P3.
Row 182: LRD, K2.
Row 183: P2tog, P1.
Row 184: LRD, fasten off.

Four units of Wheat Ears assembled into a square.

Wheat Ears Insert

Cast on 38 stitches. Knit 2 rows.

Row 1: K2, O, LRD, K34.
Row 2: P35, O, LRD, K1.
Row 3: Repeat Row 1.
Row 4: Repeat Row 2.
Row 5: K2, O, LRD, P4, (O, K1, O, P5)5x.
Row 6: K5, (P3, K5)5x, O, LRD, K1.
Row 7: K2, O, LRD, P4, (O, K3, O, P5)5x.
Rows 8, 10, 12, 14, 16, 18, 20: K5, (P5, K5)5x, O, LRD, K1.
Rows 9, 11, 13, 15, 17, 19: K2, O, LRD, P4, (O, K1, D3, K1, O, P5)5x.
Row 21: K2, O, LRD, P4, (K1, D3, K1, P5)5x.
Row 22: Repeat Row 6.
Row 23: K2, O, LRD, P4, (D3, P5)5x.
Row 24: Repeat Row 2.
Row 25: Repeat Row 1.
Row 26: Repeat Row 2.
Row 27: K2, O, LRD, P34.
Row 28: K35, O, LRD, K1.

Row 29: Repeat Row 27.
Row 30: Repeat Row 2.
Row 31: Repeat Row 1.
Row 32: Repeat Row 2.
Row 33: K2, O, LRD, (P1, Slpf)16x, P2.
Rows 34, 36, 38, 40, 42, 44: Repeat Row 2.
Row 35: K2, O, LRD, (Slpf, P1)17x.
Row 37: Repeat Row 33.
Row 39: Repeat Row 35.
Row 41: Repeat Row 33.
Row 43: Repeat Row 35.
Row 45: Repeat Row 1.
Row 46: Repeat Row 2.
Row 47: Repeat Row 27.
Row 48: Repeat Row 28.
Row 49: Repeat Row 27.
Row 50: Repeat Row 2.
Row 51: Repeat Row 1.
Row 52: Repeat Row 2.

Repeat rows 5-52 for desired length.

Lace Edging

Cast on 9 stitches.

Row 1: Sl, K4, O, LRD, K2.
Row 2: K4, (O, LRD)2x, K1.
Row 3: Sl, K1, (K1, P1 into O), K2, O, LRD, K2.
Row 4: K4, O, LRD, K4.
Row 5: Sl, K5, O, LRD, K2.
Row 6: K4, O, LRD, O, K1, O, LRD, K1.
Row 7: Sl, [K1, (K1, P1 into O)]2x, K2, O, LRD, K2.
Row 8: K4, O, LRD, K7.
Row 9: Sl, K8, O, LRD, K2.
Row 10: K4, (O, LRD)4x, K1.
Row 11: Sl, [K1, (K1, P1 into O)]3x, K2, O, LRD, K2.
Row 12: K4, O, LRD, K10.
Row 13: Cast off 7 stitches, K4, O, LRD, K2.

Repeat rows 2-13 for desired length.

Dunraven Square

I first saw this lovely pattern in 1978 in a counterpane covering a bed in Margaret Murray's house in Melbourne, Australia. Shortly afterward, I found the same pattern in a spread at Alberton, the historic Auckland, New Zealand, home of pioneering Auckland farmer and businessman Allan Kerr Taylor. In 1984, I again came across this pattern in the collection of the Welsh Folk Museum in St. Fagans, Cardiff, Wales.

I found the instructions for this somewhat difficult two-needle pattern in several nineteenth-century needlework magazines. The pattern begins with the raised-leaf motif, worked on a reverse stockinette ground. Bands of faggoting separate the raised leaves from the central band of knobs, and this central band from the cluster of knobs ending the unit. The border pattern, combining the raised leaves and knobs with a lace edging, would work well to complete other main patterns and would be a perfect trimming for towels.

Dunraven Square (shown three-quarter size) was knit with Wondersheen Cotton on size 0 needles.

Cast on 1 stitch.

Row 1: K1, P1, K1, into cast-on stitch.

Row 2: Sl, K2.

Row 3: Sl, (K1, P1, K1, in next stitch), K1.

Row 4: Sl, K4.

Row 5: Sl, (K1, O)2x, K2.

Row 6: Sl, K6.

Row 7: Sl, (K1, O)4x, K2.

Row 8: Sl, K3, P3, K4.

Row 9: Sl, K1, *O, P2, O*, K3, *-*, K2.

Row 10: Sl, K4, P5, K5.

Row 11: Sl, K1, *O, P3, O*, K5, *-*, K2.

Row 12: Sl, K5, P7, K6.

Row 13: Sl, K1, *O, P4, O*, K7, *-*, K2.

Row 14: Sl, K6, P9, K7.

Row 15: Sl, K1, O, P5, K3, D3, K3, P5, O, K2.

Row 16: Sl, K7, P7, K8.

Row 17: Sl, K1, O, P2, *O, K1, O*, P3, K2, D3, K2, P3, *-*, P2, O, K2.

Row 18: Sl, K4, P3, K3, P5, K3, P3, K5.

Row 19: Sl, K1, O, *P3, O, K3, O, P3*, K1, D3, K1, *-*, O, K2.

Row 20: Sl, K5, P5, K3, P3, K3, P5, K6.

Row 21: Sl, K1, O, P4, *O, K5, O*, P3, D3, P3, *-*, P4, O, K2.

Row 22: Sl, K6, P7, K3, P1, K3, P7, K7.

Row 23: Sl, K1, *O, P5, O*, K7, O, P3, K1, P3, O, K7, *-*, K2.

Row 24: Sl, K7, P9, K3, P1, K3, P9, K8.

Row 25: Sl, K1, O, P6, *K3, D3, K3*, P3, K1, P3, *-*, P6, O, K2.

Row 26: Sl, K8, P7, K3, P1, K3, P7, K9.

Row 27: Sl, K1, O, P3, (O, K1, O, P3, K2, D3, K2, P3)2x, O, K1, O, P3, O, K2.

Row 28: Sl, K5, (P3, K3, P5, K3)2x, P3, K6.

Row 29: Sl, K1, O, P4, (O, K3, O, P3, K1, D3, K1, P3)2x, O, K3, O, P4, O, K2.

Row 30: Sl, K6, (P5, K3, P3, K3)2x, P5, K7.

Row 31: Sl, K1, O, P5, (O, K5, O, P3, D3, P3)2x, O, K5, O, P5, O, K2.

Row 32: Sl, K7, (P7, K3, P1, K3)2x, P7, K8.

Row 33: Sl, K1, O, P6, (O, K7, O, P3, K1, P3)2x, O, K7, O, P6, O, K2.

Row 34: Sl, K8, (P9, K3, P1, K3)2x, P9, K9.

Row 35: Sl, K1, O, P7, (K3, D3, K3, P3, K1, P3)2x, K3, D3, K3, P7, O, K2.

Row 36: Sl, K9, (P7, K3, P1, K3)2x, P7, K10.

Row 37: Sl, K1, O, P4, (O, K1, O, P3, K2, D3, K2, P3)3x, O, K1, O, P4, O, K2.

Row 38: Sl, K6, P3, (K3, P5, K3, P3)3x, K7.

Row 39: Sl, K1, O, P5, (O, K3, O, P3, K1, D3, K1, P3)3x, O, K3, O, P5, O, K2.

Row 40: Sl, K7, P5, (K3, P3, K3, P5)3x, K8.

Row 41: Sl, K1, O, P6, (O, K5, O, P3, D3, P3)3x, O, K5, O, P6, O, K2.

Row 42: Sl, K8, P7, (K3, P1, K3, P7)3x, K9.

Row 43: Sl, K1, O, P7, (O, K7, O, P3, K1, P3)3x, O, K7, O, P7, O, K2.

Row 44: Sl, K9, P9, (K3, P1, K3, P9)3x, K10.

Row 45: Sl, K1, O, P8, (K3, D3, K3, P3, K1, P3)3x, K3, D3, K3, P8, O, K2.

Row 46: Sl, K10, P7, (K3, P1, K3, P7)3x, K11.

Row 47: Sl, K1, O, P9, (K2, D3, K2, P3, K1, P3)3x, K2, D3, K2, P9, O, K2.

Row 48: Sl, K11, P5, (K3, P1, K3, P5)3x, K12.

Row 49: Sl, K1, O, P10, (K1, D3, K1, P3, K1, P3)3x, K1, D3, K1, P10, O, K2.

Row 50: Sl, K12, P3, (K3, P1, K3, P3)3x, K13.

Row 51: Sl, K1, O, P11, (D3, P3, K1, P3)3x, D3, P11, O, K2.

Row 52: Sl, K13, P1, (K3, P1)6x, K14. Cluster of leaves completed.

Row 53: Sl, K1, O, K49, O, K2.

Row 54: Sl, K1, P51, K2.

Row 55: Sl, K1, O, K2, (O, LRD)24x, K1, O, K2.

Row 56: Sl, K1, P53, K2.

Four units of the Dunraven pattern assembled into a square.

Row 57: Sl, K1, O, K53, O, K2.

Row 58: Sl, K58.

Row 59: Sl, K1, O, P55, O, K2.

Row 60: Sl, K60.

Row 61: Sl, K1, O, P57, O, K2.

Row 62: Sl, K62.

Row 63: Sl, K1, O, (P5, Knob)9x, P5, O, K2.

Row 64: Sl, K64.

Row 65: Sl, K1, O, P61, O, K2.

Row 66: Sl, K66.

Row 67: Sl, K1, O, P63, O, K2.

Row 68: Sl, K68.

Row 69: Sl, K1, (P5, Knob)10x, P5, K2.

Row 70: Sl, K68.

Row 71: Sl, RLD, O, P2tog, P59, P2tog, O, LRD, K1.

Row 72: Sl, K66.

Row 73: Sl, RLD, O, P2tog, P57, P2tog, O, LRD, K1.

Row 74: Sl, K64.

Row 75: Sl, RLD, O, P2tog, P3, (Knob, P5)8x, Knob, P3, P2tog, O, LRD, K1.

Row 76: Sl, K62.

Row 77: Sl, RLD, O, P2tog, P53, P2tog, O, LRD, K1.

Row 78: Sl, K60.

Row 79: Sl, RLD, O, P2tog, P51, P2tog, O, LRD, K1.

Row 80: Sl, K58.

Row 81: Sl, RLD, O, LRD, K49, LRD, O, LRD, K1.

Row 82: Sl, K1, P53, K2.

Row 83: Sl, RLD, O, K3tog, (O, LRD)24x, O, LRD, K1.

Row 84: Sl, K1, P51, K2.

Row 85: Sl, RLD, O, LRD, K45, LRD, O, LRD, K1.

Row 86: Sl, K52.

Row 87: Sl, RLD, O, P2tog, P43, P2tog, O, LRD, K1.

Row 88: Sl, K50.

Row 89: Sl, RLD, O, LRD, K41, LRD, O, LRD, K1.

Row 90: Sl, K1, P45, K2.

Row 91: Sl, RLD, O, P2tog, P39, P2tog, O, LRD, K1.

Row 92: Sl, K46.

Row 93: Sl, RLD, O, LRD, K37, LRD, O, LRD, K1.

Row 94: Sl, K1, P41, K2.

Row 95: Sl, RLD, O, LRD, K35, LRD, O, LRD, K1.

Row 96: Sl, K42.

Row 97: Sl, RLD, O, P2tog, P33, P2tog, O, LRD, K1.

Row 98: Sl, K40.

Row 99: Sl, RLD, O, P2tog, P31, P2tog, O, LRD, K1.

Row 100: Sl, K38.

Row 101: Sl, RLD, O, P2tog, P14, Knob, P14, P2tog, O, LRD, K1.

Row 102: Sl, K36.

Row 103: Sl, RLD, O, P2tog, P27, P2tog, O, LRD, K1.

Row 104: Sl, K34.

Row 105: Sl, RLD, O, P2tog, P25, P2tog, O, LRD, K1.

Row 106: Sl, K32.

Row 107: Sl, RLD, O, P2tog, P8, Knob, P5, Knob, P8, P2tog, O, LRD, K1.

Row 108: Sl, K30.

Row 109: Sl, RLD, O, P2tog, P21, P2tog, O, LRD, K1.

Row 110: Sl, K28.

Row 111: Sl, RLD, O, P2tog, P19, P2tog, O, LRD, K1.

Row 112: Sl, K26.

Row 113: Sl, RLD, O, P2tog, P2, (Knob, P5)2x, Knob, P2, P2tog, O, LRD, K1.

Row 114: Sl, K24.

Row 115: Sl, RLD, O, P2tog, P15, P2tog, O, LRD, K1.

Row 116: Sl, K22.

The Dunraven Border (shown half-size) was knit with Wondersheen Cotton on size 0 needles.

Row 117: Sl, RLD, O, P2tog, P13, P2tog, O, LRD, K1.

Row 118: Sl, K20.

Row 119: Sl, RLD, O, P2tog, P2, Knob, P5, Knob, P2, P2tog, O, LRD, K1.

Row 120: Sl, K18.

Row 121: Sl, RLD, O, P2tog, P9, P2tog, O, LRD, K1.

Row 122: Sl, K16.

Row 123: Sl, RLD, O, P2tog, P7, P2tog, O, LRD, K1.

Row 124: Sl, K14.

Row 125: Sl, RLD, O, P2tog, P2, Knob, P2, P2tog, O, LRD, K1.

Row 126: Sl, K12.

Row 127: Sl, RLD, O, P2tog, P3, P2tog, O, LRD, K1.

Row 128: Sl, K10.

Row 129: Sl, RLD, O, P2tog, P1, P2tog, O, LRD, K1.

Row 130: Sl, K8.

Row 131: Sl, RLD, O, P3tog, O, LRD, K1.

Row 132: Sl, K6.

Row 133: Sl, K1, O, Sl-K3tog-PSSO, K1.

Row 134: Sl, K4.

Row 135: Sl, D3, K1.

Row 136: D3, fasten off.

Dunraven Border

Special Instructions:
O2 is used as the basis for 2 stitches on the following row.

Cast on 25 stitches.

Row 1: Sl, K2, O, LRD, K3, O, K1, O, K5, O, LRD, K2, O, LRD, O, K2, O2, LRD, K1.

Row 2: K3, P1, K9, O, LRD, K3, P3, K5, O, LRD, K1.

Row 3: Sl, K2, O, LRD, (K3, O)2x, K5, O, LRD, K3, O, LRD, O, K6.

Row 4: K14, O, LRD, K3, P5, K5, O, LRD, K1.

Row 5: Sl, K2, O, LRD, K3, (O, K5)2x, O, LRD, K4, O, LRD, O, K2, O2, LRD, O2, K2.

Row 6: K3, P1, K2, P1, K11, O, LRD, K3, P7, K5, O, LRD, K1.

Row 7: Sl, K2, O, LRD, K3, O, K7, O, (K5, O, LRD)2x, O, K9.

Row 8: K19, O, LRD, K3, P9, K5, O, LRD, K1.

Row 9: Sl, K2, O, LRD, K3, O, K9, O, K5, O, LRD, K6, O, LRD, O, K2 (O2, LRD)3x, K1.

Row 10: K3, P1, (K2, P1)2x, K13, O, LRD, K3, P11, K5, O, LRD, K1.

Row 11: Sl, K2, O, LRD, K7, D3, K9, O, LRD, K7, O, LRD, O, K12.

Row 12: Cast off 7 stitches, K16, O, LRD, K3, P9, K5, O, LRD, K1.

Row 13: Sl, K2, O, LRD, K6, D3, K8, O, LRD, K8, O, LRD, O, K2, O2, LRD, K1.

Row 14: K3, P1, K15, O, LRD, K3, P7, K5, O, LRD, K1.

Row 15: Sl, K2, O, LRD, K5, D3, K7, O, LRD, K9, O, LRD, O, K6.

Row 16: K20, O, LRD, K3, P5, K5, O, LRD, K1.

Row 17: Sl, K2, O, LRD, K4, D3, K6, O, LRD, K10, O, LRD, O, K2, O2, LRD, O2, K2.

Row 18: K3, P1, K2, P1, K17, O, LRD, K3, P3, K5, O, LRD, K1.

Row 19: Sl, K2, O, LRD, K3, D3, K5, O, LRD, K11, O, LRD, O, K9.

Row 20: K25, O, LRD, K3, P1, K5, O, LRD, K1.

Row 21: Sl, K2, O, LRD, K3, O, K1, O, K5, O, LRD, K12, O, LRD, O, K2, (O2, LRD)3x, K1.

Row 22: K3, P1, (K2, P1)2x, K19, O, LRD, K3, P3, K5, O, LRD, K1.

Row 23: Sl, K2, O, LRD, (K3, O)2x, K5, O, LRD, K6, Knob, K6, O, LRD, O, K12.

Row 24: Cast off 7 stitches, K22, O, LRD, K3, P5, K5, O, LRD, K1.

Row 25: Sl, K2, O, LRD, K3, O, (K5, O)2x, LRD, K14, O, LRD, O, K2, O2, LRD, K1.

Row 26: K3, P1, K21, O, LRD, K3, P7, K5, O, LRD, K1.

Row 27: Sl, K2, O, LRD, K3, O, K7, O, K5, O, LRD, K4, Knob, K3, Knob, K6, O, LRD, O, K6.

Row 28: K26, O, LRD, K3, P9, K5, O, LRD, K1.

Row 29: Sl, K2, O, LRD, K3, O, K9, O, K5, O, LRD, K16, O, LRD, O, K2, O2, LRD, O2, K2.

Row 30: K3, P1, K2, P1, K23, O, LRD, K3, P11, K5, O, LRD, K1.

Row 31: Sl, K2, O, LRD, K7, D3, K9, O, LRD, K2, (Knob, K3)3x, (LRD, O)2x, LRD, K8.

Row 32: K29, O, LRD, K3, P9, K5, O, LRD, K1.

Row 33: Sl, K2, O, LRD, K6, D3, K8, O, LRD, K13, (LRD, O)2x, LRD, K1, (O2, LRD)3x, K1.

Row 34: K3, P1, (K2, P1)2x, K21, O, LRD, K3, P7, K5, O, LRD, K1.

Row 35: Sl, K2, O, LRD, K5, D3, K7, O, LRD, K4, (Knob, K3)2x, (LRD, O)2x, LRD, K11.

Row 36: Cast off 7 stitches, K22, O, LRD, K3, P5, K5, O, LRD, K1.

Row 37: Sl, K2, O, LRD, K4, D3, K6, O, LRD, K11, (LRD, O)2x, LRD, K1, O2, LRD, K1.

Row 38: K3, P1, K19, O, LRD, K3, P3, K5, O, LRD, K1.

Row 39: Sl, K2, O, LRD, K3, D3, K5, O, LRD, K6, Knob, K3, (LRD, O)2x, LRD, K5.

Row 40: K22, O, LRD, K3, P1, K5, O, LRD, K1.

Row 41: Sl, K2, O, LRD, K3, O, K1, O, K5, O, LRD, K9, (LRD, O)2x, LRD, K1, O2, LRD, O2, K2.

Row 42: K3, P1, K2, P1, K17, O, LRD, K3, P3, K5, O, LRD, K1.

Row 43: Sl, K2, O, LRD, (K3, O)2x, K5, O, LRD, K8, (LRD, O)2x, LRD, K8.

Row 44: K23, O, LRD, K3, P5, K5, O, LRD, K1.

Row 45: Sl, K2, O, LRD, K3, (O, K5)2x, O, LRD, K7, (LRD, O)2x, LRD, K1, (O2, LRD)3x, K1.

Row 46: K3, P1, (K2, P1)2x, K15, O, LRD, K3, P7, K5, O, LRD, K1.

Row 47: Sl, K2, O, LRD, K3, O, K7, O, K5, O, LRD, K6, (LRD, O)2x, LRD, K11.

Row 48: Cast off 7 stitches, K16, O, LRD, K3, P9, K5, O, LRD, K1.

Row 49: Sl, K2, O, LRD, K3, O, K9, O, K5, O, LRD, K5, (LRD, O)2x, LRD, K1, O2, LRD, K1.

Row 50: K3, P1, K13, O, LRD, K3, P11, K5, O, LRD, K1.

Row 51: Sl, K2, O, LRD, K7, D3, K9, O, LRD, K4, (LRD, O)2x, LRD, K5.

Row 52: K16, O, LRD, K3, P9, K5, O, LRD, K1.

Row 53: Sl, K2, O, LRD, K6, D3, K8, O, LRD, K3, (LRD, O)2x, LRD, K1, O2, LRD, O2, K2.

Row 54: K3, P1, K2, P1, K11, O, LRD, K3, P7, K5, O, LRD, K1.

Row 55: Sl, K2, O, LRD, K5, D3, K7, O, LRD, K2, (LRD, O)2x, LRD, K8.

Row 56: K17, O, LRD, K3, P5, K5, O, LRD, K1.

Row 57: Sl, K2, O, LRD, K4, D3, K6, O, LRD, K1, (LRD, O)2x, LRD, K1, (O2, LRD)3x, K1.

Row 58: K3, P1, (K2, P1)2x, K9, O, LRD, K3, P3, K5, O, LRD, K1.

Row 59: Sl, K2, O, LRD, K3, D3, K5, O, (LRD)2x, (O, LRD)2x, K11.

Row 60: Cast off 7 stitches, K10, O, LRD, K3, P1, K5, O, LRD, K1.

Repeat rows 1-60 for desired length.

Acanthus Leaf

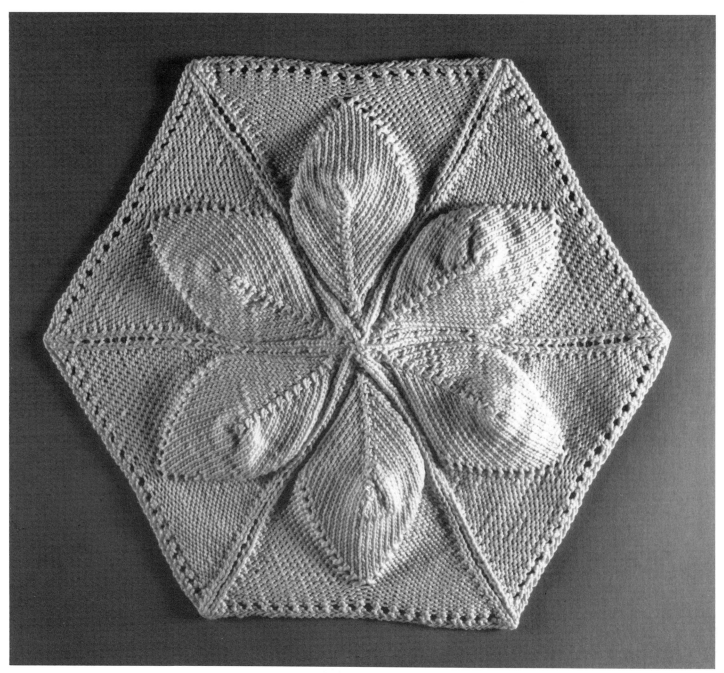

Acanthus Leaf (shown two-third size) was knit with Wondersheen Cotton on size 0 needles.

I originally found this pattern in the nineteenth-century Weldon's Practical Knitter *and later saw an example of a counterpane in this pattern at the Smithsonian Institution's National Museum of History in Washington, D.C. This particular example was beautifully worked by Mrs. Roemheld Koenigstadt and, in fact, won a blue ribbon at an exhibit in Kansas City in 1860.*

The original pattern calls for working on seven needles, but it can easily be started on a small, 24-in. circular needle. This pattern is for the experienced intermediate knitter and is the only medallion in the book knitted from the outside inward. Set on a reverse stockinette background, the leaf motif uses open increases at its edges and a central decrease begun at its midpoint.

Neither the original directions nor the Smithsonian example has a border worked with the main pattern. I suggest adding a foundation row of crocheted slip stitches along the outside edge of the assembled counterpane and tying a fringe border into the crocheted holes (see pp. 150-151).

Special Instructions:
This pattern is a hexagon, worked principally on circular needles. Each line of directions should be repeated six times around.
All even-numbered rounds between rounds 10 and 58 are worked as follows: Knit the knit stitches and purl the purl stitches of the previous round. O's are knit.

Cast on 252 stitches, using a 24-in. circular needle. Place a marker after every 42 stitches as they are cast on. There are six groups of 42 stitches. When the pattern decreases, switch from circular needles and distribute stitches evenly onto 3 double-pointed straight needles.

Round 1: Knit.
Round 2: K1, P40, K1.
Round 3: RLD, K2, (O, LRD)18x, LRD.
Round 4: K1, P38, K1.
Round 5: RLD, P36, LRD.
Round 6: RLD, P34, LRD.

Round 7: K1, P34, K1.
Round 8: RLD, P32, LRD.
Round 9: RLD, P15, O, P15, LRD.
Round 11: RLD, P14, O, K1, P14, LRD.
Round 13: RLD, P13, O, K3, O, P13, LRD.
Round 15: RLD, P12, O, K5, O, P12, LRD.
Round 17: RLD, P11, O, K7, O, P11, LRD.
Round 19: RLD, P10, O, K9, O, P10, LRD.
Round 21: RLD, P9, O, K11, O, P9, LRD.
Round 23: RLD, P8, O, K13, O, P8, LRD.
Round 25: RLD, P7, O, K15, O, P7, LRD.

Round 27: RLD, P6, O, K17, O, P6, LRD.
Round 29: RLD, P5, O, K19, O, P5, LRD.
Round 31: RLD, P4, O, K21, O, P4, LRD.
Round 33: RLD, P3, O, K23, O, P4, LRD.
Round 35: K1, P3, K11, D3, K11, P3, K1.
Round 37: K1, P3, K10, D3, K10, P3, K1.
Round 39: RLD, P2, K9, D3, K9, P2, LRD.
Round 41: K1, P2, K8, D3, K8, P2, K1.
Round 43: K1, P2, K7, D3, K7, P2, K1.
Round 45: K1, P2, K6, D3, K6, P2, K1.
Round 47: K1, P2, K5, D3, K5, P2, K1.
Round 49: K1, P2, K4, D3, K4, P2, K1.
Round 51: K1, P2, K3, D3, K3, P2, K1.
Round 53: K1, P2, K2, D3, K2, P2, K1.
Round 55: K1, P2, K1, D3, K1, P2, K1.

Round 57: K1, P2, D3, P2, K1.
Round 59: K1, P1, D3, P1, K1.
Round 60: K1, P3, K1.
Round 61: K1, D3, K1.
Round 62: K1, P1, K1.
Round 63: D3.

Two stitches remain on each needle. With a darning needle, pull thread through the six stitches and finish on the reverse side. Avoid pulling stitches too tightly.

Brooklyn Museum Pattern

The Brooklyn Museum Pattern was knit with size 3 perle cotton on size 1 needles.

This is the counterpane pattern that launched this book. I had included a photo (see p. 7)
of the counterpane from The Brooklyn Museum's collection in my 1967 book, Step-by-Step
Knitting, *and a reader wrote requesting directions for it in order to finish an incomplete*
spread she had inherited. I spent a great deal of time looking for instructions, but with no
luck. The more I looked, however, the more intrigued I became—and the more
information I began to find on counterpanes. In the end, I unearthed directions for this
pattern in two nineteenth-century needlework books—Butterick's The Art of Knitting *and*
Masters's The Work Table Companion.

I later saw several more examples of counterpanes worked in this pattern. In New
Zealand, I saw one in a private collection in Balcutha, another at the Auckland War Memorial
Museum and a third at the historic preservation of Gisbore. In Tasmania, I found yet
another example in the collection of the Van Dieman Museum.

This pattern is for the more experienced knitter. It is worked on two needles and begins
with a cluster of knobs. Unlike the knobs used elsewhere in this book, which are produced
by casting on and working extra stitches all at once in a single stitch, these knobs are
increased and decreased gradually. Bands of faggoting mark the center of the square and
lead into a series of raised-leaves worked on a reverse stockinette ground, which ends the
unit. The border pattern is the one found on the original counterpane in The Brooklyn Museum.

Special Instructions:
Pass2RN *Pass two stitches on the right needle as follows:*
Draw the two stitches before the last one on the right needle
over this last stitch (two stitches decreased).
D9 *Decrease over the following 9 stitches, as follows:*
K3, K3tog, (K1, Pass2RN)3x (8 stitches decreased).

Cast on 2 stitches.

Row 1: Knit.
Row 2: K1, O, K1.
Row 3: K1, P1, K1.
Row 4: K1, (O, K1)2x.
Row 5: K1, P3, K1.
Row 6: K1, O, K3, O, K1.
Row 7: K1, P5, K1.
Row 8: K1, (O, K2, O, K1)2x.
Row 9: K1, P9, K1.
Row 10: K1, *O, K3, O, K1*, (O, K1)2x, *-*.
Row 11: K1, P15, K1.
Row 12: *K1, O, K2, O, K1*, **O, K1, O**, K7, **-**, *-*.

Row 13: K1, P23, K1.
Row 14: K1, O, K3, (O, K1)4x, D9, (K1, O)4x, K3, O, K1.
Row 15: K1, P25, K1.
Row 16: K1, *O, K2, O, K1*, (O, K1, O, K7, [O, K1]2x)2x, *-*.
Row 17: K1, P37, K1.
Row 18: K1, O, K3, ([O, K1]4x, D9, K1)2x, (O, K1)3x, O, K3, O, K1.
Row 19: K1, P35, K1.
Row 20: K1, O, K4, (O, K7, [O, K1]3x)2x, O, K7, O, K4, O, K1.

Four units of the Brooklyn Museum Pattern assembled into
a square.

Row 21: K1, P47, K1.

Row 22: K1, O, K5, (D9, K1, [O, K1]4x)2x, D9, K5, O, K1.

Row 23: K1, P33, K1.

Row 24: : K1, *O, K8, O*, K7, (O, K1)3x, O, K7, *-*, K1.

Row 25: K1, P41, K1.

Row 26: K1, O, K9, D9, K1, (O, K1)4x, D9, K9, O, K1.

Row 27: K1, P31, K1.

Row 28: K1, *O, K12, O*, K7, *-*, K1.

Row 29: K1, P35, K1.

Row 30: K1, O, K13, D9, K13, O, K1.

Row 31: K1, P13, P2tog, P14, K1.

Row 32: K1, O, P28, O, K1.

Row 33: Knit.

Row 34: K1, O, P30, O, K1.

Row 35: K3, (O, LRD)14x, LRD, K1.

Row 36: K1, O, P31, O, K1.

Row 37: Knit.

Row 38: K1, O, P33, O, K1.

Row 39: K1, P35, K1.

Row 40: K1, O, K35, O, K1.

Row 41: K1, P37, K1.

Row 42: K1, O, P37, O, K1.

Row 43: Knit.

Row 44: K1, O, P39, O, K1.

Row 45: K3, (O, LRD)19x, K2.

Row 46: K1, O, P41, O, K1.

Row 47: Knit.

Row 48: K1, O, P43, O, K1.

Row 49: P2tog, P9, O, K1, O, (P7, O, K1, O)3x, P11.

Row 50: LRD, K9, P3, (K7, P3)3x, K10.

Row 51: P2tog, P8, O, K3, O, (P7, O, K3, O)3x, P10.

Row 52: LRD, K8, P5, (K7, P5)3x, K9.

Row 53: P2tog, (P7, O, K5, O)4x, P9.

Row 54: LRD, (K7, P7)4x, K8.

Row 55: P2tog, P6, O, K7, O, (P7, O, K7, O)3x, P8.

Row 56: LRD, K6, (P9, K7)4x.

Row 57: P2tog, P5, (O, K9, O, P7)4x.

Row 58: LRD, K5, P11, (K7, P11)3x, K6.

Row 59: P2tog, P4, K4, D3, K4, (P3, O, K1, O, P3, K4, D3, K4)3x, P6.

Row 60: LRD, K4, P9, (K3, P3, K3, P9)3x, K5.

Row 61: P2tog, P3, K3, D3, K3, (P3, O, K3, O, P3, K3, D3, K3)3x, P5.

Row 62: LRD, K3, P7, (K3, P5, K3, P7)3x, K4.

Row 63: P2tog, P2, K2, D3, K2, (P3, O, K5, O, P3, K2, D3, K2)3x, P4.

Row 64: LRD, K2, P5, (K3, P7, K3, P5)3x, K3.

Row 65: P2tog, P1, K1, D3, K1, (P3, O, K7, O, P3, K1, D3, K1)3x, P3.

Row 66: LRD, K1, P3, (K3, P9, K3, P3)3x, K2.

Row 67: P2tog, D3, (P3, O, K9, O, P3, D3)3x, P2.

Row 68: LRD, (P1, K3, P11, K3)3x, P2.

Row 69: LRD, P3, K4, D3, K4, (P3, O, K1, O, P3, K4, D3, K4)2x, P5.

Row 70: LRD, K3, P9, (K3, P3, K3, P9)2x, K4.

Row 71: P2tog, P2, K3, D3, K3, (P3, O, K3, O, P3, K3, D3, K3)2x, P4.

Row 72: LRD, K2, P7, K3, (P5, K3, P7, K3)2x.

Row 73: P2tog, P1, K2, D3, K2, P3, (O, K5, O, P3, K2, D3, K2, P3)2x.

Row 74: LRD, K1, P5, (K3, P7, K3, P5)2x, K2.

Row 75: P2tog, K1, D3, K1, (P3, O, K7, O, P3, K1, D3, K1)2x, P2.

Row 76: LRD, P3, (K3, P9, K3, P3)2x, K1.

Row 77: (LRD)2x, (P3, O, K9, O, P3, D3)2x, P1.

Row 78: P2tog, *K3, P11, K3*, P1, *-*, P2tog.

Row 79: P2tog, P2, *K4, D3, K4*, P3, O, K1, O, P3, *-*, P3, K1.

Row 80: LRD, K2, P9, K3, P3, K3, P9, K3.

Row 81: P2tog, P1, *K3, D3, K3, P3*, O, K3, O, P3, *-*.

Row 82: LRD, K1, P7, K3, P5, K3, P7, K2.

Row 83: LRD, *K2, D3, K2*, P3, O, K5, O, P3, *-*, P2.

Row 84: LRD, P5, K3, P7, K3, P5, K1.

Row 85: LRD, D3, K1, P3, O, K7, O, P3, K1, D3, K1, P1.

Row 86: P2tog, P2, K3, P9, K3, P3.

Row 87: (LRD)2x, P2, O, K9, O, P3, D3.

Row 88: LRD, K2, P11, K2, LRD.

Row 89: P2tog, P1, K4, D3, K4, P3.

Row 90: LRD, K1, P9, K2.

Row 91: P2tog, K3, D3, K3, P2.

Row 92: LRD, P7, K1.

Row 93: LRD, K1, D3, K2, P1.

Row 94: P2tog, P3, K1.

Row 95: (LRD)2x, K1.

Row 96: P3tog, fasten off.

Border Pattern

Cast on 25 stitches and knit 2 rows.

Row 1: Sl, K2, O, LRD, K3, O, K1, O, K5, O, LRD, K1, (O, LRD)3x, LRD.

Row 2: O, K10, O, LRD, K3, P3, K5, O, LRD, K1.

Row 3: Sl, K2, O, LRD, (K3, O)2x, K5, O, LRD, K2, (O, LRD)3x, K1.

Row 4: O, K11, O, LRD, K3, P5, K5, O, LRD, K1.

Row 5: Sl, K2, O, LRD, K3, O, (K5, O)2x, LRD, K3, (O, LRD)3x, K1.

Row 6: O, K12, O, LRD, K3, P7, K5, O, LRD, K1.

Row 7: Sl, K2, O, LRD, K3, O, K7, O, K5, O, LRD, K4, (O, LRD)3x, K1.

Row 8: O, K13, O, LRD, K3, P9, K5, O, LRD, K1.

Row 9: Sl, K2, O, LRD, K3, O, K9, O, K5, O, LRD, K5, (O, LRD)3x, K1.

Row 10: O, K14, O, LRD, K3, P11, K5, O, LRD, K1.

Row 11: Sl, K2, O, LRD, K7, D3, K9, O, LRD, K6, (O, LRD)3x, K1.

Row 12: O, K15, O, LRD, K3, P9, K5, O, LRD, K1.

Row 13: Sl, K2, O, LRD, K6, D3, K8, O, LRD, K7, (O, LRD)3x, K1.

Row 14: O, K16, O, LRD, K3, P7, K5, O, LRD, K1.

Row 15: Sl, K2, O, LRD, K5, D3, K7, O, LRD, K8, (O, LRD)3x, K1.

Row 16: O, K17, O, LRD, K3, P5, K5, O, LRD, K1.

Row 17: Sl, K2, O, LRD, K4, D3, K6, O, LRD, K9, (O, LRD)3x, K1.

Row 18: O, K18, O, LRD, K3, P3, K5, O, LRD, K1.

Row 19: Sl, K2, O, LRD, K3, D3, K5, O, LRD, K6, O, P1, O, K3, (O, LRD)3x, K1.

Row 20: O, K21, O, LRD, K3, P1, K5, O, LRD, K1.

Row 21: Sl, K2, O, LRD, K3, O, K1, O, K5, O, LRD, K6, (O, P1)3x, O, K4, (O, LRD)3x, K1.

Row 22: O, K26, O, LRD, K3, P3, K5, O, LRD, K1.

Row 23: Sl, K2, O, LRD, (K3, O)2x, K5, O, LRD, K4, O, P1, *O, K1, O*, P7, *-*, P1, O, K3, (O, LRD)3x, K1.

Row 24: O, K33, O, LRD, K3, P5, K5, O, LRD, K1.

Row 25: Sl, K2, O, LRD, K3, O, (K5, O)2x, LRD, K4, *(O, P1)3x*, O, K1, D9, K1, *-*, O, K4, (O, LRD)3x, K1.

Row 26: O, K34, O, LRD, K3, P7, K5, O, LRD, K1.

Row 27: Sl, K2, O, LRD, K3, O, K7, O, K5, O, LRD, K2, (O, P1, O, K1, O, P7, O, K1)2x, O, P1, O, K3, (O, LRD)3x, K1.

Row 28: O, K45, O, LRD, K3, P9, K5, O, LRD, K1.

Row 29: Sl, K2, O, LRD, K3, O, K9, O, K5, O, LRD, K2, ([O, P1]3x, O, K1, D9, K1)2x, (O, P1)3x, O, K4, (O, LRD)3x, K1.

Row 30: O, K42, O, LRD, K3, P11, K5, O, LRD, K1.

Row 31: Sl, K2, O, LRD, K7, D3, K9, O, LRD, K2, (O, P7, O, K1, O, P1, O, K1)2x, O, P7, O, K2, (LRD, O)3x, (LRD)2x.

Row 32: O, K51, O, LRD, K3, P9, K5, O, LRD, K1.

Row 33: Sl, K2, O, LRD, K6, D3, K8, O, LRD, K2, (D9, K1, [O, P1]3x, O, K1)2x, D9, K1, (LRD, O)3x, (LRD)2x.

Row 34: O, K34, O, LRD, K3, P7, K5, O, LRD, K1.

Row 35: Sl, K2, O, LRD, K5, D3, K7, O, LRD, K4, O, P7, *O, K1, O*, P1, *-*, P7, O, K2, (LRD, O)3x, (LRD)2x.

Row 36: O, K39, O, LRD, K3, P5, K5, O, LRD, K1.

Row 37: Sl, K2, *O, LRD, K4*, D3, K6, *-*, D9, K1, (O, P1)3x, O, K1, D9, K1, (LRD, O)3x, (LRD)2x.

Row 38: O, K26, O, LRD, K3, P3, K5, O, LRD, K1.

Row 39: Sl, K2, O, LRD, K3, D3, K5, O, LRD, K6, O, P7, O, K2, (LRD, O)3x, (LRD)2x.

Row 40: O, K27, O, LRD, K3, P1, K5, O, LRD, K1.

Row 41: Sl, K2, O, LRD, K3, O, K1, O, K5, O, LRD, K6, D9, K1, (LRD, O)3x, (LRD)2x.

Row 42: O, K18, O, LRD, K3, P3, K5, O, LRD, K1.

Row 43: Sl, K2, O, LRD, (K3, O)2x, K5, O, LRD, K7, (LRD, O)3x, (LRD)2x.

Row 44: O, K17, O, LRD, K3, P5, K5, O, LRD, K1.

Row 45: Sl, K2, O, LRD, K3, O, (K5, O)2x, LRD, K6, (LRD, O)3x, (LRD)2x.

Row 46: O, K16, O, LRD, K3, P7, K5, O, LRD, K1.

Row 47: Sl, K2, O, LRD, K3, O, K7, O, K5, O, LRD, K5,(LRD, O)3x, (LRD)2x.

Row 48: O, K15, O, LRD, K3, P9, K5, O, LRD, K1.

Row 49: Sl, K2, O, LRD, K3, O, K9, O, K5, O, LRD, K4, (LRD, O)3x, (LRD)2x.

Row 50: O, K14, O, LRD, K3, P11, K5, O, LRD, K1.

Row 51: Sl, K2, O, LRD, K7, D3, K9, O, LRD, K3, (LRD, O)3x, (LRD)2x.

Row 52: O, K13, O, LRD, K3, P9, K5, O, LRD, K1.

Row 53: Sl, K2, O, LRD, K6, D3, K8, O, LRD, K2, (LRD, O)3x, (LRD)2x.

Row 54: O, K12, O, LRD, K3, P7, K5, O, LRD, K1.

Row 55: Sl, K2, O, LRD, K5, D3, K7, O, LRD, K1, (LRD, O)3x, (LRD)2x.

Row 56: O, K11, O, LRD, K3, P5, K5, O, LRD, K1.

Row 57: Sl, K2, O, LRD, K4, D3, K6, O, LRD, (LRD, O)3x, (LRD)2x.

Row 58: O, K10, O, LRD, K3, P3, K5, O, LRD, K1.

Row 59: Sl, K2, O, LRD, K3, D3, K5, O, LRD, K1, (O, LRD)3x, LRD.

Row 60: O, K10, O, LRD, K3, P1, K5, O, LRD, K1.

Repeat rows 1-60 for desired length.

The Brooklyn Museum border (shown half-size) was knit size 3 perle cotton on size 1 needles.

Strip Patterns

As their name suggests, traditional strip patterns are worked and joined together in long bands the length or width of the counterpane. The individual patterns include those with both flat and embossed surfaces. Instructions for the simplest of the knit-and-purl patterns are given in charted form. (Directions for this pattern are found on pp. 126-127.)

Saxon Star

I have come across directions for numerous variations on the Saxon Star pattern, but I have never seen an actual counterpane that uses the motif. This particular version, from the nineteenth-century Weldon's Practical Knitter, is of interest because of its unusual raised-leaf border. This motif is a simple knit-and-purl pattern with a central decrease.

This two-needle pattern is a good one for beginning knitters who can work a number of repeats at one time to form a strip the length of the counterpane. (I would repeat rows 1-21 of the pattern to produce the final raised-leaf band only at the end of this strip, knitting a series of stars one after the other.) These strips could then be used alone or separated by vertical bands of an insert pattern (or patterns) from pp. 144-171. I leave the choice of a border up to you.

Cast on 52 stitches.

Row 1: Knit.

Row 2: Purl.

Row 3: Knit.

Row 4: P4, (*O, K1, O*, P6)5x, *-*, P7, *-*, P4.

Row 5: K4, P3, K7, P3, (K6, P3)5x, K4.

Row 6: P4, (*O, K3, O*, P6)5x, *-*, P7, *-*, P4.

Row 7: K4, P5, K7, P5, (K6, P5)5x, K4.

Row 8: P4, (*O, K5, O*, P6)5x, *-*, P7, *-*, P4.

Row 9: K4, P7, K7, P7, (K6, P7)5x, K4.

Row 10: P4, (*O, K7, O*, P6)5x, *-*, P7, *-*, P4.

Row 11: K4, P9, K7, P9 (K6, P9)5x, K4.

Row 12: P4, (*K3, D3, K3*, P6)5x, *-*, P7, *-*, P4.

Row 13: K4, P7, K7, P7, (K6, P7)5x, K4.

Row 14: P4, (*K2, D3, K2*, P6)5x, *-*, P7, *-*, P4.

Row 15: K4, P5, K7, P5, (K6, P5)5x, K4.

Row 16: P4, (*K1, D3, K1*, P6)5x, *-*, P7, *-*, P4.

Row 17: K4, P3, K7, P3, (K6, P3)5x, K4.

Row 18: P4, (D3, P6)5x, D3, P7, D3, P4.

Row 19: K4, P1, K7, P1, (K6, P1)5x, K4.

Rows 20 and 22: Purl.

Rows 21 and 23: Knit.

Row 24: P9, K34, P9.

Row 25: K9, P9, K1, P14, K1, P9, K9.

Row 26: *P4, O, K1, O, P4*, K34, *-*.

Row 27: *K4, P3, K4,*, P9, K2, P12, K2, P9, *-*.

Row 28: *P4, O, K3, O, P4*, K34, *-*.

Row 29: *K4, P5, K4*, P9, K3, P10, K3, P9, *-*.

Row 30: *P4, O, K5, O, P4*, K34, *-*.

Row 31: *K4, P7, K4*, P9, K4, P8, K4, P9, *-*.

Row 32: *P4, O, K7, O, P4*, K34, *-*.

Row 33: (K4, P9)2x, K5, P6, K5, (P9, K4)2x.

Row 34: *P4, K3, D3, K3, P4*, K34, *-*.

Row 35: *K4, P7, K4*, P9, K6, P4, K6, P9, *-*.

Row 36: *P4, K2, D3, K2, P4*, K34, *-*.

Row 37: *K4, P5, K4*, P9, K7, P2, K7, P9, *-*.

Row 38: *P4, K1, D3, K1, P4*, K34, *-*.

Row 39: *K4, P3, K4*, P9, K16, P9, *-*.

Row 40: *P4, D3, P4*, K34, *-*.

Row 41: (K4, P1)2x, K15, P2, K15, (P1, K4)2x.

Row 42: P9, K34, P9.

Row 43: K9, P2, K13, P4, K13, P2, K9.

Row 44: P9, K34, P9.

Row 45: K9, P3, K11, P6, K11, P3, K9.

Row 46: P9, K15, P4, K15, P9.

Row 47: *K9, P4, K9*, P2, K4, P2, *-*.

Row 48: *P4, O, K1, O, P4*, K15, P4, K15, *-*.

Row 49: *K4, P3, K4*, P5, K7, P3, K4, P3, K7, P5, *-*.

Row 50: *P4, O, K3, O, P4*, K15, P4, K15, *-*.

Row 51: *K4, P5, K4*, P6, K5, P4, K4, P4, K5, P6, *-*.

Row 52: *P4, O, K5, O, P4*, K15, P4, K15, *-*.

Row 53: (K4, P7)2x, K3, P1, K4, P4, K4, P1, K3, (P7, K4)2x.

Row 54: *P4, O, K7, O, P4*, K11, P4,K4, P4, K11, *-*.

Row 55: *K4, P9, K4*, P8, K1, P2, K4, P4, K4, P2, K1, P8, *-*.

Row 56: *P4, K3, D3, K3, P4*, K11, P4, K4, P4, K11, *-*.

Row 57: *K4, P7, K4*, P8, K1, P2, K4, P4, K4, P2, K1, P8, *-*.

Row 58: *P4, K2, D3, K2, P4*, K11, P4, K4, P4, K11, *-*.

Row 59: *K4, P5, K4*, P7, K3, P1, K4, P4, K4, P1, K3, P7, *-*.

Row 60: *P4, K1, D3, K1, P4*, K10, P1, K4, P4, K4, P1, K10, *-*.

Row 61: *K4, P3, K4*, P6, K5, P4, K4, P4, K5, P6, *-*.

Row 62: *P4, D3, P4*, K15, P4, K15, *-*.

Row 63: *K4, P1, K4*, P5, K7, P3, K4, P3, K7, P5, *-*.

Row 64: P9, K15, P4, K15, P9.

Row 65: *K9, P4, K9*, P2, K4, P2, *-*.
Row 66: P9, K15, P4, K15, P9.
Row 67: K9, P3, K11, P6, K11, P3, K9.
Row 68: P9, K34, P9.
Row 69: K9, P2, K13, P4, K13, P2, K9.
Row 70: *P4, O, K1, O, P4*, K34, *-*.
Row 71: *K4, P3, K4*, P1, K15, P2, K15, P1, *-*.
Row 72: *P4, O, K3, O, P4*, K34, *-*.
Row 73: *K4, P5, K4*, P9, K16, P9, *-*.
Row 74: *P4, O, K5, O, P4*, K34, *-*.
Row 75: *K4, P7, K4*, P9, K7, P2, K7, P9, *-*.
Row 76: *P4, O, K7, O, P4*, K34, *-*.
Row 77: (K4, P9)2x, K6, P4, K6, (P9, K4)2x.
Row 78: *P4, K3, D3, K3, P4*, K34, *-*.
Row 79: *K4, P7, K4*, P9, K5, P6, K5, P9, *-*.
Row 80: *P4, K2, D3, K2, P4*, K34, *-*.
Row 81: *K4, P5, K4*, P9, K4, P8, K4, P9, *-*.
Row 82: *P4, K1, D3, K1, P4*, K34, *-*.
Row 83: *K4, P3, K4*, P9, K3, P10, K3, P9, *-*.
Row 84: *P4, D3, P4*, K34, *-*.
Row 85: *K4, P1, K4*, P9, K2, P12, K2, P9, *-*.
Row 86: P9, K34, P9.
Row 87: K9, P9, K1, P14, K1, P9, K9.
Row 88: P9, K34, P9.

Repeat rows 1-88 for desired length. Then work rows 1-21 and cast off following Row 22.

Saxon Star (shown two-third size) was worked in size 3 perle cotton on size 1 needles.

Godey's Pattern

This extremely simple knit-and-purl pattern is drawn from the nineteenth-century Godey's Lady's Book and Magazine. If I were to make a counterpane with this pattern, I would knit three repeats at one time, side by side, using the unit's vertical garter-stitch border only to begin and end the group of three repeats. Knitting several repeats at once decreases the number of strips to be sewn together. Finally, I would add a wide garter-stitch border or a fringe border like the one used with An Old Time Favorite (see p. 109) to complete the counterpane.

Godey's Pattern was worked with Antique Bedspread Cotton on size 0 needles.

Note: repeat rows 1-36 of chart on facing page for pattern. For information on using chart, see pp. 34-35.

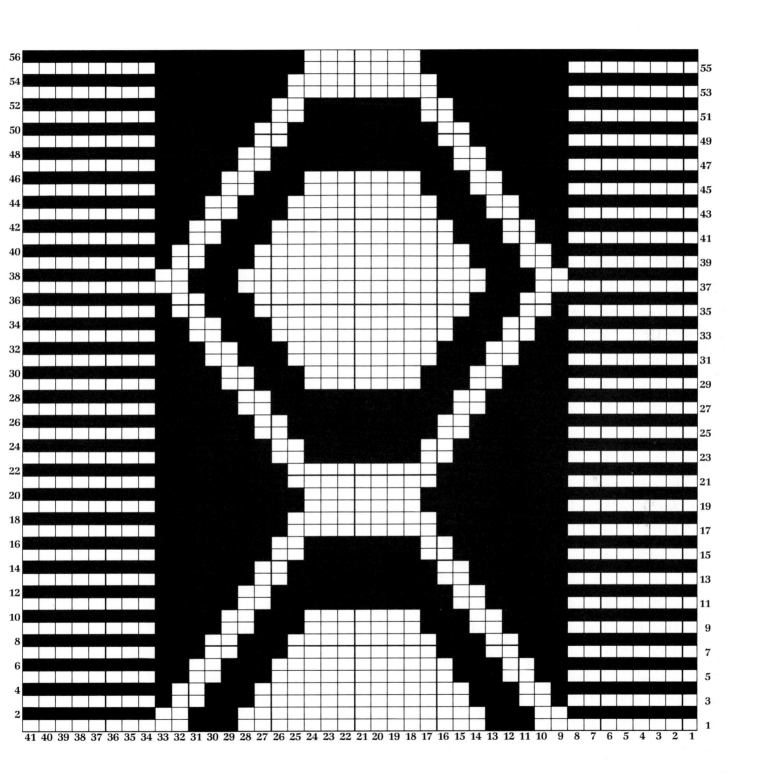

Triangles

This pattern is an old one, which I have found in several nineteenth-century publications but have never seen used for an actual counterpane. It can be combined with a variety of patterns. Used alone, it would make a handsome table mat, which I would surround on all four sides with a simple seed-stitch border.

This is an exceptionally simple, two-needle pattern made of yarn-over increases and decreases. Any number of borders (pp. 144-171) can be used with it.

Special Instructions:
This pattern is worked on a multiple of 7 plus 2 stitches. The instructions in the brackets should be repeated once for each 7 stitches. However, because of the pattern shift, bracketed instructions in rows 14, 16, 18, 20 and 22 should be repeated the number of patterns being worked minus one.
The sample is worked on 39 stitches: 5 repeats plus 2 stitches, plus 1 stitch on each side for a garter-stitch border. Note that the border stitches are not included in the instructions.

Cast on. Knit 1 row; purl 1 row.

Row 1: K1, [K5, LRD, O], K1.
Row 2: K1, [K1, P6], K1.
Row 3: K1, [K4, LRD, P1, O], K1.
Row 4: K1, [K2, P5], K1.
Row 5: K1, [K3, LRD, P2, O], K1.
Row 6: K1, [K3, P4], K1.

Row 7: K1, [K2, LRD, P3, O], K1.
Row 8: K1, [K4, P3], K1.
Row 9: K1, [K1, LRD, P4, O], K1.
Row 10: K1, [K5, P2], K1.
Row 11: K1, [LRD, P5, O], K1.
Row 12: K1, [P7], K1.
Row 13: K2, [O, RLD, K5].
Row 14: K1, P5, [K1, P6], K1, P1, K1.
Row 15: K2, [O, P1, RLD, K4].
Row 16: K1, P4, [K2, P5], K2, P1, K1.
Row 17: K2, [O, P2, RLD, K3].
Row 18: K1, P3, [K3, P4], K3, P1, K1.
Row 19: K2, [O, P3, RLD, K2].
Row 20: K1, P2, [K4, P3], K4, P1, K1.
Row 21: K2, [O, P4, RLD, K1].
Row 22: K1, P1, [K5, P2], K5, P1, K1.
Row 23: K2, [O, P5, RLD].
Row 24: K1, [P7], K1.

Repeat rows 1-24 for desired length.

The Triangles sample was worked with Parisian Cotton on size 1 needles.

Close Strip

Taken from the nineteenth-century Godey's Lady's Book and Magazine, *this is a very easy, overall knit-and-purl pattern of flat and raised triangles. I have never seen a full counterpane worked in this pattern and imagine it would be boring to work a full spread in this motif alone. Instead, if I wanted to use this pattern, I would combine it with another, probably the Northern Star (see p. 110), and I would choose a nice fringe for a border.*

Note: Repeat rows 3-18 of chart below for pattern. For information on using chart, see pp. 34-35.

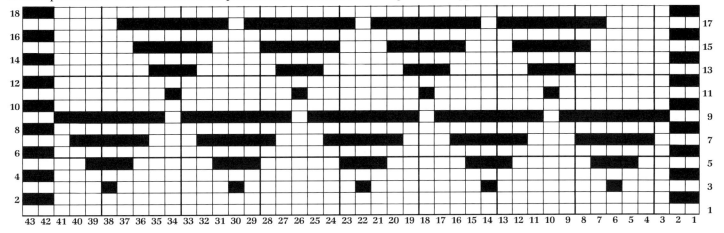

Close Strip was knit with Antique Bedspread Cotton on size 0 needles.

Falling Leaves

This version of the classic diamond pattern gains interest by alternating the texture of the rows of diamonds—one stockinette stitch, the next garter stitch. All the leaves carry a central raised vein, produced by a D3 decrease (see Glossary of Knitting Terms, p. 20).

This pattern might be a good one to experiment with. Instead of always using a central decrease for the leaf vein, for example, you could work one leaf with central decreases and its neighbor with paired edge decreases. I would like to see the effect of this seemingly minor change on the pattern.

Special Instructions:
This pattern is worked on a multiple of 14 plus 9 stitches. On most rows, the stitch sequence in the parentheses is repeated 1 time less than the number of patterns being worked. On rows 4, 6, 18, 19, 20 and 21, the repeat number is the same as the number of patterns being worked.
The sample is worked on 65 stitches: 4 repeats plus 9 stitches.

Cast on 65 stitches and knit 2 rows.

Row 1: Sl, K3, RLD, K5, O, K1, O, (K5, D3, K5, O, K1, O)3x, K5, RLD, K4.

Row 2: Sl, K9, (P3, K11)3x, P3, K10.

Row 3: Sl, K3, RLD, K4, O, K3, O, (K4, D3, K4, O, K3, O)3x, K4, RLD, K4.

Row 4: Sl, K8, (P5, K9)4x.

Row 5: Sl, K3, RLD, K3, O, K5, O, (K3, D3, K3, O, K5, O)3x, K3, RLD, K4.

Row 6: Sl, (K7, P7)4x, K8.

Row 7: Sl, K3, RLD, K2, O, K7, O, (K2, D3, K2, O, K7, O)3x, K2, RLD, K4.

Row 8: Sl, K6, (P9, K5)3x, P9, K7.

Row 9: Sl, K3, RLD, K1, O, K9, O, (K1, D3, K1, O, K9, O)3x, K1, RLD, K4.

Row 10: Sl, K5, (P11, K3)3x, P11, K6.

Row 11: Sl, K3, RLD, O, K11, O, (D3, O, K11, O)3x, RLD, K4.

Row 12: Sl, K4, (P13, K1)3x, P13, K5.

Row 13: Sl, K4, (O, K5, D3, K5, O, K1)3x, O, K5, D3, K5, O, K5.

Row 14: Sl, K5, (P11, K3)3x, P11, K6.

Row 15: Sl, K5, (O, K4, D3, K4, O, K3)3x, O, K4, D3, K4, O, K6.

Row 16: Sl, K6, (P9, K5)3x, P9, K7.

Row 17: Sl, K6, (O, K3, D3, K3, O, K5)3x, O, K3, D3, K3, O, K7.

Row 18: Sl, (K7, P7)4x, K8.

Row 19: Sl, (K7, O, K2, D3, K2, O)4x, K8.

Row 20: Sl, K8, (P5, K9)4x.

Row 21: Sl, K8, (O, K1, D3, K1, O, K9)4x.

Row 22: Sl, K9, (P3, K11)3x, P3, K10.

Row 23: Sl, K9, (O, D3, O, K11)3x, O, D3, O, K10.

Row 24: Sl, K10, (P1, K13)3x, P1, K11

Repeat rows 1-24 for desired length. Cast off knitting all stitches.

Falling Leaves (shown two-third size) was worked with size 3 perle cotton on size 1 needles.

An Old-Time Favorite

This pattern from the nineteenth-century Godey's Lady's Book and Magazine *produces a simple but handsome counterpane. The sixth and seventh rows of the pattern can be repeated any number of times to lengthen the unit, with rows 1-5 worked to break it up.*

This pattern might be interesting knitted in color. The first five rows could be worked in one color and the last two rows in another. A pair of colors could be used throughout, or the shades could change with each new unit.

As a border for this pattern, I suggest fringe, worked only at the top and bottom points of the zigzag edges. I would then knit a garter-stitch border an inch or two wide for the straight sides of the piece.

Special Instructions:
The pattern is worked on a multiple of 21 plus 2 stitches. The bracketed instructions should be repeated once for each 21 stitches. The sample is worked on 65 stitches: 3 repeats plus 2 stitches.

Cast on.

Rows 1, 3, 5: Knit.
Rows 2, 4: Purl.
Row 6: Sl, [(LRD, K7, O, K1, O, K9, RLD)5x], K1.
Row 7: Purl.

Repeat rows 6 and 7 for desired length. Then repeat rows 1-5 and cast off.

An Old-Time Favorite (shown two-third size) was worked with Antique Bedspread Cotton on size 0 needles.

Northern Star

If you have learned only to knit and purl, the Northern Star is the perfect pattern for you. Set on a stockinette background, the star is worked in garter stitch, the cross in reverse stockinette, and the border in double-moss stitch—all simple combinations of knit and purl.

To use this pattern in a counterpane, I suggest eliminating the border from the top edge, repeating the pattern the length of the counterpane and then completing the final unit with the missing border. If you like the stars separated from each other top and bottom by the double-moss band, knit a continuous strip of full pattern units. Knitting strips the length of the counterpane minimizes the tedious job of sewing together numerous individual units. To complete the counterpane, I would use a fringe border.

Northern Star (shown two-third size) was worked with Antique Bedspread Cotton on size 0 needles.

Note: For information on using chart on facing page, see pp. 34-35.

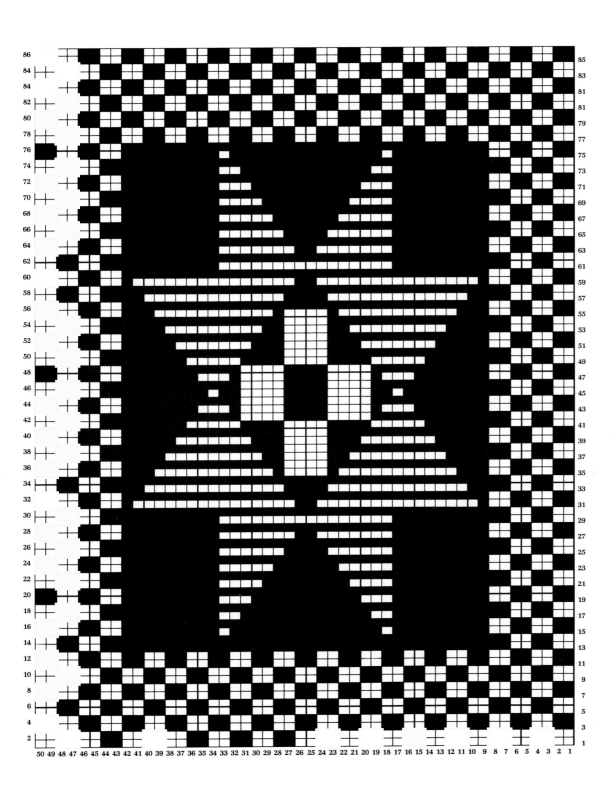

Hexagons

This popular pattern, found in many nineteenth-century needlework magazines, was often used as the square section of tidy patterns (it could, in fact, easily substitute for the square pattern in the Double Star on p. 44 and the Star Tidy on p. 50). I have seen a full counterpane knit entirely of the Hexagon pattern in a private collection in Newcastle on Tyne, England, but I think it would be more interesting to combine this motif with another, perhaps one of the insert patterns from pp. 144-171. The pattern can also be knit in color, with the honeycomb outline in one shade and the background in another. This pattern would also be perfect for pillow covers. The hexagon is a very easy pattern for the beginning knitter. It uses simple knit, purl and slip stitches. I think the Cherry Leaf border on p. 154 would nicely finish off a counterpane worked in this pattern.

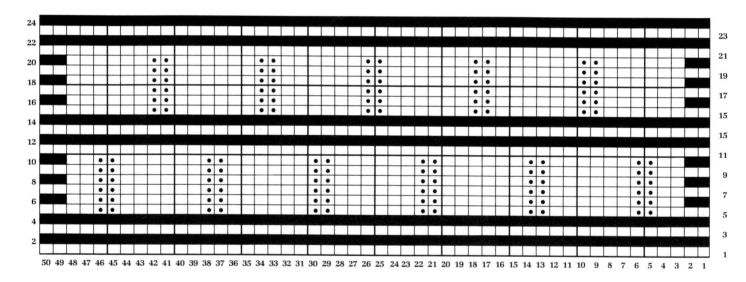

The Hexagons sample (shown three-quarter size) was worked with Antique Bedspread Cotton on size 0 needles.

Legend for chart (above):

● = slip stitch as if to purl.

For information on using chart, see pp. 34-35.

Betty Fogel's Pattern

This pattern was named for a friend I met some years ago at Penland School in Penland, North Carolina. When she heard of my interest in counterpanes, she sent me a slide of one she had bought at a flea market 25 years earlier. After searching through my library, I finally found written instructions for the pattern in one of my nineteenth-century sources.

This is a simple two-needle pattern. It involves yarn-overs and decreases, with a purl stitch separating the vertical columns of decreases. I leave the choice of border (see pp. 144-171) up to you.

Special Instructions:
This sample has a 7-stitch border on each side, which is worked as follows:
Rows 1 and 2: Knit.
Row 3: The first 7 stitches: K2, (O, LRD)2x, K1.
The last 7 stitches: K1, (LRD, O)2x, K2.
Rows 4-14: Knit.
Row 15: Repeat Row 3.
Rows 16-24: Knit.
The directions for the border pattern are not included in the instructions below.
The pattern is worked on a multiple of 14 plus 1 stitch. The instructions in the brackets should be repeated once for each 14 stitches with the exception of Row 11, where the instructions should be repeated one time less than the multiple of 14. The sample is worked on 57 stitches: 4 repeats plus 1 stitch. The D3 in Row 11 is worked over the last stitch of one pattern and the first two stitches of the next pattern.

Cast on and knit 2 rows.

Row 1: [P1, RLD, K4, O, K1, O, K4, LRD], P1.

Rows 2, 4, 6, 8, 10: [K1, P13], K1.

Row 3: [P1, RLD, (K3, O)2x, K3, LRD], P1.

Row 5: [P1, RLD, K2, O, K5, O, K2, LRD], P1.

Row 7: [P1, RLD, K1, O, K7, O, K1, LRD], P1.

Row 9: [P1, RLD, O, K9, O, LRD], P1.

Row 11: LRD, [O, K11, O, D3]—last repeat ends O, K11, O, RLD.

Row 12: Purl.

Row 13: [K1, O, K4, LRD, P1, RLD, K4, O], K1.

Rows 14, 16, 18, 20, 22: P7, [K1, P13]—last repeat ends P7 instead of P13.

Row 15: K2, [O, K3, LRD, P1, RLD, K3, O, K3]—last repeat ends K2.

Row 17: K3, [O, K2, LRD, P1, RLD, K2, O, K5]—last repeat ends K3.

Row 19: K4, [O, K1, LRD, P1, RLD, K1, O, K7]—last repeat ends K4.

Row 21: K5, [O, LRD, P1, RLD, O, K9]—last repeat ends K4.

Row 23: K6, [O, D3, O, K11]—last repeat ends K6.

Row 24: Purl.

Repeat rows 1-24 for desired length.

Betty Fogel's Pattern (shown two-third size) was worked with Parisian Cotton on size 1 needles.

A Bit of Scotland

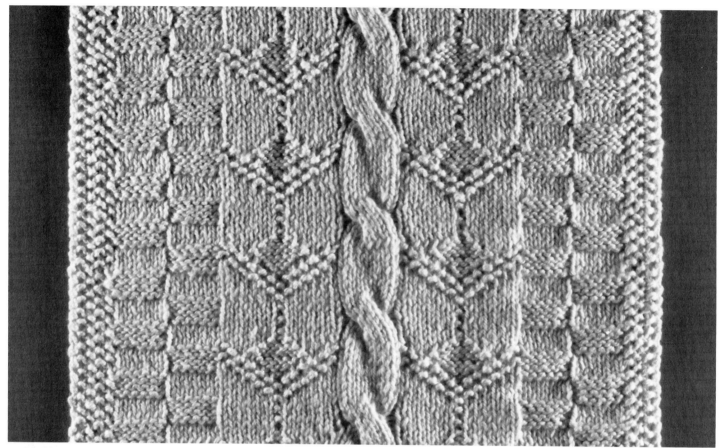

A Bit of Scotland (shown three-quarter size) was worked with Antique Bedspread Cotton on size 0 needles.

Note: Repeat rows 5-20 of chart below for pattern.
For information on using chart, see pp. 34-35.

Legend for chart (below):
= seven-stitch, front-cross cable.

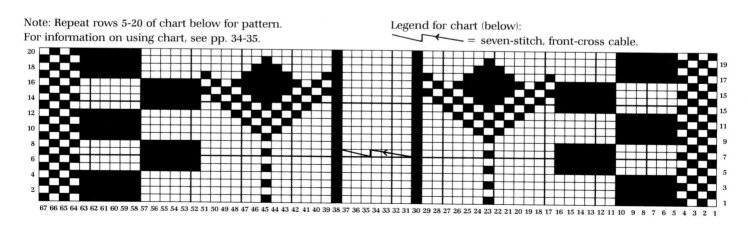

I saw an example of this pattern in the counterpane collection of the National Museums of Scotland in Edinburgh and later worked from a photo of the spread to write directions for it. The pattern's cable is worked on an odd number of stitches, which was quite common in nineteenth-century patterns. Today we generally work cables on an even number of stitches, which produces more tension in the twist than does the odd-numbered method.

A Bit of Scotland is a very simple two-needle, knit-and-purl pattern. Good for the beginner, it uses stockinette, seed and garter stitches with a seven-stitch cable and horizontal ribbing. The fringe border I have presented is similar to the one on the original counterpane, but a lace border (pp. 144-171) can be substituted.

The fringe border (shown here full-size and, like its chart, turned sideways) was worked with the same yarn and needle size as the main pattern.

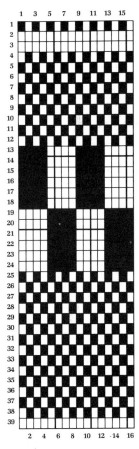

Note: For information on using chart above, see pp. 34-35.

Leaves and Zigzags

The raised-leaf motif appears in many nineteenth-century patterns. This particular version of the pattern, from Butterick's Fancy and Practical Knitting, is different from most. Although its upper half is conventionally worked in solid stockinette stitch and shaped with paired decreases, the openwork pattern in its lower half is unexpected. Simple yarn-overs and decreases combine to create both this open patterning and the unusual zigzag openwork piercing the garter-stitch background.

This two-needle pattern is for the intermediate knitter. It would be nicely completed with any of the straight border patterns (pp. 144-171).

Cast on 48 stitches; knit 2 rows.

Setup Row 1: Sl, K14, O, K1, O, K32.

Setup Row 2: Sl, (O, LRD) 2x, K23, (O, LRD)2x, P3, K11, (O, LRD)2x.

Setup Row 3: Sl, K15, O, K1, O, K33.

Setup Row 4: Sl, K1, (O, LRD)2x, K21, (O, LRD)2x, K1, P5, K10, (O, LRD)2x, K1.

Setup Row 5: Sl, K16, O, K1, O, K34.

Setup Row 6: Sl, K2, (O, LRD)2x, K19, (O, LRD)2x, K2, P7, K9, (O, LRD)2x, K2.

Setup Row 7: Sl, K15, O, LRD, O, K1, O, RLD, O, K33.

Setup Row 8: Sl, K3, (O, LRD)2x, K17, (O, LRD)2x, K3, P9, K8, (O, LRD)2x, K3.

Setup Row 9: Sl, K15, O, LRD, K1, (O, K1)2x, RLD, O, K33.

Skip to Row 10 of pattern.

On all subsequent repeats, work rows 1-9 as follows:

Row 1: Sl, K14, O, K1, O, K16, RLD, K7, LRD, K15.

Leaves and Zigzags (shown three-quarter size) was knit with Parisian Cotton on size 1 needles.

Row 2: Sl, (O, LRD)2x, K10, P9, K12, (O, LRD)2x, P3, K11, (O, LRD)2x.

Row 3: Sl, K15, O, K1, O, K17, RLD, K5, LRD, K15.

Row 4: Sl, K1, (O, LRD)2x, K9, P7, K11, (O, LRD)2x, K1, P5, K10, (O, LRD)2x, K1.

Row 5: Sl, K16, O, K1, O, K18, RLD, K3, LRD, K15.

Row 6: Sl, K2, (O, LRD)2x, K8, P5, K10, (O, LRD)2x, K2, P7, K9, (O, LRD)2x, K2.

Row 7: Sl, K15, O, LRD, O, K1, O, RLD, O, K17, RLD, K1, LRD, K15.

Row 8: Sl, K3, (O, LRD)2x, K7, P3, K9, (O, LRD)2x, K3, P9, K8, (O, LRD)2x, K3.

Row 9: Sl, K15, O, LRD, K1, (O, K1)2x, RLD, O, K17, D3, K15.

Row 10: Sl, K4, (O, LRD)2x, K15, (O, LRD)2x, K4, P11, K7, (O, LRD)2x, K4.

Row 11: Sl, K15, (O, LRD)2x, O, K1, (O, RLD)2x, O, K33.

Row 12: Sl, K5, (O, LRD)2x, K13, (O, LRD)2x, K5, P13, K6, (O, LRD)2x, K5.

Row 13: Sl, K15, (O, LRD)2x, K1, (O, K1)2x, (RLD, O)2x, K33.

Row 14: Sl, K4, (O, LRD)2x, K13, (O, LRD)2x, K6, P15, K7, (O, LRD)2x, K4.

Row 15: Sl, K15, (O, LRD)3x, O, K1, O, (RLD, O)3x, K33.

Row 16: Sl, K3, (O, LRD)2x, K13, (O, LRD)2x, K7, P17, K8, (O, LRD)2x, K3.

Row 17: Sl, K15, (O, LRD)3x, (K1, O)2x, K1, (RLD, O)3x, K33.

Row 18: Sl, K2, (O, LRD)2x, K13, (O, LRD)2x, K8, P19, K9, (O, LRD)2x, K2.

Row 19: Sl, K14, RLD, K15, LRD, K32.

Row 20: Sl, K1, (O, LRD)2x, K13, (O, LRD)2x, K9, P17, K10, (O, LRD)2x, K1.

Row 21: Sl, K14, RLD, K13, LRD, K32.

Row 22: Sl, (O, LRD)2x, K13, (O, LRD)2x, K10, P15, K11, (O, LRD)2x.

Row 23: Sl, K14, RLD, K11, LRD, K32.

Row 24: Sl, K1, [(O, LRD)2x, K11]2x, P13, K10, (O, LRD)2x, K1.

Row 25: Sl, K14, RLD, K9, LRD, K32.

Row 26: Sl, K2, (O, LRD)2x, K9, (O, LRD)2x, K12, P11, K9, (O, LRD)2x, K2.

Row 27: Sl, K14, RLD, K7, LRD, K16, O, K1, O, K15.

Row 28: Sl, K3, (O, LRD)2x, K7, P3, K1, (O, LRD)2x, K11, P9, K8, (O, LRD)2x, K3.

Row 29: Sl, K14, RLD, K5, LRD, K17, O, K1, O, K16.

Row 30: Sl, K4, (O, LRD)2x, K6, P5, K2, (O, LRD)2x, K10, P7, K7, (O, LRD)2x, K4.

Row 31: Sl, K14, RLD, K3, LRD, K18, O, K1, O, K17.

Row 32: Sl, K3, (O, LRD)2x, K7, P7, K3, (O, LRD)2x, K9, P5, K8, (O, LRD)2x, K3.

Row 33: Sl, K14, RLD, K1, LRD, K17, O, LRD, O, K1, O, RLD, O, K16.

Row 34: Sl, K2, (O, LRD)2x, K8, P9, K4, (O, LRD)2x, K8, P3, K9, (O, LRD)2x, K2.

Row 35: Sl, K14, D3, K17, O, LRD, K1, (O, K1)2x, RLD, O, K16.

Row 36: Sl, K1, (O, LRD)2x, K9, P11, K5, (O, LRD)2x, K18, (O, LRD)2x, K1.

Row 37: Sl, K32, (O, LRD)2x, O, K1, (O, RLD)2x, O, K16.

Row 38: Sl, (O, LRD)2x, K10, P13, K6, (O, LRD)2x, K18, (O, LRD)2x.

Row 39: Sl, K32, (O, LRD)2x, K1, (O, K1)2x, (RLD, O)2x, K16.

Row 40: Sl, K1, (O, LRD)2x, K9, P15, K7, (O, LRD)2x, K16, (O, LRD)2x, K1.

Row 41: Sl, K32, (O, LRD)3x, O, K1, (O, RLD)3x, O, K16.

Row 42: Sl, K2, (O, LRD)2x, K8, P17, K8, (O, LRD)2x, K14, (O, LRD)2x, K2.

Row 43: Sl, K32, (O, LRD)3x, K1, (O, K1)2x, (RLD, O)3x, K16.

Row 44: Sl, K3, (O, LRD)2x, K7, P19, K9, (O, LRD)2x, K12, (O, LRD)2x, K3.

Row 45: Sl, K31, RLD, K15, LRD, K15.

Row 46: Sl, K4, (O, LRD)2x, K6, P17, K10, (O, LRD)2x, K10, (O, LRD)2x, K4.

Row 47: Sl, K31, RLD, K13, LRD, K15.

Row 48: Sl, K3, (O, LRD)2x, K7, P15, K11, (O, LRD)2x, K10, (O, LRD)2x, K3.

Row 49: Sl, K31, RLD, K11, LRD, K15.

Row 50: Sl, K2, (O, LRD)2x, K8, P13, K12, (O, LRD)2x, K10, (O, LRD)2x, K2.

Row 51: Sl, K31, RLD, K9, LRD, K15.

Row 52: Sl, K1, (O, LRD)2x, K9, P11, K13, (O, LRD)2x, K10, (O, LRD)2x, K1.

Repeat rows 1-52 for desired length, then end with the following rows.

Row 1: Sl, K31, RLD, K7, LRD, K15.

Row 2: Sl, (O, LRD)2x, K10, P9, K12, (O, LRD)2x, K12, (O, LRD)2x.

Row 3: Sl, K31, RLD, K5, LRD, K15.

Row 4: Sl, K1, (O, LRD)2x, K9, P7, K11, (O, LRD)2x, K12, (O, LRD)2x, K1.

Row 5: Sl, K31, RLD, K3, LRD, K15.

Row 6: Sl, K2, (O, LRD)2x, K8, P5, K10, (O, LRD)2x, K12, (O, LRD)2x, K2.

Row 7: Sl, K31, RLD, K1, LRD, K15.

Row 8: Sl, K3, (O, LRD)2x, K7, P3, K9, (O, LRD)2x, K12, (O, LRD)2x, K3.

Row 9: Sl, K31, D3, K15.

Row 10: Knit 48.

Cast off.

Alma's Pattern

This pattern was named for my friend Alma Selkirk, because it was at her house in Pennsylvania that I first saw a pair of counterpanes using this motif. Since then, I have seen spreads knitted in this pattern in a variety of places—at the Baltimore Museum of Art; at Bassett Hall in Colonial Williamsburg in Virginia; at Historic Cherry Hill in Albany, New York; and in several private collections. Most use the strips of double cables to separate the bands of diamonds, but the Cherry Hill version uses the Lyre Pattern rather than the cable with the Diamond Strip. I have given directions for all three elements.

The Lyre Pattern alone also makes a lovely counterpane. Examples of such counterpanes can be found in the Royal Ontario Museum in Toronto, Ontario, and in the Hennepin County Historical Society in Minneapolis, Minnesota.

This two-needle pattern is a good one for an advanced beginner. It is principally a knit-and-purl pattern and is entirely logical in its progression. The border, which I selected from the nineteenth-century Butterick's The Art of Knitting, *resembles the border on the Cherry Hill counterpane. It would make a superb border for many of the main patterns in this book.*

The Diamond Strip sample (shown at two-third size) was knit with cotton warp on size 1 needles.

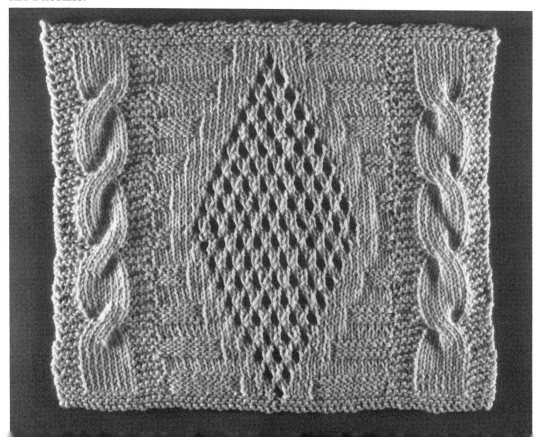

Assembly Diagram

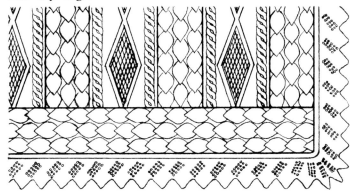

Diamond Strip

Special Instructions:
O2 is used as the basis for one stitch, drop one wrap on following row.

Cast on 63 stitches and knit 4 rows.

Row 1: K16, P11, K4, O2, LRD, K3, P11, K16.

Row 2: K4, P8, K15, P9, K15, P8, K4.

Row 3: K16, P11, K9, P11, K16.

Row 4: Repeat Row 2.

Row 5: K30, (O2, LRD)2x, K29.

Row 6: K4, P8, K4, P31, K4, P8, K4.

Row 7: Knit.

Row 8: Repeat Row 6.

Row 9: K16, P9, K4, (O2, LRD)3x, K3, P9, K16.

Row 10: K4, P8, K13, P13, K13, P8, K4.

Row 11: K16, P9, K13, P9, K16.

Row 12: Repeat Row 10.

Row 13: K28, (O2, LRD)4x, K27.

Row 14: Repeat Row 6.

Row 15: Knit.

Row 16: Repeat Row 6.

Row 17: K4, CF8, K4, P7, K4, (O2, LRD)5x, K3, P7, K4, CB8, K4.

Row 18: K4, P8, K11, P17, K11, P8, K4.

Row 19: K16, P7, K17, P7, K16.

Row 20: Repeat Row 18.

Row 21: K26, (O2, LRD)6x, K25.

Row 22: Repeat Row 6.

Row 23: Knit.

Row 24: Repeat Row 6.

Row 25: K16, P5, K4, (O2, LRD)7x, K3, P5, K16.

Row 26: K4, P8, K9, P21, K9, P8, K4.

Row 27: K16, P5, K21, P5, K16.

Row 28: Repeat Row 26.

Row 29: K24, (O2, LRD)8x, K23.

Row 30: Repeat Row 6.

Row 31: Knit.

Row 32: Repeat Row 6.

Row 33: K4, CF8, K4, P3, K4, (O2, LRD)9x, K3, P3, K4, CB8, K4.

Row 34: K4, P8, K7, P25, K7, P8, K4.

Row 35: K16, P3, K25, P3, K16.

Row 36: Repeat Row 34.

Row 37: K22, (O2, LRD)10x, K21.

Row 38: Repeat Row 6.

Row 39: Knit.

Row 40: Repeat Row 6.

Row 41: K16, P3, K4, (O2, LRD)9x, K3, P3, K16.

Row 42: Repeat Row 34.

Row 43: Repeat Row 35.

Row 44: Repeat Row 34.

Row 45: Repeat Row 29.

Row 46: Repeat Row 6.

Row 47: Knit.

Row 48: Repeat Row 6.

Row 49: K4, CF8, K4, P5, K4, (O2, LRD)7x, K3, P5, K4, CB8, K4.

Row 50: Repeat Row 26.

Row 51: Repeat Row 27.

Row 52: Repeat Row 26.

Row 53: Repeat Row 21.

Row 54: Repeat Row 6.

Row 55: Knit.

Row 56: Repeat Row 6.

Row 57: K16, P7, K4, (O2, LRD)5x, K3, P7, K16.

Row 58: Repeat Row 18.

Row 59: Repeat Row 19.

Row 60: Repeat Row 18.

Row 61: Repeat Row 13.

Row 62: Repeat Row 6.

Row 63: Knit.

Row 64: Repeat Row 6.

Row 65: K4, CF8, K4, P9, K4, (O2, LRD)3x, K3, P9, K4, CB8, K4.

Row 66: Repeat Row 10.

Row 67: Repeat Row 11.

Row 68: Repeat Row 10.

Row 69: Repeat Row 5.

Row 70: Repeat Row 6.

Row 71: Knit.

Row 72: Repeat Row 6.

Repeat rows 1-72 for desired length. Then repeat rows 1-4, knit 4 rows and cast off.

Lyre Pattern

Special Instructions:
O2 is used as the basis for one stitch, with one wrap dropped on following row.
The pattern begins with a multiple of 20 plus 19 stitches. (minimum 39 stitches) and ends with a multiple of 21 plus 19 stitches. All repeats are worked on a multiple of 21 plus 19 stitches. The number of stitches per row varies.
The bracketed instructions should be repeated once for each 20 stitches added. They are not repeated when the pattern is worked on the minimum number of stitches.
The sample is worked on 41 stitches: 1 repeat plus 19 stitches, plus 1 stitch on each side for a garter-stitch border. Note that the border stitches are not included in the row instructions.

Cast on.

Row 1: [*P2, K13, LRD, P2*, O2, K1, O2], *-*.
Row 2: [*K2, P14, K2*, P3], *-*.
Row 3: [*P2, RLD, K10, LRD, P2*, K1, (O, K1)2x], *-*.
Row 4: [*K2, P12, K2*, P5], *-*.
Row 5: [*P2, RLD, K8, LRD, P2*, K2, O, K1, O, K2], *-*.
Row 6: [*K2, P10, K2*, P7], *-*.
Row 7: [*P2, RLD, K6, LRD, P2*, K3, O, K1, O, K3], *-*.
Row 8: [*K2, P8, K2*, P9], *-*.
Row 9: [*P2, RLD, K4, LRD, P2*, K4, O, K1, O, K4], *-*.
Row 10: [*K2, P6, K2*, P11], *-*.
Row 11: [*P2, RLD, K2, LRD, P2*, K5, O, K1, O, K5], *-*.
Row 12: [*K2, P4, K2*, P13], *-*.
Row 13: [*P2, RLD, LRD, P2*, K6, O, K1, O, K6], *-*.
Row 14: [*K2, P2, K2*, P15], *-*.
Row 15: [*P2, O2, RLD, O2, P2*, K13, LRD], *-*.
Row 16: [*K2, P3, K2*, P14], *-*.
Row 17: [*P2, K1, (O, K1)2x, P2*, RLD, K10, LRD], *-*.
Row 18: [*K2, P5, K2*, P12], *-*.

Row 19: [*P2, K2, O, K1, O, K2, P2*, RLD, K8, LRD], *-*.
Row 20: [*K2, P7, K2*, P10], *-*.
Row 21: [*P2, K3, O, K1, O, K3, P2*, RLD, K6, LRD], *-*.
Row 22: [*K2, P9, K2*, P8], *-*.
Row 23: [*P2, K4, O, K1, O, K4, P2*, RLD, K4, LRD], *-*.
Row 24: [*K2, P11, K2*, P6], *-*.
Row 25: [*P2, K5, O, K1, O, K5, P2*, RLD, K2, LRD], *-*.
Row 26: [*K2, P13, K2*, P4], *-*.
Row 27: [*P2, K6, O, K1, O, K6, P2*, RLD, LRD], *-*.
Row 28: [*K2, P15, K2*, P2], *-*.
Row 29: [*P2, K13, LRD, P2*, O2, RLD, O2], *-*.

Repeat rows 2-29 for desired length. On the last repeat, cast off following Row 14 or Row 28.

Pointed Edging

Cast on 22 stitches and knit 1 row.

Row 1: Sl, K1, O, K1, D3, K1, O, K2, (O, LRD)2x, O, K9.

Row 2 and all even-numbered rows through Row 14: Sl, K.
Row 3: Sl, K1, O, K1, D3, K1, O, K3, (O, LRD)2x, O, K9.
Row 5: Sl, K1, O, K1, D3, K1, O, K4, (O, LRD)2x, O, K9.
Row 7: Sl, K1, O, K1, D3, K1, O, K5, (O, LRD)2x, O, K9.
Row 9: Sl, K1, O, K1, D3, K1, O, K6, (O, LRD)2x, O, K9.
Row 11: Sl, K1, O, K1, D3, K1, O, K7, (O, LRD)2x, O, K9.
Row 13: Sl, K1, O, K1, D3, K1, O, K8, (O, LRD)2x, O, K9.
Row 15: Sl, K1, O, K1, D3, K1, O, K9, (O, LRD)2x, O, K9.
Row 16: Cast off 8, K21.

Repeat rows 1-16 for desired length. Cast off remaining stitches.

The Lyre Pattern and edging (shown three-quarter size) were knit with cotton warp on size 1 needles.

Diamond-Clematis Strip

Before going to Australia, Tasmania and New Zealand in 1978, I spent a great deal of time knitting counterpane swatches from books in my collection and from the library. This particular pattern I found in the nineteenth-century publication The Young Ladies Journal. *During my trip, I was delighted to find this pattern used in a counterpane in the Van Dieman Museum in Hobart, Tasmania. That version had the double-cable panel worked on either side of the clematis strip. Later, in the Canterbury Museum in Christchurch, New Zealand, and in the Welsh Folk Museum in Cardiff, Wales, I saw counterpanes worked in the main diamond-strip pattern without the clematis and double-cable patterns.*

This two-needle pattern is moderately difficult but excellent for teaching beginning knitters new skills. The diamond-strip pattern contains raised-leaf motifs in the center, which are created with yarn-overs and paired decreases. The unusual feather-and-fan pattern, worked in both an inset strip and in the border, increases on the front side of the work and decreases every row on the front and back sides.

If you use the double cable on either side of the clematis strip, the two patterns can be knitted at the same time. This will eliminate the need to sew the three pieces together.

Diamond Strip

Special Instructions:
"Follow pattern" means knit the knit stitches and purl the purl stitches as they face you.
Purl the O of previous row.

Cast on 53 stitches.

Row 1: (P1, K1)10x, P3, K3, P1, K3, P3, (K1, P1)10x.
Row 2: Follow pattern.
Row 3: Follow pattern.
Row 4: (P1, K1)9x, P1, K3, P3, K1, P1, K1, P3, K3, P1, (K1, P1)9x.
Row 5: Follow pattern.
Row 6: Follow pattern.
Row 7: (P1, K1)9x, P3, K3, P1, K3, P1, K3, P3, (K1, P1)9x.
Row 8: Follow pattern.
Row 9: Follow pattern.

Row 10: (P1, K1)8x, P1, K3, P3, K1, P5, K1, P3, K3, P1, (K1, P1)8x.
Row 11: Follow pattern.
Row 12: Follow pattern.
Row 13: (P1, K1)8x, P3, K3, (P1, K3)3x, P3, (K1, P1)8x.
Row 14: Follow pattern.
Row 15: Follow pattern.
Row 16: (P1, K1)7x, P1, (K3, P3, K1, P3)2x, K3, P1, (K1, P1)7x.
Row 17: Follow pattern.
Row 18: Follow pattern.
Row 19: (P1, K1)7x, P3, *K3, P1, K3*, P5, *-*, P3, (K1, P1)7x.

Row 20: Follow pattern.
Row 21: Follow pattern.
Row 22: (P1, K1)6x, P1, K3, *P3, K1, P3*, K7, *-*, K3, P1, (K1, P1)6x.
Row 23: Follow pattern.
Row 24: Follow pattern.
Row 25: (P1, K1)6x, P3, *K3, P1, K3*, P9, *-*, P3, (K1, P1)6x.
Row 26: Follow pattern.
Row 27: Follow pattern.
Row 28: (P1, K1)5x, P1, K3, *P3, K1, P3*, K11, *-*, K3, P1, (K1, P1)5x.
Row 29: Follow pattern.
Row 30: Follow pattern.
Row 31: (P1, K1)5x, P3, *K3, P1, K3*, P6, O, K1, O, P6, *-*, P3, (K1, P1)5x.
Row 32: Follow pattern, purling O of previous row.
Row 33: (P1, K1)5x, P3, *K3, P1, K3*, P6, K1, (O, K1)2x, P6, *-*, P3, (K1, P1)5x.

Row 34: (P1, K1)4x, P1, K3, *P3, K1, P3*, K7, P5, K7, *-*, K3, P1, (K1, P1)4x.
Row 35: (K1, P1)4x, K1, P3, *K3, P1, K3*, P7, K2, O, K1, O, K2, P7, *-*, P3, K1, (P1, K1)4x.
Row 36: Follow pattern.
Row 37: (P1, K1)4x, P3, *K3, P1, K3*, P8, K3, O, K1, O, K3, P8, *-*, P3, (K1, P1)4x.
Row 38: Follow pattern.
Row 39: (P1, K1)4x, P3, *K3, P1, K3*, P8, RLD, K5, LRD, P8, *-*, P3, (K1, P1)4x.
Row 40: (P1, K1)3x, P1, K3, *P3, K1, P3*, K9, P7, K9, *-*, K3, P1, (K1, P1)3x.
Row 41: (K1, P1)3x, K1, P3, *K3, P1, K3*, P9, RLD, K3, LRD, P9, *-*, P3, K1, (P1, K1)3x.
Row 42: Follow pattern.

The Diamond Strip pattern (shown half-size) was knit with size 3 perle cotton on size 1 needles.

Row 43: (P1, K1)3x, P3, *K3, P1, K3*, P10, RLD, K1, LRD, P10, *-*, P3, (K1, P1)3x.
Row 44: Follow pattern.
Row 45: (P1, K1)3x, P3, *K3, P1, K3*, P10, D3, P10, *-*, P3, (K1, P1)3x.
Row 46: (P1, K1)2x, P1, K3, *P3, K1, P3*, K23, *-*, K3, P1, (K1, P1)2x.
Row 47: Follow pattern.
Row 48: Follow pattern.
Row 49: (P1, K1)2x, P3, *K3, P1, K3*, P6, **O, K1, O**, P11, **-**, P6, *-*, P3, (K1, P1)2x.
Row 50: Follow pattern.
Row 51: (P1, K1)2x, P3, *K3, P1, K3*, P6, **K1, (O, K1)2x**, P11, **-**, P6, *-*, P3, (K1, P1)2x.
Row 52: P1, K1, P1, K3, *P3, K1, P3* K7, P5, K11, P5, K7, *-*, K3, P1, K1, P1.
Row 53: K1, P1, K1, P3, *K3, P1, K3*, P7, **K2, O, K1, O, K2**, P11, **-**, P7, *-*, P3, K1, P1, K1.
Row 54: Follow pattern.
Row 55: P1, K1, P3, *K3, P1, K3*, P8, **K3, O, K1, O, K3**, P11, **-**, P8, *-*, P3, K1, P1.
Row 56: Follow pattern.
Row 57: P1, K1, P3, *K3, P1, K3*, P8, **RLD, K5, LRD**, P11, **-**, P8, *-*, P3, K1, P1.
Row 58: P1, K1, P1, K3, *P3, K1, P3*, K7, P7, K11, P7, K7, *-*, K3, P1, K1, P1.
Row 59: K1, P1, K1, P3, *K3, P1, K3*, P7, **RLD, K3, LRD**, P11, **-**, P7, *-*, P3, K1, P1, K1.
Row 60: Follow pattern.
Row 61: (P1, K1)2x, P3, *K3, P1, K3*, P6, **RLD, K1, LRD**, P11, **-**, P6, *-*, P3, (K1, P1)2x.
Row 62: Follow pattern.
Row 63: (P1, K1)2x, P3, *K3, P1, K3*, P6, D3, P11, D3, P6, *-*, P3, (K1, P1)2x.

Row 64: (P1, K1)2x, P1, K3, *P3, K1, P3*, K23, *-*, K3, P1, (K1, P1)2x.
Row 65: Follow pattern.
Row 66: Follow pattern.
Row 67: (P1, K1)3x, P3, *K3, P1, K3*, P10, O, K1, O, P10, *-*, P3, (K1, P1)3x.
Row 68: Follow pattern.
Row 69: (P1, K1)3x, P3, *K3, P1, K3*, P10, K1, (O, K1)2x, P10, *-*, P3, (K1, P1)3x.
Row 70: (P1, K1)3x, P1, K3, *P3, K1, P3*, K9, P5, K9, *-*, K3, P1, (K1, P1)3x.
Row 71: (K1, P1)3x, K1, P3, *K3, P1, K3*, P9, K2, O, K1, O, K2, P9, *-*, P3, K1, (P1, K1)3x.
Row 72: Follow pattern.
Row 73: (P1, K1)4x, P3, *K3, P1, K3*, P8, K3, O, K1, O, K3, P8, *-*, P3, (K1, P1)4x.
Row 74: Follow pattern.
Row 75: (P1, K1)4x, P3, *K3, P1, K3*, P8, RLD, K5, LRD, P8, *-*, P3, (K1, P1)4x.
Row 76: (P1, K1)4x, P1, K3, *P3, K1, P3*, K7, P7, K7, *-*, K3, P1, (K1, P1)4x.
Row 77: (K1, P1)4x, K1, P3, *K3, P1, K3*, P7, RLD, K3, LRD, P7, *-*, P3, K1, (P1, K1)4x.
Row 78: Follow pattern.
Row 79: (P1, K1)5x, P3, *K3, P1, K3*, P6, RLD, K1, LRD, P6, *-*, P3, (K1, P1)5x.
Row 80: Follow pattern.
Row 81: (P1, K1)5x, P3, *K3, P1, K3*, P6, D3, P6, *-*, P3, (K1, P1)5x.
Row 82: (P1, K1)5x, P1, K3, *P3, K1, P3*, K11, *-*, K3, P1, (K1, P1)5x.
Row 83: Follow pattern.
Row 84: Follow pattern.

Row 85: (P1, K1)6x, P3, *K3, P1, K3*, P9, *-*, P3, (K1, P1)6x.
Row 86: Follow pattern.
Row 87: Follow pattern.
Row 88: (P1, K1)6x, P1, K3, *P3, K1, P3*, K7, *-*, K3, P1, (K1, P1)6x.
Row 89: Follow pattern.
Row 90: Follow pattern.
Row 91: (P1, K1)7x, P3, *K3, P1, K3*, P5, *-*, P3, (K1, P1)7x.
Row 92: Follow pattern.
Row 93: Follow pattern.
Row 94: (P1, K1)7x, P1, K3, (P3, K1, P3, K3)2x, P1, (K1, P1)7x.
Row 95: Follow pattern.
Row 96: Follow pattern.
Row 97: (P1, K1)8x, P3, *K3, P1, K3*, P1, *-*, P3, (K1, P1)8x.

Row 98: Follow pattern.
Row 99: Follow pattern.
Row 100: (P1, K1)8x, P1, K3, P3, K1, P5, K1, P3, K3, P1, (K1, P1)8x.
Row 101: Follow pattern.
Row 102: Follow pattern.
Row 103: (P1, K1)9x, P3, (K3, P1)2x, K3, P3, (K1, P1)9x.
Row 104: Follow pattern.
Row 105: Follow pattern.
Row 106: (P1, K1)9x, P1, K3, P3, K1, P1, K1, P3, K3, P1, (K1, P1)9x.
Row 107: Follow pattern.
Row 108: Follow pattern.

Repeat rows 1-108 for desired length. Cast off on Row 108 following pattern.

Assembly Diagram

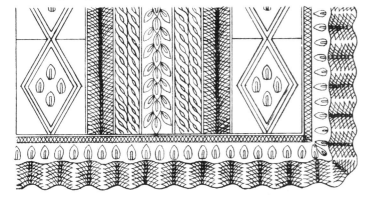

Feather and Fan Pattern

Cast on 25 stitches.

Row 1: P4, K3, LRD, (O, K1)7x, O, RLD, K3, P4.
Row 2: K4, P2, PRD, P15, P2tog, P2, K4.
Row 3: P4, K1, LRD, K15, RLD, K1, P4.
Row 4: K4, PRD, P15, P2tog, K4.
Repeat rows 1-4 for desired length.

The Feather and Fan Pattern was knit with the same yarn and needle size as the Diamond Strip.

Clematis Strip

Special Instructions:
The pattern is worked on a multiple of 29 stitches. Each line of instructions should be repeated once for each 29 stitches. The sample, worked on 29 stitches, is one repeat.

Cast on. Knit 1 row; purl 1 row.

Row 1: K14, O, RLD, K13.
Row 2: K2, P25, K2.
Row 3: K12, LRD, O, K1, O, RLD, K12.
Row 4: Repeat Row 2.
Row 5: K11, LRD, O, K1, P1, K1, O, RLD, K11.
Row 6: K1, (K1, P12)2x, K2.
Row 7: K5, O, K4, D3, O, K2, P1, K2, O, D3, K4, O, K5.
Row 8: Repeat Row 6.

Row 9: *K3, LRD, O, K1, O, RLD, K3*, O, K1, LRD, P1, RLD, K1, O, *-*.
Row 10: Repeat Row 6.
Row 11: K4, *O, K1, P1, K1, O*, D3, **K1, O, K1**, LRD, P1, RLD, **-**, D3, *-*, K4.
Row 12: K2, P4, K1, (P7, K1)2x, P4, K2.
Row 13: K4, O, LRD, P1, K2, *O, LRD, O*, K1, LRD, P1, RLD, K1, *-*, K2, P1, RLD, O, K4.

Row 14: Repeat Row 12.
Row 15: K4, O, K2, P1, RLD, K1, O, *RLD, O, LRD*, P1, *-*, O, K1, LRD, P1, K2, O, K4.
Row 16: K2, P5, K1, (P6, K1)2x, P5, K2.
Row 17: K4, *O, K1, LRD, P1, RLD, K1, O*, K2, O, D3, O, K2, *-*, K4.
Row 18: K2, P5, K1, P13, K1, P5, K2.
Row 19: K5, O, LRD, P1, RLD, K1, O, K7, O, K1, LRD, P1, RLD, O, K5.
Row 20: K2, P25, K2.
Row 21: K6, O, (RLD)2x, K1, O, K3, O, RLD, K2, O, K1, (LRD)2x, O, K6.
Row 22: Repeat Row 20.

Row 23: K7, O, D3, O, K2, LRD, O, K1, O, RLD, K2, O, D3, O, K7.
Row 24: Repeat Row 20.
Row 25: K8, O, *RLD, K1, LRD*, O, K1, P1, K1, O, *-*, O, K8.
Row 26: K1, (K1, P12)2x, K2.

Repeat rows 7-26 for desired length.

Cable Pattern

Cast on 24 stitches.

Row 1: K1, LRD, O, (P2, K6)2x, P2, O, LRD, K1.
Row 2 and all even-numbered rows: K5, P6, K2, P6, K5.
Row 3: Repeat Row 1.
Row 5: K1, LRD, O, (P2, CF6)2x, P2, O, LRD, K1.
Row 7: Repeat Row 1.
Row 8: Repeat Row 2.

Repeat rows 1-8 for desired length.

The Clematis Strip (left) and the Cable Pattern (right), shown two-third size, were knit with size 3 perle cotton on size 1 needles.

Border Pattern
FEATHER SECTION

Special Instructions:
The pattern is worked on a multiple of 21 plus 3 stitches. The instructions in brackets should be repeated once for each 21 stitches.
This sample is worked on 66 stitches: 3 repeats plus 3 stitches.

Cast on.

Row 1: [P3, K3, LRD, (O, K1)8x, RLD, K3], P3.
Row 2: [K3, P2, PRD, P16, P2tog, P2], K3.
Row 3: [P3, K1, LRD, K16, RLD, K1], P3.
Row 4: [K3, PRD, P16, P2tog], K3.
Rows 5-24: Repeat rows 1-4 five more times.
Row 25: Knit.
Row 26: Knit.
Row 27: Purl.
Row 28: Knit.

Repeat rows 1-28 for desired length.

RAISED SECTION

Row 29: P11, *O, K1, O*, (P10, *-*, P9, *-*)2x, P12.
Row 30: K12, (P3, K9, P3, K10)2x, P3, K11.
Row 31: P11, *K1, O, K1, O, K1*, (P10, *-*, P9, *-*)2x, P12.
Row 32: K12, (P5, K9, P5, K10)2x, P5, K11.
Row 33: P11, *K2, O, K1, O, K2*, (P10, *-*, P9, *-*)2x, P12.
Row 34: K12, (P7, K9, P7, K10)2x, P7, K11.
Row 35: P11, *K3, O, K1, O, K3*, (P10, *-*, P9, *-*)2x, P12.
Row 36: K12, (P9, K9, P9, K10)2x, P9, K11.
Row 37: P11, *RLD, K5, LRD*, (P10, *-*, P9, *-*)2x, P12.
Row 38: K12, (P7, K9, P7, K10)2x, P7, K11.
Row 39: P11, *RLD, K3, LRD*, (P10, *-*, P9, *-*)2x, P12.
Row 40: K12, (P5, K9, P5, K10)2x, P5, K11.
Row 41: P11, *RLD, K1, LRD*, (P10, *-*, P9, *-*)2x, P12.
Row 42: K12, (P3, K9, P3, K10)2x, P3, K11.
Row 43: P11, D3, (P10, D3, P9, D3)2x, P12.

Row 44: Knit.
Row 45: Purl.
Row 46: Purl.
Row 47: K1, (O, LRD)32x, K1.
Row 48: Purl.
Row 49: (O, LRD)33x.
Row 50: Purl.
Row 51: Repeat Row 19.
Row 52: Purl.
Row 53: Knit.
Row 54: Knit.
Row 55: Purl.

Cast off knitting.

Crocheted Edging

Working from right to left, *work 1 single crochet in each of next 2 stitches, then work 3 double crochet stitches in next stitch*, repeat from *, being sure to follow the contour of the pattern as shown in the photo below.

The Border Pattern (shown two-third size) was knit with the same yarn and needle size as the other units. The crocheted edging was worked with a C/2 (2.5mm) crochet hook.

Nangle Shells and Cables

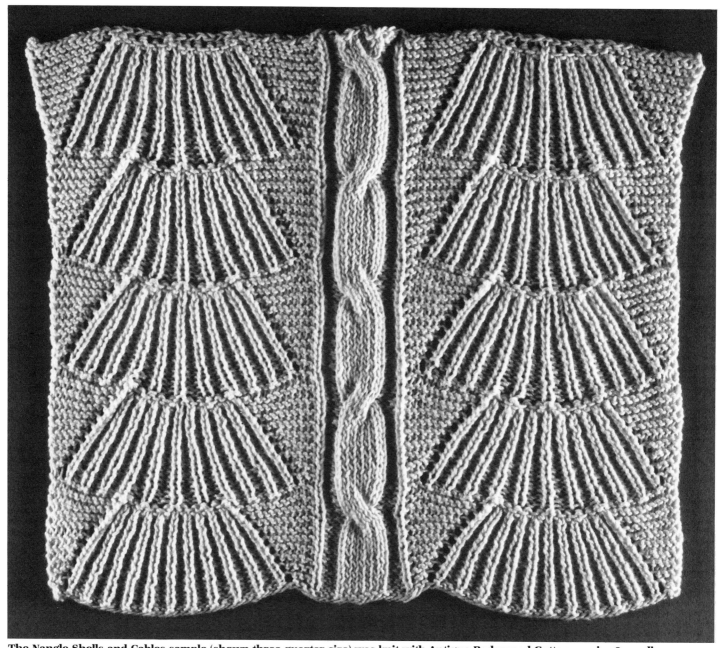

The Nangle Shells and Cables sample (shown three-quarter size) was knit with Antique Bedspread Cotton on size 0 needles.

This pattern, from the nineteenth-century Weldon's Practical Needlework, *is the last one I knitted up and selected for this book. Now it is one of my favorites.*

The pattern's two bands of shells are divided by a seven-stitch mock cable (working cables on an uneven number of stitches was a typical nineteenth-century technique). The shell patterns are knit-and-purl ribbing, with all the decreasing used to shape them worked in the last row of the repeat.

This intermediate pattern would make a beautiful afghan. If worked in a heavier-weight cotton or wool, it would be more three-dimensional. Because the pattern itself is strong, I would suggest using a fairly narrow border (see pp. 144-171) with it. Alternatively, you could add several more garter stitches to the outside edge of the first and last strip and also add a narrow garter-stitch border to the top and bottom of the counterpane.

Special Instructions:
This pattern is actually two different patterns worked in combination. The shell pattern is worked on 35 stitches; the cable pattern, on 15 stitches. The sample is worked on 85 stitches as follows: shell, cable, shell. There are no extra border stitches included in the directions.
Abbreviated Patterns #1 and #2 are worked on the 15 stitches of the cable pattern as follows:
AP1 *K1, P3, K7, P3, K1.*
AP2 *P1, K3, P7, K3, P1.*
The cable crosses are worked as follows:
C7F *Slip 4 stitches onto a cable needle and hold in front of work. Knit the next 3 stitches; knit the 4 stitches from the cable needle.*
C7B *Slip 3 stitches onto a cable needle and hold in back of work. Knit the next 4 stitches; knit the 3 stitches from the cable needle.*
Cross the cable on the center 7 stitches of AP1 every 17th row. The first time the cable crosses, use C7F. The second time the cable crosses, use C7B. Continue to alternate the direction of the cross each time Row 17 is worked.
Note that one half of the cable stays on top of the other half.
The first shell pattern is worked on the stitches between the asterisks. The pair of asterisks at the end of each row identifies the stitches of the second shell pattern.

Cast on 85 stitches.

Row 1: *K2, O, K1, (P2, K1)10x, O, K2*, AP1, *-*.
Row 2: *K3, P1, (K2, P1)10x, K3*, AP2, *-*.
Row 3: *K3, O, K1, (P2, K1)10x, O, K3*, AP1, *-*.
Row 4: *K4, P1, (K2, P1)10x, K4*, AP2, *-*.
Row 5: *K4, O, K1, (P2, K1)10x, O*, K4, AP1, *-*.
Row 6: *K5, P1, (K2, P1)10x, K5*, AP2, *-*.
Row 7: *K5, O, K1, (P2, K1)10x, O, K5*, AP1, *-*.
Row 8: *K6, P1, (K2, P1)10x, K6*, AP2, *-*.
Row 9: *K6, O, K1, (P2, K1)10x, O, K6*, AP1, *-*.
Row 10: *K7, P1, (K2, P1)10x, K7*, AP2, *-*.
Row 11: *K7, O, K1, (P2, K1)10x, O, K7*, AP1, *-*.
Row 12: *K8, (P1, K2)10x, P1, K8*, AP2, *-*.

Row 13: *K8, O, K1, (P2, K1)10x, O, K8*, AP1, *-*.
Row 14: *K9, P1, (K2, P1)10x, K9*, AP2, *-*.
Row 15: *K9, O, K1, (P2, K1)10x, O, K9*, AP1, *-*.
Row 16: *K10, P1, (K2, P1)10x, K10*, AP2, *-*.
Row 17: *K10, O, K1, (P2, K1)10x, O, K10*, K1, P3, C7F/C7B, P3, K1, *-*.
Row 18: *K11, P1, (K2, P1)10x, K11*, AP2, *-*.
Row 19: *K11, O, K1, (P2, K1)10x, O, K11*, AP1, *-*.
Row 20: *K12, (D3)5x, K1, (D3)5x, K12*, AP2, *-*.

Repeat rows 1-20 for desired length. Cast off, knitting the knit stitches and purling the purl stitches.

Leaves, Melons and Lace

The Leaf and Melon pattern (left) and its Melon and Lace Border (right), shown three-quarter size, were knit with Parisian Cotton on size 1 needles.

When working with the Cooper-Hewitt Museum's textile collection several years ago, I found in the files a copy of the nineteenth-century publication The New Knitter or Lady's Worktable Companion. *Included in this book were directions for the melon pattern, an elegant pattern that has since become one of my favorites. I later found an embossed-leaf pattern in a nineteenth-century book by Butterick,* The Art of Knitting, *and more recently in Barbara Abbey's* The Complete Book of Knitting. *I decided that this pair of moderately difficult two-needle patterns belonged together and have combined them here.*

Special Instructions:

AP1 *Abbreviated Pattern #1 is worked as follows:*
Slp, K2, O, LRD, K8, O, LRD, K1.

AP2 *Abbreviated Pattern #2 is worked as follows:*
P1, K2, O, LRD, P6, K2, O, LRD, K1.

P6O2 *Wrap yarn around needle twice when purling these 6 stitches.*

MPC *Melon pattern cross, shown in the drawing below, is worked as follows:*
Slip the next 6 stitches to the right-hand needle, dropping the extra loops formed by P6O2 in the previous row. Transfer stitches back to the left-hand needle, being careful not to twist them. Draw the 4th stitch over the 1st stitch and knit, draw the 5th stitch over the 1st stitch and knit, draw the 6th stitch over the 1st stitch and knit. Then knit stitches 1, 2, 3 in order.

Cast on 47 stitches.

Setup Row 1: Slp, K46.
Setup Row 2: Slp, K6, (P1, K7)3X, P1, K15.

Row 1: AP1, (P7, K1)3x, P6, K1.
Row 2: Slp, K6, (P1, K7)3x, AP2.
Row 3: Repeat Row 1.
Row 4: Repeat Row 2.
Row 5: Repeat Row 1.
Row 6: Repeat Row 2, working P6O2 in place of P6 in AP2.

Row 7: Slp, K2, O, LRD, MPC, K2, O, LRD, K1, *P7, M1R, K1, M1L*, P7, K1, *-*, P6, K1.
Row 8: Slp, K6, P3, K7, P1, K7, P3, K7, AP2.
Row 9: AP1, *P7, M1R, K3, M1L*, P7, K1, *-*, P6, K1.
Row 10: Slp, K6, P5, K7, P1, K7, P5, K7, AP2.
Row 11: AP1, *P7, M1R, K1, RLD, K2, M1L*, P7, K1, *-*, P6, K1.
Row 12: Slp, K6, P6, K7, P1, K7, P6, K7, AP2.

Row 13: AP1, *P7, M1R, K2, RLD, K2, M1L*, P7, K1, *-*, P6, K1.
Row 14: Slp, K6, P7, K7, P1, K7, P7, K7, AP2 working P6O2 in place of P6 in AP2.
Row 15: Slp, K2, O, LRD, MPC, K2, O, LRD, K1, *P7, M1R, K3, RLD, K2, M1L*, P7, K1, *-*, P6, K1.
Row 16: Slp, K6, P8, K7, P1, K7, P8, K7, AP2.
Row 17: AP1, *P7, K4, RLD, K2*, P7, K1, *-*, P6, K1.
Row 18: Slp, K6, P7, K7, P1, K7, P7, K7, AP2.
Row 19: AP1, *P7, RLD, K1, RLD, LRD*, P7, K1, *-*, P6, K1.

Row 20: Slp, K6, P4, K7, P1, K7, P4, K7, AP2.
Row 21: AP1, *P7, RLD, LRD*, P7, K1, *-*, P6, K1.
Row 22: Slp, K6, P2tog, K7, P1, K7, P2tog, K7, AP2, working P6O2 in place of P6 in AP2.

Repeat rows 7-22 for desired length. Notice that the embossed leaf pattern is worked in the middle only on the next repeat. In subsequent repeats, leaf alternates as indicated in the photo on the facing page.

Melon and Lace Border

Special Instructions:

AP1 *Abbreviated Pattern #1 is worked as follows:*
Slp, K4, O, LRD, K8, O, LRD.

AP2 *Abbreviated Pattern #2 is worked as follows:*
K2, O, LRD, P6, K2, O, LRD.

K2togB *Knit two stitches together through the backs of the stitches. This decrease slants from right to left (one stitch decreased).*

Cast on 37 stitches.

Setup Row 1: K7, P1, K11, P15, K3.
Setup Row 2: AP1, K20.

Row 1: O, K7, P1, K1, (O, LRD)5x, P1, AP2, K3.
Row 2: AP1, K21.
Row 3: O, K8, P1, (O, LRD)5x, K1, P1, AP2, K3.
Row 4: AP1, K22.
Row 5: O, K9, P1, K1, (O, LRD)5x, P1, AP2, K3.
Row 6: AP1, K23.
Row 7: O, K10, P1, (O, LRD)5x, K1, P1, (AP2, working P6O2 in place of P6), K3.

Row 8: Slp, K4, O, LRD, MPC, K2, O, LRD, K24.
Row 9: K2togB, K9, P1, K1, (O, LRD)5x, P1, AP2, K3.
Row 10: AP1, K23.
Row 11: K2togB, K8, P1, (O, LRD)5x, K1, P1, AP2, K3.
Row 12: AP1, K22.
Row 13: K2togB, K7, P1, K1, (O, LRD)5x, P1, AP2, K3.
Row 14: AP1, K21.
Row 15: K2togB, K6, P1, (O, LRD)5x, K1, P1, (AP2, working P6O2 in place of P6), K3.
Row 16: Slp, K4, O, LRD, MPC, K2, O, LRD, K20.

Repeat rows 1-16 for desired length.

Melon Pattern Cross

Note: first six stitches on right needle show finished cross. Remaining stitches show cross being worked.

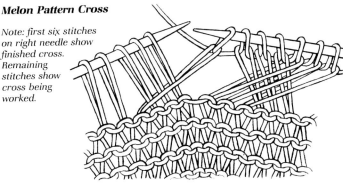

Alsacian Scallops

One of the pleasures of my 1978 visit to Christchurch, New Zealand, was meeting Jean Double, an avid knitter who presented me with a handsome knitted scallop pattern for a dress. I liked the pattern so much that I isolated its basic unit and began experimenting with it. To define the pattern better, I added the gathering stitch, which is used in many nineteenth-century patterns. Several years later, when visiting the Alsacian Museum in Strasbourg, France, I saw (in a wonderful collection of knitted white cotton petticoats) a pattern very similar to my version of the original dress pattern. For this reason, I have dubbed the pattern Alsacian Scallops. I am sure it would make an elegant counterpane.

This is a relatively easy two-needle pattern. The only unusual part of the pattern is the gathering stitch, shown in the drawing below, which involves a simple wrapping on the purl side of a designated group of stitches.

Purl Wrap (P4 wrap)

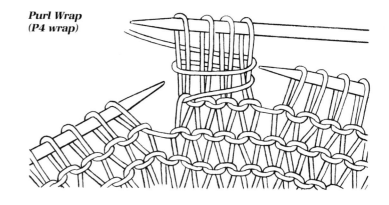

Special Instructions:
As shown in the drawing at right, the purl wrap (P4 wrap) is worked as follows:
Purl 4 stitches, transfer from the right-hand needle to a double-pointed needle and hold apart from the two knitting needles. Wrap the knitting yarn around the 4 stitches counterclockwise (covering the purl surface first). Make 3 complete wraps. Return stitches to right needle and continue with the row.
The pattern is worked on a multiple of 21 plus 3 stitches. The instructions in the brackets should be repeated once for each 21 stitches. The sample is worked on 68 stitches: 3 repeats plus 3 stitches, plus 1 stitch on each side for a garter-stitch border. The border stitches are not included in the directions.

Cast on.

Row 1 and 3: Knit.
Row 2 (front): Purl.
Row 4: K1, [O, K21], K2.
Row 5: P2, [(P1, K3)5x, P2], P1.
Row 6: K1, [K1, O, K1, (P3, K1)5x, O], K2.

Row 7: P2, [P2, (K3, P1)5x, P2], P1.
Row 8: K1, [(K1, O)2x, (RLD, P2)5x, (K1, O)2x], K2.
Row 9: P2, [P4, (K2, P1)5x, P4], P1.
Row 10: K1, [(K1, O)4x, (RLD, P1)5x, (K1, O)4x], K2.

Row 11: P2, [P8, (K1, P1)5x, P8], P1.
Row 12: K1, [K8, (RLD)5x, K8], K2.
Row 13: P2, [P8, P4 wrap, P9], P1.
Row 14: Knit.

Repeat rows 1-14 for desired length.

The Alsacian Scallops sample was knit with size 3 perle cotton on size 1 needles.

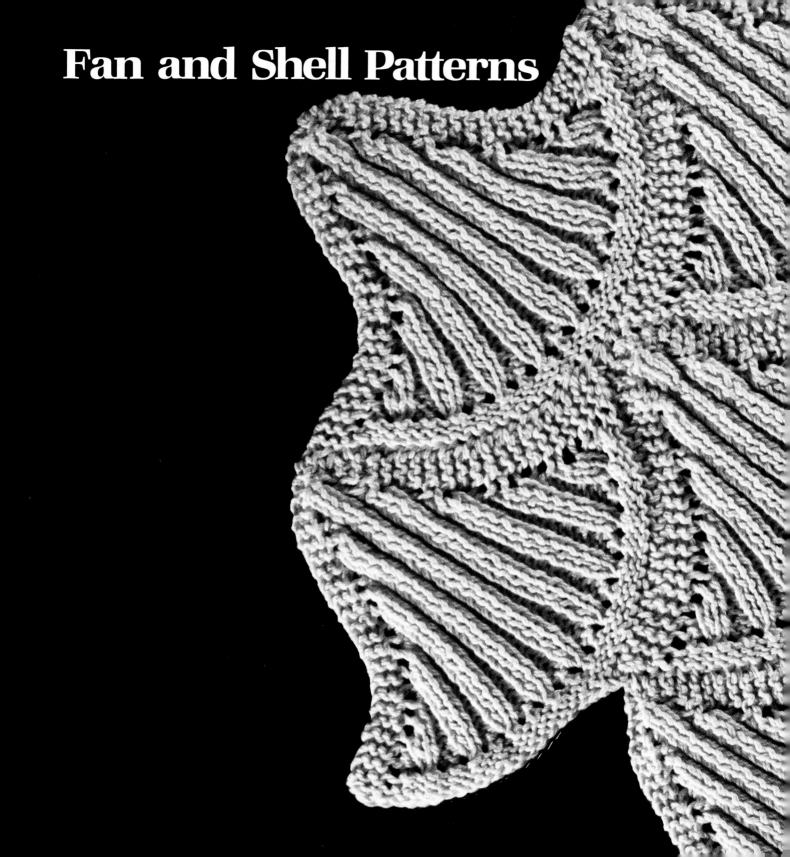

Fan and Shell Patterns

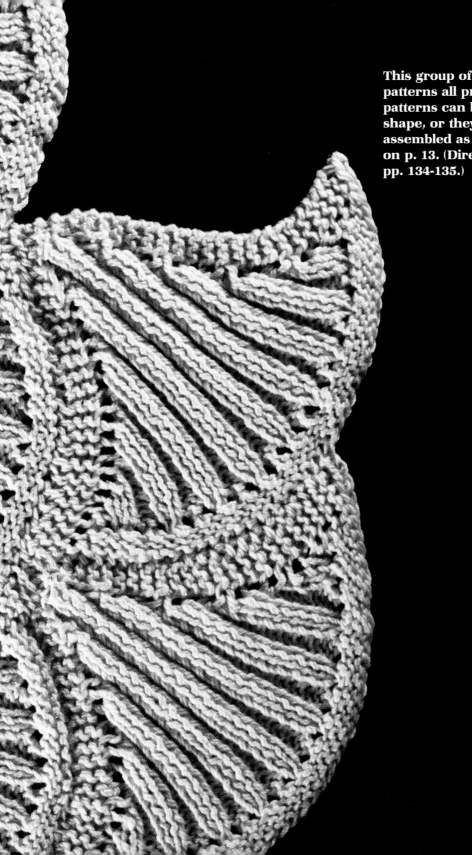

This group of relatively simple but elegant patterns all produce fan or shell shapes. These patterns can be blocked to retain their teardrop shape, or they can be blocked as triangles and assembled as four-unit squares, as shown on p. 13. (Directions for this pattern are found on pp. 134-135.)

Scallop Shells

This pattern is one of my all-time favorites. Its sheer simplicity is endlessly appealing.
I have seen only one counterpane worked in this pattern, an 1881 example that is now part
of the collection of the Canterbury Museum in Christchurch, New Zealand. I wrote directions
for the pattern and only later realized that I had overlooked printed instructions for it in
the nineteenth-century Weldon's Practical Needlework because the pattern units had been
assembled as four-unit squares rather than as the series of cascading fan shapes used in
the Canterbury Museum example. The choice of assembly is up to you.

This is just the pattern for a beginning knitter. It is worked on two needles and involves
only knit, purl and garter stitches, with yarn-overs for the increases.

The original counterpane uses no half-pattern units around the edges, but instead squeezes
full units in around the inside edge of the border. The edges of the counterpane therefore
undulate like waves. I like this effect and have therefore provided no half-patterns.

To complete the counterpane, I have used a modified version of the Barberry Leaf
border pattern from Weldon's Practical Knitter. You may want to make further changes in
this pattern or choose another lace edging from pp. 144-171.

Cast on 2 stitches.

Rows 1-5: B1, knit remaining stitches. When Row 5 is completed there will be 7 stitches.

Row 6: B1, K1, O, K2, O, K3.

Row 7: K4, P2, K4.

Row 8: K3, O, P1, K2, P1, O, K3.

Row 9: K5, P2, K5.

Row 10: K3, O, P2, K2, P2, O, K3.

Row 11: K3, P1, K2, P2, K2, P1, K3.

Row 12: K3, O, K1, P2, K2, P2, K1, O, K3.

Row 13: K3, (P2, K2)2x, P2, K3.

Row 14: K3, O, (K2, P2)2x, K2, O, K3.

Row 15: K4, (P2, K2)2x, P2, K4.

Row 16: K3, O, P1, (K2, P2)2x, K2, P1, O, K3.

Row 17: K5, (P2, K2)2x, P2, K5.

Row 18: K3, O, (P2, K2)3x, P2, O, K3.

Row 19: K3, P1, (K2, P2)3x, K2, P1, K3.

Row 20: K3, O, K1, (P2, K2)3x, P2, K1, O, K3.

Row 21: K3, (P2, K2)4x, P2, K3.

Row 22: K3, O, (K2, P2)4x, K2, O, K3.

Row 23: K4, (P2, K2)4x, P2, K4.

Row 24: K3, O, P1, (K2, P2)4x, K2, P1, O, K3.

Row 25: K5, (P2, K2)5x, K3.

Row 26: K3, O, (P2, K2)5x, P2, O, K3.

Row 27: K3, P1, (K2, P2)5x, K2, P1, K3.

Row 28: K3, O, K1, (P2, K2)5x, P2, K1, O, K3.

Row 29: K3, (P2, K2)6x, P2, K3.

Row 30: K3, O, (K2, P2)6x, K2, O, K3.

Row 31: K4, (P2, K2)6x, P2, K4.

Row 32: K3, O, P1, (K2, P2)6x, K2, P1, O, K3.

Row 33: K5, (P2, K2)7x, K3.

Row 34: K3, O, (P2, K2)7x, P2, O, K3.

Assembly Diagrams

This and the other fan and shell patterns can be assembled as a series of
fan shapes (1), or as squares (2). The fan shapes can also be turned 90° to the
right or left, or turned 180°. See pp. 13-14 for blocking information.

1
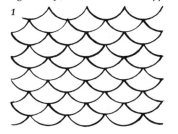

2
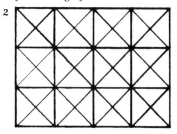

Row 35: K3, P1, (K2, P2)7x, K2, P1, K3.
Row 36: K3, O, K1, (P2, K2)7x, P2, K1, O, K3.
Row 37: K3, (P2, K2)8x, P2, K3.
Row 38: K3, O, (K2, P2)8x, K2, O, K3.
Row 39: K4, (P2, K2)8x, P2, K4.

Row 40: K3, O, P1, (K2, P2)8x, K2, P1, O, K3.
Row 41: K5, (P2, K2)9x, K3.
Row 42: K3, (O, LRD)19x, O, K3.
Row 43: Knit.
Row 44: K3, O, P39, O, K3.
Row 45: Knit.

Cast off knitting.

Barberry Leaf Border

Special Instructions:
O2 is used as the basis for 2 stitches on the following row.

Cast on 25 stitches, knit 1 row.

Row 1: Slp, *K2, O, LRD*, K1, O, LRD, *-*, K5, O, LRD, K1, (O2, LRD)2x, K1.

Row 2: K3, P1, K2, P1, K3, O, LRD, K12, O, LRD, K1.
Row 3: Slp, (K2, O, LRD)3x, K4, O, LRD, K3, (O2, LRD)2x, K1.
Row 4: K3, P1, K2, P1, K5, O, LRD, K12, O, LRD, K1.
Row 5: Slp, (K2, O, LRD, K3, O, LRD)2x, K5, (O2, LRD)2x, K1.
Row 6: K3, P1, K2, P1, K7, O, LRD, K12, O, LRD, K1.
Row 7: Slp, *K2, O, LRD*, K4, O, LRD, (*-*)2x, K12.
Row 8: Cast off 6 stitches, K7, O, LRD, K12, O, LRD, K1.

Repeat rows 1-8 for desired length.

The Scallop Shells samples (shown two-third size) were knit with a doubled strand of Knit-Cro-Sheen cotton on size 2 needles.

Interlocking Ribs

This simple yet compelling pattern is drawn from the collection of Historic Cherry Hill in Albany, New York. I have never seen another example of a counterpane worked in this pattern, nor have I ever found any written instructions for it. It consists only of reverse stockinette ribbing bordered on each side by a band of faggoting. The insert pattern is a cable on a seed-stitch ground; the border is a garter-stitch edging rhythmically broken by curving columns of faggoting. The original counterpane bears the 1862 date of its completion in one corner, worked in purl stitches on stockinette ground. You, too, can personalize your counterpane with such a notation. You might also try working this pattern in several colors.

Cast on 30 stitches.

Row 1: Knit.
Row 2: Purl.
Row 3: K1, (O, LRD)14x, K1.
Row 4: Purl.
Row 5: Purl.
Row 6: Knit.

Row 7: Purl.
Rows 8-31: Repeat rows 5-7 eight more times.
Row 32: Purl.
Row 33: Repeat Row 3.
Row 34: Purl.
Row 35: Knit.

Cast off by purling.

Half-Pattern

Cast on 30 stitches.

Row 1: Knit.
Row 2: Purl.
Row 3: LRD, (O, LRD)14x.
Row 4: P29.
Row 5: P2tog, P27.
Row 6: K28.
Row 7: P2tog, P26.
Row 8: P27.
Row 9: LRD, K25.
Row 10: P26.
Row 11: P2tog, P24.
Row 12: K25.
Row 13: P2tog, P23.
Row 14: P24.
Row 15: LRD, K22.
Row 16: P23.
Row 17: P2tog, P21.
Row 18: K22.
Row 19: P2tog, P20.
Row 20: P21.
Row 21: LRD, K19.
Row 22: P20.
Row 23: P2tog, P18.
Row 24: K19.
Row 25: P2tog, P17.
Row 26: P18.
Row 27: LRD, K16

Row 28: P17.
Row 29: P2tog, P15.
Row 30: K16.
Row 31: P2tog, P14.
Row 32: P15.
Row 33: LRD, K13.
Row 34: P14.
Row 35: P2tog, P12.
Row 36: K13.
Row 37: P2tog, P11.
Row 38: P12.
Row 39: LRD, K10.
Row 40: P11.
Row 41: P2tog, P9.
Row 42: K10.
Row 43: P2tog, P8.
Row 44: P9.
Row 45: LRD, K7.
Row 46: P8.
Row 47: P2tog, P6.
Row 48: K7.
Row 49: P2tog, P5.
Row 50: P6.
Row 51: LRD, K4.
Row 52: P5.
Row 53: P2tog, P3.
Row 54: K4.
Row 55: P2tog, P2
Row 56: P3.
Row 57: LRD, K1.
Row 58: P2tog, fasten off.

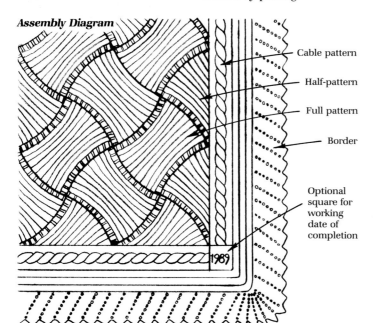

Assembly Diagram

Cable pattern

Half-pattern

Full pattern

Border

Optional square for working date of completion

Cable Pattern

Cast on 14 stitches.

Row 1: (K1, P1)2x, K6, (P1, K1)2x.
Row 2: *K1, P1, K1,* P8, *-*.
Rows 3-6: Repeat rows 1 and 2 two more times.
Row 7: (K1, P1)2x, CF6, (P1, K1)2x.
Row 8: Repeat Row 2.

Repeat rows 1-8 for desired length.

Interlocking Ribs Border

Special Instructions:
AP1 Abbreviated pattern #1 is worked as follows:
Slp, K2, (O, LRD)2x, K1.
AP2 Abbreviated pattern #2 is worked as follows:
K2, (O, LRD)2x, K2.

Cast on 23 stitches.

Row 1: AP1, (put marker on needle), O, K1, (O, LRD)7x.
Row 2: K16, AP2.

Row 3: AP1, O, K16.
Row 4: K17, AP2.
Row 5: AP1, O, K17.
Row 6: K18, AP2.

Row 7: AP1, O, K18.
Row 8: K19, AP2.
Row 9: AP1, O, K19.
Row 10: K20, AP2.
Row 11: AP1, O, K20.
Row 12: Cast off 5 stitches, (O, LRD)7x, K1, AP2.

Repeat rows 3-12 for desired length. On the last repeat, work rows 3-11 and then cast off all stitches.

The Interlocking Ribs samples (shown half-size) were worked with a doubled strand of Knit-Cro-Sheen Cotton on size 2 needles.

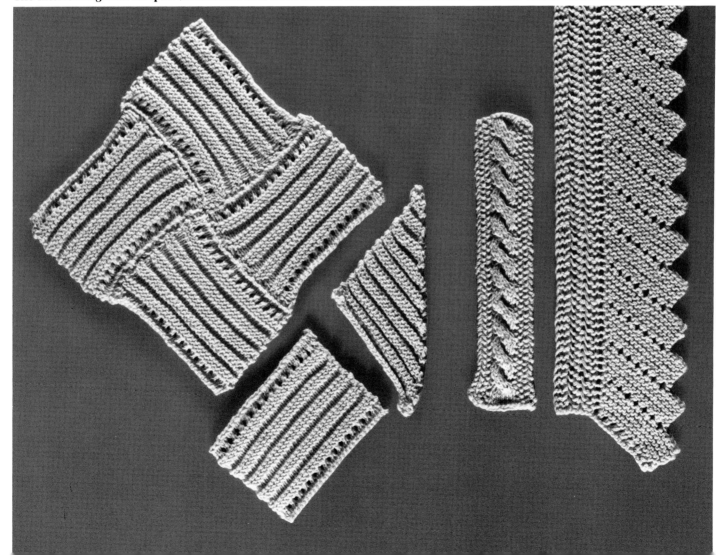

Bay Leaves

This is a popular nineteenth-century pattern, which shows up with variations from example to example. The version for which I have given instructions is in the Royal Ontario Museum in Toronto, Canada, and is the first example I saw of a counterpane worked in this pattern. The modifications of the pattern usually involve working the tapered back area of the fan shape with a different motif. The museum at the Rhode Island School of Design has a handsome variation worked with horizontal ribbing in place of the slip-knit stitch used here.

In an issue of Architectural Digest from the late 1970s, I came across a picture of a bedroom with twin beds covered with counterpanes, one in this pattern, the other in an entirely different pattern. Why not? How dull to knit a pair of counterpanes in the same pattern!

For the intermediate knitter, the Bay Leaves pattern is worked on two needles and involves knit, purl, slip and garter stitches, with yarn-overs and central decreases. The units can be assembled as fan shapes, using the half-unit to complete the sides, or as four-unit squares (see Assembly Diagram on p. 134). I suggest using the Cherry Leaf border (see p. 154) to complete this counterpane.

Special Instructions:
Slpf   slip stitch purlwise, holding yarn to front.

Cast on 3 stitches.

Row 1: K1, (O, K1)2x.
Row 2: K5.
Row 3: K2, O, K1, O, K2.
Row 4: K7.
Row 5: K3, O, K1, O, K3.
Row 6: K9.
Row 7: K4, O, K1, O, K4.
Row 8: K11.
Row 9: K5, O, K1, O, K5.
Row 10: K13.
Row 11: K5, O, P2tog, P1, O, K5.
Row 12: K5, P1, Slpf, P2, K5.
Row 13: K5, O, P2tog, P2, O, K5.
Row 14: K5, (P1, Slpf)2x, P1, K5.

Row 15: K5, O, P2tog, P3, O, K5.
Row 16: K5, (P1, Slpf)2x, P2, K5.
Row 17: K5, O, P2tog, P4, O, K5.
Row 18: K5, (P1, Slpf)3x, P1, K5.
Row 19: K5, O, P2tog, P5, O, K5.
Row 20: K5, (P1, Slpf)3x, P2, K5.
Row 21: K5, O, P2tog, P6, O, K5.
Row 22: K5, (P1, Slpf)4x, P1, K5.
Row 23: K5, O, P2tog, P7, O, K5.

Row 24: K5, (P1, Slpf)4x, P2, K5.
Row 25: K5, O, P2tog, P8, O, K5
Row 26: K5, (P1, Slpf)5x, P1, K5.
Row 27: K5, O, P2tog, P9, O, K5.
Row 28: K5, (P1, Slpf)5x, P2, K5.
Row 29: K5, O, P2tog, P10, O, K5.
Row 30: K5, (P1, Slpf)6x, P1, K5.
Row 31: K5, O, P2tog, P11, O, K5.
Row 32: K5, (P1, Slpf)6x, P2, K5.
Row 33: K5, O, P2tog, P12, O, K5.
Row 34: K5, (P1, Slpf)7x, P1, K5.
Row 35: K5, O, P2tog, P13, O, K5.

Row 36: K5, (P1, Slpf)7x, P2, K5.
Row 37: K5, O, P2tog, P14, O, K5.
Row 38: K5, (P1, Slpf)8x, P1, K5.
Row 39: K5, O, P2tog, P15, O, K5.
Row 40: K5, (P1, Slpf)8x, P2, K5.
Row 41: K5, O, P2tog, P16, O, K5.
Row 42: K5, (P1, Slpf)9x, P1, K5.
Row 43: K5, O, P2tog, P17, O, K5.
Row 44: K5, (P1, Slpf)9x, P2, K5.
Row 45: K5, O, P2tog, P18, O, K5.
Row 46: K5, (P1, Slpf)10x, P1, K5.
Row 47: K5, O, P2tog, P19, O, K5.

Row 48: K5, (P1, Slpf)10x, P2, K5.

Row 49: K5, O, P2tog, P20, O, K5.

Row 50: K5, (P1, Slpf)11x, P1, K5.

Row 51: K5, O, P2tog, P21, O, K5.

Row 52: K5, (P1, Slpf)11x, P2, K5.

Row 53: K5, O, P2tog, P22, O, K5

Row 54: K5, P3, (O, K1, O, P6)2x, O, K1, O, P7, K5.

Row 55: K5, O, LRD, K5, (P3, K6)2x, P3, K3, O, K5.

Row 56: K5, P4, (O, K3, O, P6)2x, O, K3, O, P7, K5.

Row 57: K5, O, LRD, K5, (P5, K6)2x, P5, K4, O, K5.

Row 58: K5, P5, (O, K5, O, P6)2x, O, K5, O, P7, K5.

Row 59: K5, O, LRD, K5, (P7, K6)2x, P7, K5, O, K5.

Row 60: K5, P6, (O, K7, O, P6)2x, O, K7, O, P7, K5.

Row 61: K5, O, LRD, K5, (P9, K6)3x, O, K5.

Row 62: K5, P7, (K3, D3, K3, P6)2x, K3, D3, K3, P7, K5.

Row 63: K5, O, LRD, K5, (P7, K6)2x, P7, K7, O, K5.

Row 64: K5, P8, (K2, D3, K2, P6)2x, K2, D3, K2, P7, K5.

Row 65: K5, O, LRD, K5, (P5, K6)2x, P5, K8, O, K5.

Row 66: K5, P9, (K1, D3, K1, P6)2x, K1, D3, K1, P7, K5.

Row 67: K5, O, LRD, K5, (P3, K6)2x, P3, K9, O, K5.

Row 68: K5, P10, (D3, P6)2x, D3, P7, K5.

Row 69: K5, (O, P2tog)16x· O, K5.

Row 70: K43.

Row 71: K5, P33, K5.

Cast off.

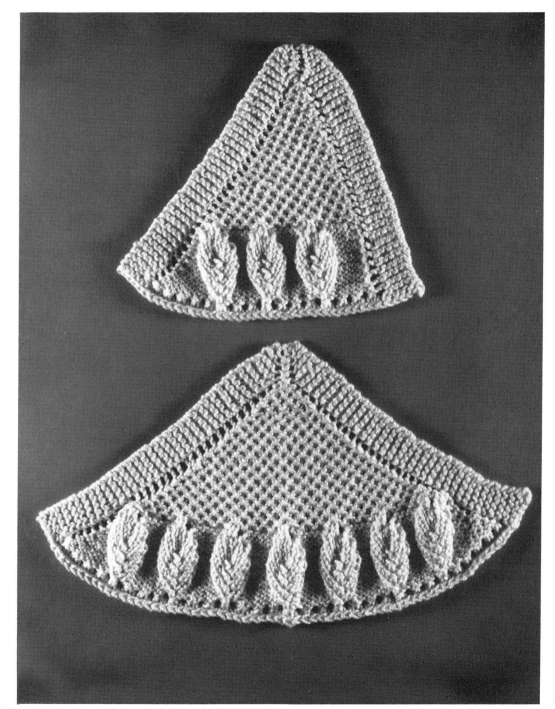

The Bay Leaves samples (shown half-size) were worked with size 3 perle cotton on size 1 needles.

Bay Leaves Half-Pattern
LEFT SIDE

Special Instructions:
Slpf *slip stitch purlwise, holding yarn to front.*

Cast on 3 stitches.

Row 1: K1, (O, K1)2x.
Row 2: K5.
Row 3: K2, O, K1, O, K2.
Row 4: K7.
Row 5: K3, O, K1, O, K3.
Row 6: K9.
Row 7: K4, O, K1, O, K4.
Row 8: K11.
Row 9: K5, O, K1, O, K5.
Row 10: K13.
Row 11: K5, O, P2tog, P1, O, K5.
Row 12: K5, P1, Slpf, P2, K5.
Row 13: K5, O, P2tog, P2, O, K5.
Row 14: K4, (P1, Slpf)2x, P1, K5.
Row 15: K5, O, P2tog, P3, O, K5.
Row 16: K5, (P1, Slpf)2x, P2, K5.
Row 17: K5, P2tog, P4, O, K5.
Row 18: K5, (P1, Slpf)3x, P1, K5.
Row 19: K5, O, P2tog, P5, O, K5.
Row 20: K5, (P1, Slpf)3x, P2, K5.
Row 21: K5, O, P2tog, P6, O, K5.
Row 22: K5, (P1, Slpf)4x, P1, K5.

Row 23: K5, O, P2tog, P7, O, K5.
Row 24: K5, (P1, Slpf)4x, P2, K5.
Row 25: K5, O, P2tog, P8, O, K5
Row 26: K5, (P1, Slpf)5x, P1, K5.
Row 27: K5, O, P2tog, P9, O, K5.
Row 28: K5, (P1, Slpf)5x, P2, K5.
Row 29: K5, O, P2tog, P10, O, K5.
Row 30: K5, (P1, Slpf)6x, P1, K5.
Row 31: K5, O, P2tog, P11, O, K5.
Row 32: K5, (P1, Slpf)6x, P2, K5.
Row 33: K5, O, P2tog, P12, O, K5.
Row 34: K5, (P1, Slpf)7x, P1, K5.
Row 35: K5, O, P2tog, P13, O, K5.
Row 36: K5, (P1, Slpf)7x, P2, K5.
Row 37: K5, O, P2tog, P14, O, K5.
Row 38: K5, (P1, Slpf)8x, P1, K5.
Row 39: K5, O, P2tog, P15, O, K5.
Row 40: K5, (P1, Slpf)8x, P2, K5.
Row 41: K5, O, P2tog, P16, O, K5.
Row 42: K5, (P1, Slpf)9x, P1, K5.

Row 43: K5, O, P2tog, P17, O, K5.
Row 44: K5, (P1, Slpf)9x, P2, K5.
Row 45: K5, O, P2tog, P18, O, K5.
Row 46: K5, (P1, Slpf)10x, P1, K5.
Row 47: K5, O, P2tog, P19, O, K5.
Row 48: K5, (P1, Slpf)10x, P2, K5.
Row 49: K5, O, P2tog, P20, O, K5.
Row 50: K5, (P1, Slpf)11x, P1, K5.
Row 51: K5, O, P2tog, P21, O, K5.
Row 52: K5, (P1, Slpf)11x, P2, K5.
Row 53: K5, O, P2tog, P22, O, K5.
Row 54: K5, P3, (O, K1, O, P6)2x, O, K1, O, P7, K5.
Row 55: K5, O, LRD, K5, (P3, K6)2x, P3, K3, O, K5.
Row 56: K5, P4, (O, K3, O, P6)2x, O, K3, O, P7, K5.
Row 57: K5, O, LRD, K5, (P5, K6)2x, P5, K4, O, K5.
Row 58: K5, P5, (O, K5, O, P6)2x, O, K5, O, P7, K5.
Row 59: K5, O, LRD, K5, (P7, K6)2x, P7, K5, O, K5.
Row 60: K5, P6, (O, K7, O, P6)2x, O, K7, O, P7, K5.
Row 61: K5, O, LRD, K5, (P9, K6)3x, O, K5.
Row 62: K5, P7, (K3, D3, K3, P6)2x, K3, D3, K3, P7, K5.
Row 63: K5, O, LRD, K5, (P7, K6)2x, P7, K7, O, K5.
Row 64: K5, P8, (K2, D3, K2, P6)2x, K2, D3, K2, P7, K5.
Row 65: K5, O, LRD, K5, (P5, K6)2x, P5, K8, O, K5.
Row 66: K5, P9, (K1, D3, K1, P6)2x, K1, D3, K1, P7, K5.

Row 67: K5, O, LRD, K5, (P3, K6)2x, P3, K9, O, K5.
Row 68: K5, P10, (D3, P6)2x, D3, P7, K5.
Row 69: K5, (O, P2tog)16x, O, K5.
Row 70: K43.
Row 71: K5, P33, K5.

Cast off.

To reverse shaping for right-side half-pattern, work rows 1-10 as above and then, beginning with Row 11, read instructions from right to left.

Wilma's Pattern

I have found this very old pattern under various names in many nineteenth-century needlework magazines, and have seen numerous examples of counterpanes worked in it. I named the pattern here for my friend Wilma Smith Leland, who has a lovely counterpane in this motif made by her grandmother. This very easy pattern is worked on two needles and involves knit, purl and garter stitches, with eyelet faggoting on the top edge. The pattern can be assembled as squares or as cascading fan shapes (see Assembly Diagram on p. 134). The original counterpane used the fan shapes, with no half-pattern units at the sides. I like the scalloped edges of the original and hence have provided no half-pattern. The Florence Border (see p. 152) or the Frisby Edging (see p. 155) would nicely complete this counterpane.

Wilma's Pattern (shown two-third size) was worked with size 3 perle cotton on size 1 needles.

Cast on 53 stitches.

Rows 1 and 3 (front side): Knit.
Rows 2 and 4: K2, (O, LRD)25x, K1.
Rows 5 and 6: Knit.
Row 7: K4, RLD, K47.
Row 8: K4, P2tog, P42, K4.
Row 9: K4, RLD, K45.
Row 10: K4, P2tog, P40, K4.
Row 11: K4, P2tog, P39, K4.
Row 12: K4, RLD, K42.
Row 13: K4, P2tog, P37, K4.
Row 14: K4, RLD, K40.
Row 15: K4, RLD, K39.
Row 16: K4, P2tog, P34, K4.
Row 17: K4, RLD, K37.
Row 18: K4, P2tog, P32, K4.
Row 19: K4, P2tog, P31, K4.
Row 20: K4, RLD, K34.
Row 21: K4, P2tog, P29, K4.
Row 22: K4, RLD, K32.
Row 23: K4, RLD, K31.
Row 24: K4, P2tog, P26, K4.
Row 25: K4, RLD, K29.
Row 26: K4, P2tog, P24, K4.
Row 27: K4, P2tog, P23, K4.
Row 28: K4, RLD, K26.
Row 29: K4, P2tog, P21, K4

Row 30: K4, RLD, K24.
Row 31: K4, RLD, K23.
Row 32: K4, P2tog, P18, K4.
Row 33: K4, RLD, K21.
Row 34: K4, P2tog, P16, K4.
Row 35: K4, P2tog, P15, K4.
Row 36: K4, RLD, K18.
Row 37: K4, P2tog, P13, K4.
Row 38: K4, RLD, K16.
Row 39: K4, RLD, K15.
Row 40: K4, P2tog, P10, K4.
Row 41: K4, RLD, K13.
Row 42: K4, P2tog, P8, K4.
Row 43: K4, P2tog, P7, K4.
Row 44: K4, RLD, K10.
Row 45: K4, P2tog, P5, K4.
Row 46: K4, RLD, K8.
Row 47: K4, RLD, K7.
Row 48: K4, P2tog, P2, K4.
Row 49: K4, RLD, K5.
Row 50: K4, P2tog, K4.
Row 51: K3, D3C, K3.
Row 52: K3, P1, K3.
Row 53: K2, D3C, K2.
Row 54: K2, P1, K2.
Row 55: K1, D3C, K1.
Row 56: K1, P1, K1.
Row 57: D3C, fasten off.

Gauffre Fan

I first came across directions for this simple but elegant pattern in an 1837 edition of the British publication, The Ladies Knitting and Netting Book. The only example I have ever found of a counterpane knitted in this pattern is one in the collection of the Welsh Folk Museum in St. Fagans, Cardiff, Wales. That counterpane handsomely combined the Gauffre Fan pattern with Wilma's Pattern (see p. 141).

This two-needle pattern is a good one for the advanced beginner. It involves knit, purl, slip and garter stitches as well as decreases. The original counterpane I saw was assembled with four-unit squares, but you can also join the units as a series of cascading fans (see Assembly Diagram on p. 134). If you decide to use the second assembly method, you will need to work out half-units to make straight sides, unless you, too, like the scalloped edges produced when the half-units are absent. A fringe border or a simple knitted lace edging (pp. 144-171) would work well with this pattern.

The Gauffre Fan sample was knit with Parisian Cotton on size 1 needles.

Special Instructions:
S2 is used throughout the pattern to mean slip the next 2 stitches as if to purl, holding yarn in back.

Cast on 72 stitches.

Rows 1-3: Sl, K.
Row 4: Sl, K3, LRD, K60, RLD, K4.
Row 5: Sl, K.
Row 6: Sl, K3, LRD, K58, RLD, K4.
Row 7: Sl, K.
Row 8: Sl, K3, P2tog, P56, P2tog, K4.
Row 9: Sl, K.
Row 10: Sl, K3, LRD, K2, (S2, K4)8x, S2, K2, RLD, K4.
Row 11: Sl, K4, P2, S2, (P4, S2)8x, P2, K5.
Row 12: Sl, K3, LRD, K1, (S2, K4)8x, S2, K1, RLD, K4.
Row 13: Sl, K4, P1, (S2, P4)8x, S2, P1, K5.
Row 14: Sl, K3, LRD, (S2, K4)8x, S2, RLD, K4.
Row 15: Sl, K.
Row 16: Sl, K3, P2tog, P48, P2tog, K4.
Row 17: Sl, K.
Row 18: Sl, K3, LRD, K1, (S2, K4)7x, S2, K1, RLD, K4.
Row 19: Sl, K4, P1, (S2, P4)7x, S2, P1, K5.
Row 20: Sl, K3, LRD, (S2, K4)7x, S2, RLD, K4.
Row 21: Sl, K4, (S2, P4)7x, S2, K5.
Row 22: Sl, K4, S2, LRD, K2, (S2, K4)5x, S2, K2, RLD, S2, K5.
Row 23: Sl, K.
Row 24: Sl, K3, P2tog, P40, P2tog, K4.

Row 25: Sl, K.
Row 26: Sl, K3, LRD, (S2, K4)6x, S2, RLD, K4.
Row 27: Sl, K3, P1, (S2, P4)6x, S2, P1, K4.
Row 28: Sl, K3, LRD, Sl, (K4, S2)5x, K4, Sl, RLD, K4.
Row 29: Sl, K4, Sl, (P4, S2)5x, P4, Sl, K5.
Row 30: Sl, K3, LRD, (K4, S2)5x, K4, RLD, K4.
Row 31: Sl, K.
Row 32: Sl, K3, P2tog, P32, P2tog, K4.
Row 33: Sl, K.
Row 34: Sl, K3, LRD, Sl, (K4, S2)4x, K4, Sl, RLD, K4.
Row 35: Sl, K4, Sl, (P4, S2)4x, P4, Sl, K5.
Row 36: Sl, K3, LRD, (K4, S2)4x, K4, RLD, K4.
Row 37: Sl, K4, (P4, S2)4x, P4, K5.
Row 38: Sl, K3, LRD, K3, (S2, K4)3x, S2, K3, RLD, K4.
Row 39: Sl, K.
Row 40: Sl, K3, P2tog, P24, P2tog, K4.
Row 41: Sl, K.
Row 42: Sl, K3, LRD, (K4, S2)3x, K4, RLD, K4.
Row 43: Sl, K4, (P4, S2)3x, P4, K5.
Row 44: Sl, K3, LRD, K3, (S2, K4)2x, S2, K3, RLD, K4.
Row 45: Sl, K4, P3, (S2, P4)2x, S2, P3, K5.
Row 46: Sl, K3, LRD, K2, (S2, K4)2x, S2, K2, RLD, K4.
Row 47: Sl, K.
Row 48: Sl, K3, P2tog, P16, P2tog, K4.

Row 49: Sl, K.
Row 50: Sl, K3, LRD, K3, S2, K4, S2, K3, RLD, K4.
Row 51: Sl, K4, P3, S2, P4, S2, P3, K5.
Row 52: Sl, K3, LRD, K2, S2, K4, S2, K2, RLD, K4.
Row 53: Sl, K4, P2, S2, P4, S2, P2, K5.
Row 54: Sl, K3, LRD, K1, S2, K4, S2, K1, RLD, K4.
Row 55: Sl, K.
Row 56: Sl, K3, P2tog, P8, P2tog, K4.
Row 57: Sl, K.
Row 58: Sl, K3, LRD, K2, S2, K2, RLD, K4.
Row 59: Sl, K4, P2, S2, P4, S2, P2, K5.
Row 60: Sl, K3, LRD, K1, S2, K1, RLD, K4.
Row 61: Sl, K4, P1, S2, P1, K5.

Row 62: Sl, K3, LRD, S2, RLD, K4.
Row 63: Sl, K.
Row 64: Sl, K3, LRD, RLD, K4.
Row 65: Sl, K.
Row 66: Sl, K2, LRD, RLD, K3.
Row 67: Sl, K.
Row 68: Sl, K1, LRD, RLD, K2.
Row 69: Sl, K.
Row 70: Sl, LRD, RLD, K1.
Row 71: Sl, K.
Row 72: LRD, RLD.
Row 73: LRD, fasten off.

Four units of the Gauffre Fan assembled into a square.

Lace and Border Patterns

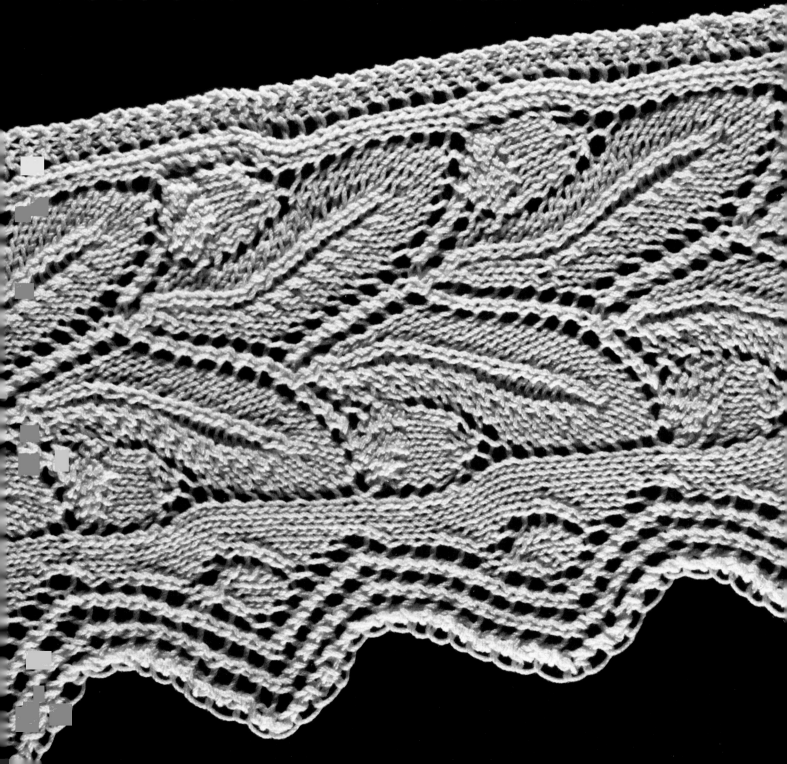

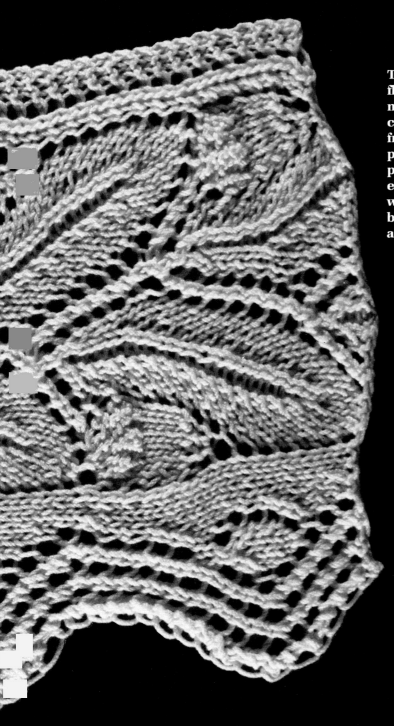

These lace and border patterns include both flat and embossed edgings and inserts. Although many of the main patterns in the previous chapters include a border pattern, other edgings from this chapter can be substituted. An insert pattern can also be combined with any border pattern to produce a wider, more elaborate edging for a counterpane. Many of these patterns would make a handsome edging on household bed and table linens. (Directions for this pattern are found on pp. 170-171.)

Valenciennes Lace

Special Instructions:
O2 counts as 2 stitches on following row. Loops that should be dropped will be indicated by the abbreviation DL.

Cast on 16 stitches.

Setup Row 1: K3, O2, P2tog, K2, (O2, LRD)2x, K5.

Row 1: K3, O2, P2tog, DL, K2, (O2, LRD)2x, K5.
Row 2: K7, (P1, K2)2x, O2, P2tog, DL, K3.
Row 3: K3, O2, P2tog, DL, K13.
Row 4: K13, O2, P2tog, DL, K3.

Row 5: K3, O2, P2tog, DL, K2, (O2, LRD)3x, K5.
Row 6: K7, (P1, K2)3x, O2, P2tog, DL, K3.
Row 7: K3, O2, P2tog, DL, K16.
Row 8: Cast off 5 stitches, K10, (11 stitches on right needle), O2, P2tog, DL, K3.

Repeat rows 1-8 for desired length. Cast off all stitches on Row 8.

The Valenciennes Lace sample was worked with size 5 perle cotton on size 0 needles.

Wave Lace Border

Special Instructions:
AP1   Abbreviated Pattern #1 is worked as follows:
Sl, K1, O, LRD

Cast on 16 stitches and knit 1 row.

Row 1: AP1, K8, LRD, O, K2.
Row 2: O, K16.
Row 3: AP1, K7, LRD, O, K4.
Row 4: O, K17.
Row 5: AP1, K6, LRD, O, K6.
Row 6: O, K18.
Row 7: AP1, K5, LRD, O, K8.
Row 8: O, K19.
Row 9: AP1, K4, LRD, O, K10.
Row 10: O, K20.
Row 11: AP1, K3, LRD, O, K12.
Row 12: O, K21.

Wave Lace Border was knit with Antique Bedspread Cotton on size 0 needles.

Row 13: AP1, K2, LRD, O, K14.
Row 14: O, K22.
Row 15: AP1, K1, LRD, O, K16.

Row 16: O, LRD, K21.
Row 17: AP1, K3, O, LRD, K14.
Row 18: O, (LRD)2x, K19.
Row 19: AP1, K4, O, LRD, K12.
Row 20: O, (LRD)2x, K18.
Row 21: AP1, K5, O, LRD, K10.
Row 22: O, (LRD)2x, K17.
Row 23: AP1, K6, O, LRD, K8.
Row 24: O, (LRD)2x, K16.
Row 25: AP1, K7, O, LRD, K6.
Row 26: O, (LRD)2x, K15.
Row 27: AP1, K8, O, LRD, K4.
Row 28: O, (LRD)2x, K14.
Row 29: AP1, K9, O, LRD, K2.
Row 30: O, (LRD)2x, K13.

Repeat rows 1-30 for desired length.

Eyelet Scallop Edgings

VERSION 1

Special Instructions:
The even-numbered rows are the front side of the work.

Cast on 8 stitches.

Row 1: Slp, K5, O, K2.
Row 2: O, LRD, K7.
Row 3: Slp, K4, O, LRD, O, K2.
Row 4: O, LRD, K8.
Row 5: Slp, K3, (O, LRD)2x, O, K2.
Row 6: O, LRD, K9.
Row 7: Slp, K2, (O, LRD)3x, O, K2.
Row 8: O, LRD, K10.
Row 9: Slp, K2, LRD, (O, LRD)3x, K1.
Row 10: O, LRD, K9.
Row 11: Slp, K3, LRD, (O, LRD)2x, K1.
Row 12: O, LRD, K8.
Row 13: Slp, K4, LRD, O, LRD, K1.
Row 14: O, LRD, K7.
Row 15: Slp, K5, LRD, K1.
Row 16: O, LRD, K6.

Repeat rows 1-16 for desired length.

VERSION 2

Special Instructions:
This pattern is a variation of Version 1. The odd-numbered rows are identical.
The odd-numbered rows are the front side of the work.

Cast on 8 stitches.

Row 1: Slp, K5, O, K2.
Row 2: O, LRD, P6, K1.
Row 3: Slp, K4, O, LRD, O, K2.
Row 4: O, LRD, P7, K1.
Row 5: Slp, K3, (O, LRD)2x, O, K2.
Row 6: O, LRD, P8, K1.
Row 7: Slp, K2, (O, LRD)3x, O, K2.
Row 8: O, LRD, P9, K1.
Row 9: Slp, K2, LRD, (O, LRD)3x, K1.
Row 10: O, LRD, P8, K1.
Row 11: Slp, K3, LRD, (O, LRD)2x, K1.
Row 12: O, LRD, P7, K1.
Row 13: Slp, K4, LRD, O, LRD, K1.
Row 14: O, LRD, P6, K1.
Row 15: Slp, K5, LRD, K1.
Row 16: O, LRD, P5, K1.

Repeat rows 1-16 for desired length.

Eyelet Scallop Edgings were worked with size 5 perle cotton on size 0 needles.

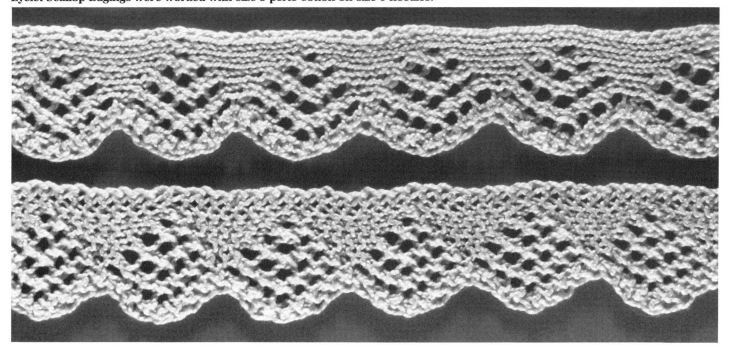

Panel Lace

Special Instructions:
AP1 Abbreviated Pattern #1 is worked as follows:
Sl, K2, O, LRD, K1, O, LRD.
AP2 Abbreviated Pattern #2 is worked as follows:
K1, O, LRD, K2, O, LRD, K1B.

Cast on 26 stitches and knit 1 row.

Row 1: AP1, K12, (O, LRD)3x.
Row 2: O, K6, P12, AP2.
Row 3: AP1, K1, (O, LRD)5x, K1, O, LRD, K1, (O, LRD)2x.
Row 4: O, K7, P12, AP2.
Row 5: AP1, *K1, O, LRD*, K6, O, LRD, *-*, K2, (O, LRD)2x.

Row 6: O, K8, P12, AP2.
Row 7: AP1, K1, (O, LRD)5x, K1, O, LRD, K3, (O, LRD)2x.
Row 8: O, K9, P12, AP2.

Row 9: AP1, K12, O, LRD, K4, (O, LRD)2x.
Row 10: O, K22, AP2.
Row 11: AP1, P12, O, LRD, K5, (O, LRD)2x.
Row 12: O, K23, AP2.
Row 13: AP1, P12, O, LRD, K6, (O, LRD)2x.
Row 14: Cast off 6 stitches, K17, AP2.

Repeat rows 1-14 for desired length.

The Panel Lace sample was knit with size 3 perle cotton on size 1 needles.

Sawtooth Edgings

VERSION 1

Special Instructions:
AP1   Abbreviated Pattern #1 is worked as follows:
K2, (O, LRD)2X

Cast on 9 stitches.

Row 1: AP1, O, K3.
Row 2 and all even-numbered rows: Knit.
Row 3: AP1, O, K4.
Row 5: AP1, O, K5.

Row 7: AP1, O, K6.
Row 9: AP1, O, K7.
Row 11: AP1, O, K8.
Row 12: Cast off 6 stitches, K8.

Repeat rows 1-12 for desired length.

VERSION 2

Special Instructions:
This pattern is a variation of Version 1. The odd-numbered rows are identical.
AP1   Abbreviated Pattern #1 is worked as follows:
K2, (O, LRD)2x.

Cast on 9 stitches.

Row 1: AP1, O, K3.
Row 2: Slp, P9.
Row 3: AP1, O, K4.

Row 4: Slp, P10.
Row 5: AP1, O, K5.
Row 6: Slp, P11.
Row 7: AP1, O, K6.
Row 8: Slp, P12.
Row 9: AP1, O, K7.
Row 10: Slp, P13.
Row 11: AP1, O, K8.
Row 12: Slp, P14.
Row 13: Cast off 6 stitches, K8.
Row 14: Slp, P8.

Repeat rows 1-14 for desired length.

Sawtooth Edgings were worked with size 5 perle cotton on size 0 needles.

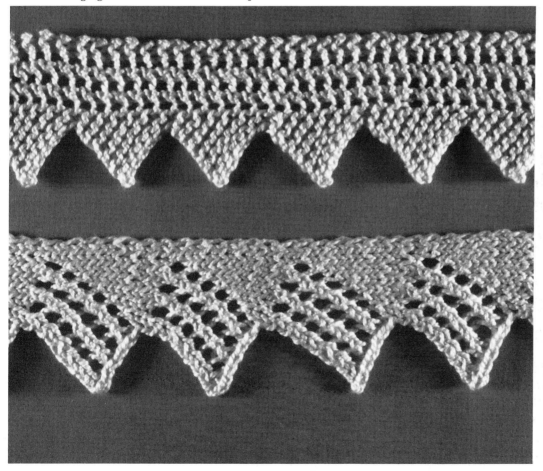

Knitted and Tied Fringe Border

Special Instructions:
The length of the fringe is determined by the number of stitches added to the 8-stitch border shown below. The directions call for the fringe portion of the pattern to be worked on 17 stitches. For a longer or shorter fringe, adjust this number accordingly.

Cast on 25 stitches (8 of these stitches will serve as the border).

Row 1: Slp, K2, O, LRD, K1, O, LRD, K17.
Row 2: Knit.

Repeat rows 1 and 2 for desired length. Then cast off 7 stitches and pass the yarn through the stitch remaining on the right needle. Break yarn. Unravel the remaining stitches. Knot the fringe according to one of the drawings on the facing page.

Knitted and Tied Fringe Borders were worked with Wondersheen Cotton on size 3 needles.

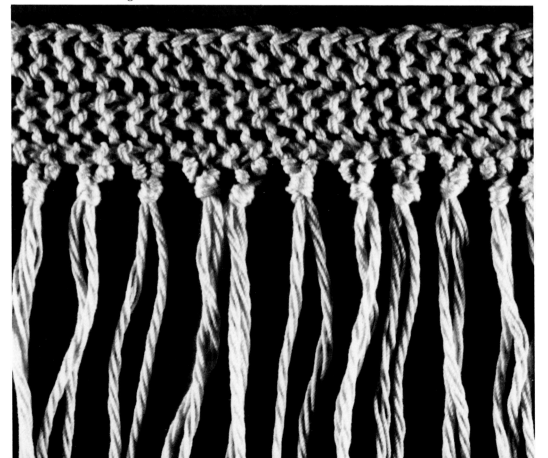

Simple Tied-Fringe Border

When tying fringe directly to a counterpane, first add two rows of single crochet around the entire edge of the counterpane. Rather than crochet around the full perimeter twice, I find it easier to attach two balls of yarn and crochet the pair of rows about 12 in. at a time, working my way in this fashion to the end. The fringe can then be tied and knotted with the crochet hook, as shown in the drawing below. The tied fringe can then be more elaborately knotted if desired.

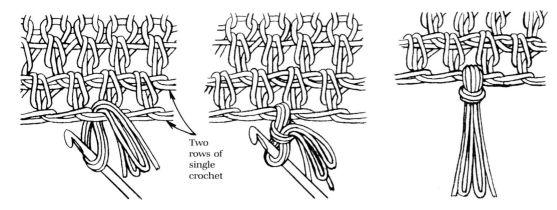

Two rows of single crochet

Basic Knots for Fringe Border

Two basic tied knots for fringe are shown below. For more elaborate knots, consult Step by Step Macrame *(see Bibliography, pp. 176-177).*

Square Knot

1. Make left-right half-knot.

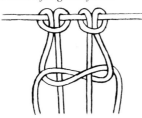

2. Complete square knot with right-left half-knot. Continue, if desired, with series of square knots.

Overhand Knot

Favorite Open Lace

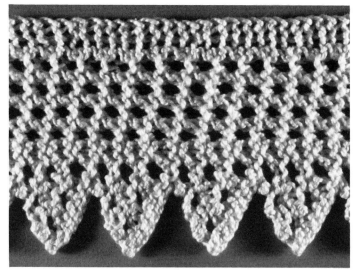

Special Instructions:
O2 is the basis for 2 stitches on following row.
KP means knit and purl into the O2.
AP1   Abbreviated Pattern #1 is worked as follows:
Sl, K1, (O, LRD)5x, K1.
AP2   Abbreviated Pattern #2 is worked as follows:
Sl, K1, O, LRD.

Cast on 15 stitches.

Row 1: AP1, O2, LRD.
Rows 2, 4, 6, 8 and 10:
Knit all stitches except KP
into the O2's.
Row 3: AP2, K12.
Row 5: AP1, O2, LRD, O2,
K1.

Row 7: AP2, K15.
Row 9: AP1, (O2, LRD)3x.
Row 11: AP2, K18.
Row 12: Cast off 7 stitches,
K14.

Repeat rows 1-12 for
desired length.

The Favorite Open Lace sample was knit with size 5 perle
cotton on size 0 needles.

Florence Border

Florence Border was worked with size 5 perle cotton on
size 0 needles.

Special Instructions:
O2 is the basis for 2 stitches on following row.
KP means knit and purl into the O2.

Cast on 10 stitches and
knit 1 row.

Row 1: K2, O, P2tog, K1,
(O2, LRD)2x, K1.
Row 2: K2, (KP, K1)2x, O,
P2tog, K2.
Row 3: K2, O, P2tog, K3,
(O2, LRD)2x, K1.
Row 4: K2, KP, K1, KP, K3,
O, P2tog, K2.
Row 5: K2, O, P2tog, K5,
(O2, LRD)2x, K1.

Row 6: K2, KP, K1, KP, K5,
O, P2tog, K2.
Row 7: K2, O, P2tog, K7,
(O2, LRD)2x, K1.
Row 8: K2, KP, K1, KP, K7,
O, P2tog, K2.
Row 9: K2, O, P2tog, K14.
Row 10: Cast off 8 stitches,
K5, O, P2tog, K2.

Repeat rows 1-10 for
desired length. Cast off on
Row 10.

Myrtle Leaf Lace

Special Instructions:
The number of stitches on the needle increases on Row 5 to 31 stitches and on Row 9 to 34 stitches. O2 is the basis for 2 stitches on the following row.

Cast on 26 stitches.

Row 1: *K2, O, LRD* (K1, O, K2, D3, K2, O)2x, *-*, O2, K2.

Row 2: K3, P1, *K1, O, LRD*, P17, *-*, K1.

Row 3: K2, O, LRD, K2, (O, K1, D3, K1, O, K3)2x, O, LRD, K4.

Row 4: K5, O, LRD, P17, K1, O, LRD, K1.

Row 5: K2, O, LRD, K3, *O, D3, O*, K5, *-*, K4, O, (LRD, O2)2x, K2.

Row 6: K3, P1, K2, P1, *K1, O, LRD*, P17, *-*, K1.

Row 7: K2, O, (LRD)2x, *K2, O, K1, O, K2*, D3, *-*, RLD, K1, O, LRD, K7.

Row 8: K8, O, LRD, P17, K1, O, LRD, K1.

Row 9: K2, O, (LRD)2x, *K1, O, K3, O, K1*, D3, *-*, RLD, K1, O, LRD, (O2, LRD)3x, K1.

Row 10: K3, P1, (K2, P1)2x, *K1, O, LRD*, P17, *-*, K1.

Row 11: K2, O, (LRD)2x, *O, K5, O*, D3, *-*, RLD, K1, O, LRD, K10.

Row 12: Cast off 8 stitches, K2, O, LRD, P17, K1, O, LRD, K1.

Repeat rows 1-12 for desired length and cast off.

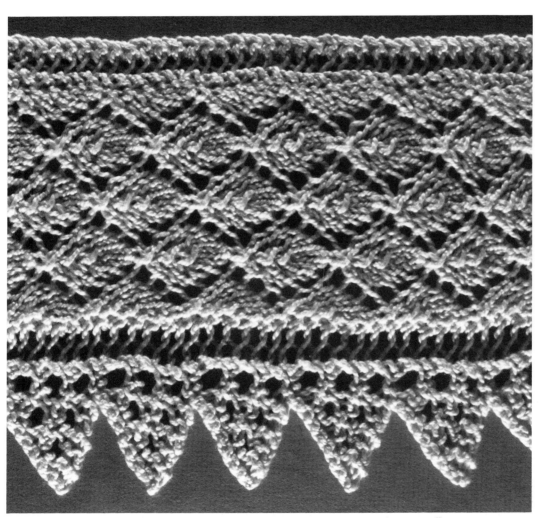

The Myrtle Leaf Lace sample was worked with size 5 perle cotton on size 0 needles.

Cherry Leaf Border

Special Instructions:

AP1   *Abbreviated Pattern #1 is worked as follows:*
Sl, K2, O, LRD, K1, O, LRD.

AP2   *Abbreviated Pattern #2 is worked as follows:*
K3, P1, K2, P1.

AP3   *Abbreviated Pattern #3 is worked as follows:*
(O2, LRD)2x, K1.

AP4   *Abbreviated Pattern #4 is worked as follows:*
(O, LRD, K1)2x.

Cast on 24 stitches and knit two rows.

Row 1: AP1, K2, (O, LRD)2x, K5, AP3.

Row 2: AP2, K13, AP4.

Row 3: AP1, K3, (O, LRD)2x, K6, AP3.

Row 4: AP2, K15, AP4.

Row 5: AP1, K4, (O, LRD)2x, K7, AP3.

Row 6: AP2, K17, AP4.

Row 7: AP1, K5, (O, LRD)2x, K8, AP3.

Row 8: AP2, K19, AP4.

Row 9: AP1, K6, (O, LRD)2x, K9, AP3.

Row 10: AP2, K21, AP4.

Row 11: AP1, K26.

Row 12: Cast off 10 stitches, K17, AP4.

Repeat rows 1-12 for desired length.

Cherry Leaf Border was knit with size 5 perle cotton on size 0 needles.

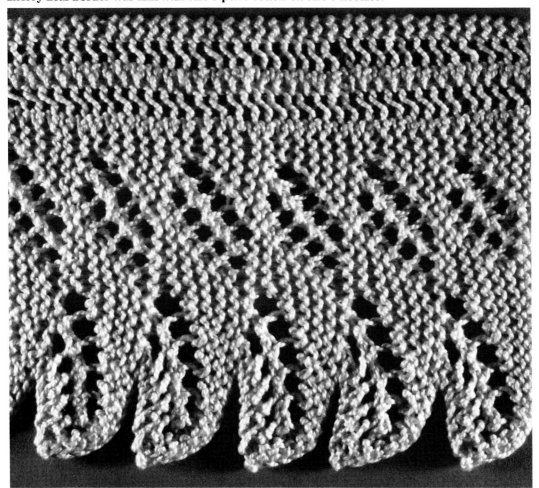

Frisby Edging

Special Instructions:
O2 is the basis for 2 stitches on following row.
AP1 Abbreviated Pattern #1 is worked as follows:
Sl, K2, O, LRD.

Cast on 15 stitches and knit 1 row.

Row 1: AP1, K1, (O2, LRD)4x, K1.
Row 2: K3, P1, (K2, P1)3x, K3, O, LRD, K1.

Row 3: AP1, K14.
Row 4: Cast off 4 stitches, K11, O, LRD, K1.

Repeat rows 1-4 for desired length.

Frisby Edging was worked with Parisian Cotton on size 1 needles.

Christchurch Border

Special Instructions:
AP1 Abbreviated Pattern #1 is worked as follows:
K2, O, LRD, O, K2.
AP2 Abbreviated Pattern #2 is worked as follows:
LRD, O, K2, LRD, (O, LRD)2x, K1.

Cast on 12 stitches.

Row 1: Sl, K3, O, LRD, AP1.
Row 2: O, LRD, K11.
Row 3: Sl, K2, (O, LRD)2x, AP1.
Row 4: O, LRD, K12.
Row 5: Sl, K3, (O, LRD)2x, AP1.
Row 6: O, LRD, K13.
Row 7: Sl, K2, (O, LRD)3x, AP1.
Row 8: O, LRD, K14.
Row 9: Sl, K2, LRD, O, AP2.
Row 10: O, LRD, K13.
Row 11: Sl, K1, LRD, O, AP2.
Row 12: O, LRD, K12.
Row 13: Sl, K2, AP2.
Row 14: O, LRD, K11.
Row 15: Sl, K1, AP2.
Row 16: O, LRD, K10.

Repeat rows 1-16 for desired length.

Christchurch Border was knit with size 3 perle cotton on size 1 needles.

Raised Leaf Insert

Special Instructions:
This pattern is presented in three versions, which differ only in the decrease methods used to create the motif. The first version (at bottom in photo) uses a center stitch decrease. The second (at center) uses decreases that slant toward the center stitch, and the last version (at top) uses decreases that slant away from the center stitch. On all versions repeat rows 1-20 for desired length.

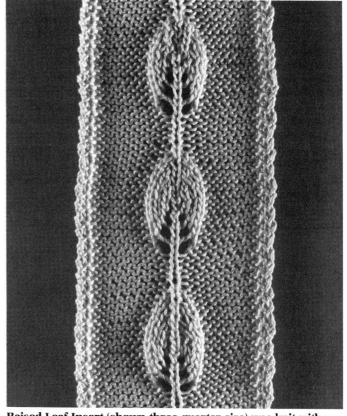

Raised Leaf Insert (shown three-quarter size) was knit with Marisa Swiss Cotton on size 0 needles.

VERSION 1

Cast on 21 stitches and knit 4 rows.

Rows 1 and 3: K2, P8, K1, P8, K2.
Rows 2 and 4: K10, P1, K10.
Row 5: K2, P8, O, K1, O, P8, K2.
Row 6: K10, P3, K10.
Row 7: K2, P8, (K1, O)2x, K1, P8, K2.
Row 8: K10, P5, K10.
Row 9: K2, P8, K2, (O, K1)2x, K1, P8, K2.
Row 10: K10, P7, K10.
Row 11: K2, P8, K3, O, K1, O, K3, P8, K2.
Row 12: K10, P9, K10.
Row 13: K2, P8, K3, D3C, K3, P8, K2.
Row 14: K10, P7, K10.
Row 15: K2, P8, K2, D3C, K2, P8, K2.
Row 16: K10, P5, K10.
Row 17: K2, P8, K1, D3C, K1, P8, K2.
Row 18: K10, P3, K10.
Row 19: K2, P8, D3C, P8, K2.
Row 20: K10, P1, K10.

VERSION 2

Work like Version 1, substituting the following rows:

Row 13: K2, P8, K2, RLD, K1, LRD, K2, P8, K2.

Row 15: K2, P8, K1, RLD, K1, LRD, K1, P8, K2.
Row 17: K2, P8, RLD, K1, LRD, P8, K2.
Rows 18, 19 and 20: Same as above.

VERSION 3

Work like Version 1, substituting the following rows:

Row 13: K2, P8, K2, LRD, K1, RLD, K2, P8, K2.
Row 15: K2, P8, K1, LRD, K1, RLD, K1, P8, K2.
Row 17: K2, P8, LRD, K1, RLD, P8, K2.
Rows 18, 19 and 20: Same as above.

Purse and Garter-Stitch Insert

Cast on 21 stitches.

Row 1: K5, (O, P2tog)3x, K3, (O, P2tog)2x, K3.
Row 2: K3, (O, P2tog)2x, K3, (O, P2tog)3x, K5.

Repeat rows 1 and 2 for desired length.

Purse and Garter-Stitch Insert was knit with warp cotton on size 1 needles.

Checkered Raised-Leaf Border

Special Instructions:
AP1 *Abbreviated Pattern #1 is worked as follows:*
K3, O, LRD, K3, P7, K3.
AP2 *Abbreviated Pattern #2 is worked as follows:*
K3, O, LRD, P3, K7, P3.

Cast on 37 stitches and knit 1 row.

Row 1: AP1, O, LRD, O, K17.
Row 2: K20, P3, K7, P3, K5.
Row 3: AP1, O, LRD, K1, O, K17.
Row 4: K21, P13, K5.
Row 5: AP2, (O, LRD)2x, O, K8, O, K1, O, K8.
Row 6: K8, P3, K16, P7, K8.
Row 7: AP2, O, LRD, K1, O, LRD, O, K9, O, K1, O, K9.
Row 8: K8, P5, K14, P13, K5.
Row 9: AP1, (O, LRD)3x, O, K10, O, K1, O, K10.
Row 10: K8, P7, K15, P3, K7, P3, K5.
Row 11: AP1, O, LRD, K1, (O, LRD)2x, O, K11, O, K1, O, K11.
Row 12: K8, P9, K16, P13, K5.
Row 13: AP2, (O, LRD)4x, O, K12, O, K1, O, K12.
Row 14: K8, P11, K20, P7, K8.
Row 15: AP2, O, LRD, K1, (O, LRD)3x, O, K8, RLD, K7, LRD, K8.
Row 16: K8, P9, K18, K13, K5.
Row 17: AP1, (O, LRD)5x, O, K8, RLD, K5, LRD, K8.
Row 18: K8, P7, K19, P3, K7, P3, K5.
Row 19: AP1, O, LRD, K1, (O, LRD)4x, O, K8, RLD, K3, LRD, K8.

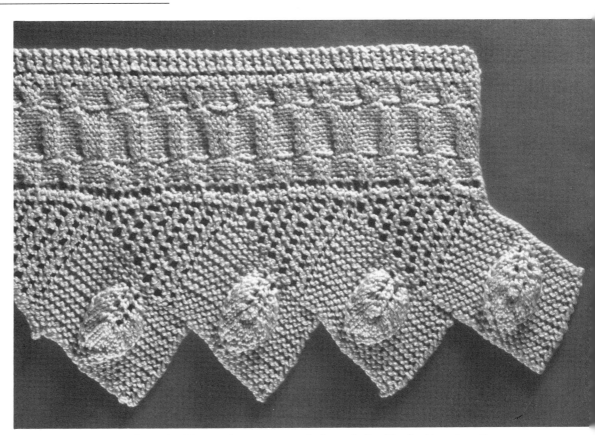

Checkered Raised-Leaf Border (shown three-quarter size) was knit with size 5 perle cotton on size 0 needles.

Row 20: K8, P5, K20, K13, K5.
Row 21: AP2, (O, LRD)6x, O, K8, RLD, K1, LRD, K8.
Row 22: K8, P3, K24, P7, K8.
Row 23: AP2, O, LRD, K1, (O, LRD)5x, O, K8, D3, K8.

Row 24: K31, P13, K5.
Row 25: AP1, (O, LRD)7x, O, K17.
Row 26: Cast off 13 stitches, K18, P3, K7, P3, K5.

Repeat rows 1-26 for desired length.

Traveling Diamonds

Traveling Diamonds (shown two-third size) was worked with size 5 cotton on size 0 needles.

Special Instructions:
AP1 *Abbreviated Pattern #1 is worked as follows:*
Slp, K1, O, LRD.
AP2 *Abbreviated Pattern #2 is worked as follows:*
O, LRD, K1.

Cast on 21 stitches.

Setup Row 1: Knit 21.
Setup Row 2: P20, K1.

Row 1: AP1, K3, O, LRD, O, D3, O, RLD, O, K4, AP2.
Row 2 and all even-numbered rows: Slp, P19, K1.
Row 3: AP1, K1, (LRD, O)2x, K3, (O, RLD)2x, K2, AP2.

Row 5: AP1, (LRD, O)2x, K5, (O, RLD)2x, K1, AP2.
Row 7: Slp, K1, O, D3, O, LRD, O, K7, (O, RLD)2x, AP2.
Row 9: AP1, K1, (O, RLD)2x, K3, (LRD, O)2x, K2, AP2.
Row 11: AP1, K2, (O, RLD)2x, K1, (LRD, O)2x, K3, AP2.
Row 12: Repeat Row 2.

Work rows 1-12 for desired length. Repeat rows 1 and 2, then cast off.

Diamond Lace

Special Instructions:
O2 is the basis for 2 stitches on following row.

Cast on 34 stitches and knit 2 rows (optional).

Row 1: K3, (O, RLD)2x, *K5, LRD, O, K1*, O, RLD, *-*, (O, RLD)2x, O2, K5.
Row 2: K6, P27, K3.
Row 3: K3, O, D3C, (O, RLD, K3, LRD, O, K3)2x, (O, RLD)2x, O2, K6.

Row 4: K7, P27, K3.
Row 5: K3, O, D3C, (O, RLD, K1, LRD, O, K5)2x, (O, RLD)2x, O2, K7.
Row 6: K8, P27, K3.
Row 7: K3, (O, D3C)2x, O, K7, O, D3C, O, K7, (O, RLD)2x, O2, K8.

The Diamond Lace sample (shown three-quarter size) was knit with size 5 perle cotton on size 0 needles.

Row 8: Cast off 5 stitches, K3, P27, K3.
Row 9: K3, O, D3C, (O, K1, O, RLD, K5, LRD)2x, (O, RLD)2x, O2, K4.
Row 10: K5, P27, K3.
Row 11: K3, O, LRD, (O, K3, O, RLD, K3, LRD)2x, (O, LRD)2x, O2, K6.
Row 12: K7, P27, K3.
Row 13: K3, O, LRD, (O, K5, O, RLD, K1, LRD)2x, (O, LRD)2x, O, K8.
Row 14: K8, P27, K3.
Row 15: K3, O, LRD, (O, K7, O, D3C)2x, (O, LRD)2x, O2, LRD, K7.
Row 16: Cast off 5 stitches, K3, P27, K3.

Repeat rows 1-16 for desired length.

Eureka Lace Insert

Special Instructions:
D5 Decrease over the next 5 stitches as follows:
Slip the next 5 stitches onto a crochet hook that matches the needle size and draw the working yarn through the stitches. Transfer the loop onto the right needle and continue working. O2 is the basis for 2 stitches on following row.

Cast on 25 stitches and knit 2 rows.

Row 1: *LRD, O2, LRD*, K7, O, D3, O, K7, *-*.
Row 2: Slp, K11, P1, K12.
Row 3: Slp, K1, *LRD, O2, LRD*, K3, LRD, O, K3, O, LRD, K3, *-*, K2.
Row 4: Slp, K10, P3, K11.
Row 5: *LRD, O2, LRD*, K4, LRD, O, K5, O, LRD, K4, *-*.
Row 6: Slp, K9, P5, K10.
Row 7: Slp, *K1, LRD, O2, LRD*, K1, LRD, O, K7, O, LRD, *-*, K2.
Row 8: Slp, K8, P7, K9.
Row 9: *LRD, O2, LRD*, K2, LRD, O, K9, O, LRD, K2, *-*.
Row 10: Slp, K7, P2, O2, D5, O2, P2, K8.
Row 11: Slp, K1, *LRD, O2, LRD, K2*, O, RLD, K5, LRD, O, K2, *-*.
Row 12: Slp, K8, P7, K9.
Row 13: *LRD, O2, LRD*, K5, O, RLD, K3, LRD, O, K5, *-*.
Row 14: Slp, K9, P5, K10.
Row 15: Slp, K1, *LRD, O2, LRD*, K4, O, RLD, K1, LRD, O, K4, *-*, K2.
Row 16: Slp, K10, P3, K11.

Repeat rows 1-16 for desired length. Then repeat rows 1 and 2 and cast off.

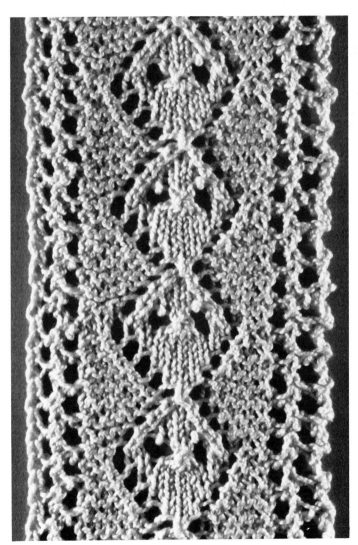

Eureka Lace Insert was knit with size 5 perle cotton on size 0 needles.

Diamond Rib Insert

Special Instructions:
The sample shows a different number of rows between 2nd and 3rd repeat. The number of rows between repeats is arbitrary.

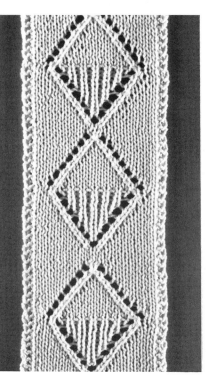

Diamond Rib Insert (shown half-size) was knit with Parisian Cotton on size 1 needles.

Cast on 24 stitches; knit 1 row, purl 1 row.

Row 1: K10, LRD, O, RLD, K10.
Row 2: K2, P19, K2.
Row 3: K9, LRD, O, K1, O, RLD, K9.
Row 4: K2, P8, K1, P1, K1, P8, K2.
Row 5: K8, LRD, O, P1, K1, P1, O, RLD, K8.

Row 6: Repeat Row 4.
Row 7: K7, LRD, O, (K1, P1)2x, K1, O, RLD, K7.
Row 8: K2, P6, (K1, P1)3x, K1, P6, K2.
Row 9: K6, LRD, O, (P1, K1)3x, P1, O, RLD, K6.
Row 10: Repeat Row 8.
Row 11: K5, LRD, O, (K1, P1)4x, K1, O, RLD, K5.
Row 12: K2, P4, (K1, P1)5x, K1, P4, K2.
Row 13: K4, LRD, O, (P1, K1)5x, P1, O, RLD, K4.
Row 14: Repeat Row 12.
Row 15: K4, O, RLD, K11, LRD, O, K4.
Rows 16, 18, 20, 22, 24, 26: K2, P19, K2.
Row 17: K5, O, RLD, K9, LRD, O, K5.
Row 19: K6, O, RLD, K7, LRD, O, K6.
Row 21: K7, O, RLD, K5, LRD, O, K7.
Row 23: K8, O, RLD, K3, LRD, O, K8.
Row 25: K9, O, RLD, K1, LRD, O, K9.
Row 27: K10, O, D3, O, K10.
Row 28: K2, P9, LCO, P10, K2.
Row 29: Knit, closing the loop of the LCO.
Row 30: K2, P20, K2.

Repeat rows 1-30 for desired length. If desired, additional rows of stocking stitch may be worked between Row 28 and Row 1 of the next repeat.

Coral Lace Insert

Special Instructions:
The pattern is worked on a multiple of 21 stitches. The sample is worked on 63 stitches, or 3 repeats.

Cast on. Knit 2 rows (optional).

Row 1: *LRD, K3, LRD, (K1, O)2x*, K1, *-*, K2.
Row 2 and all even-numbered rows: Purl.
Row 3: *(LRD, K1)2x, O, K3, O*, K1, *-*, K2.
Row 5: *D3, K1, O, K5, O*, K1, *-*, K2.

Row 7: K2, *(O, K1)2x, LRD, K3, LRD*, K1, *-*.
Row 9: K2, *O, K3, O, (K1, LRD)2x*, K1, *-*.
Row 11: K2, *O, K5, O, K1, D3*, K1, *-*.
Row 12: Purl.

Repeat rows 1-12 for desired length.

Coral Lace Insert (shown three-quarter size) was worked with Antique Bedspread Cotton on size 0 needles.

Hoop and Van Dyke Edging

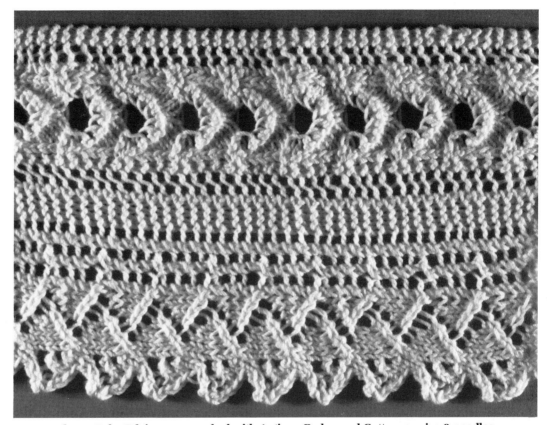

Hoop and Van Dyke Edging was worked with Antique Bedspread Cotton on size 0 needles.

Special Instructions:
O2 is the basis for 2 stitches on following row.

Cast on 32 stitches.

Row 1: K3, O, LRD, K3, LCO6, K5, O, LRD, K3, (O, P2tog)2x, O, PRD3, O, P5, O2, P2tog.

Row 2: O, K2, P1, K3, LRD, O, K12, O, LRD, K3, (O, K1)6x, K5, O, LRD, K1.

Row 3: K3, O, (LRD)2x, K14, LRD, K2, O, LRD, K3, (O, P2tog)3x, P2, O, P2tog, P2, (O2, P2tog)2x.

Row 4: (K2, P1)2x, K1, LRD, O, K14, O, (LRD)2x, K12, LRD, K2, O, LRD, K1.

Row 5: K3, O, LRD, P2tog, P10, PRD, K2, O, LRD, K3, (O, P2tog)3x, P4, O, P2tog, P4, O, P2tog.

Row 6: Cast off 4 stitches, K3, O, RLD, K13, O, LRD, RLD, K8, LRD, K2, O, LRD, K1.

Row 7: K3, O, LRD, P2tog, P6, PRD, K2, O, LRD, K3, (O, P2tog)3x, P1, PRD, O, P5.

Row 8: K6, O, RLD, K2, O, LRD, K7, O, LRD, RLD, K4, LRD, K2, O, LRD, K1.

Repeat rows 1-8 for desired length. Purl 1 row, then cast off.

Pine-Tree and Bobble Insert

Pine-Tree and Bobble Insert was knit with size 3 perle cotton on size 1 needles.

Special Instructions:
This pattern is worked on a multiple of 12 stitches plus 1 stitch. The instructions in the brackets should be repeated once for each 12 stitches.
The sample is worked on 39 stitches—3 repeats, plus 1 stitch, plus a 1-stitch garter border on each side. The border stitches are not included in the directions.
This pattern is equally attractive with or without the bobble worked in the center of each pattern. The bobble should be worked on the bold-faced knit stitch in Row 5.

Cast on.

Row 1: [K1, O, K1, RLD, K5, LRD, K1, O], K1.
Row 2 and all even-numbered rows: Purl.
Row 3: [K2, O, K1, RLD, K3, LRD, K1, O, K1], K1.
Row 5: [K3, O, K1, RLD, **K1**, LRD, K1, O, K2], K1.

Row 7: [K4, O, K1, D3, K1, O, K3], K1.
Row 8: Purl.

Repeat rows 1-8 for desired length.

Leaves and Knobs

Leaves and Knobs Insert (shown two-third size) was knit with size 5 perle cotton on size 0 needles.

Special Instructions:
AP1 *Abbreviated Pattern #1 is worked as follows:*
Sl, K2, O, LRD, K1, O.
AP2 *Abbreviated Pattern #2 is worked as follows:*
O, K2, O, LRD, K2.
D4R *Decrease over the next 4 stitches as follows:*
Sl, K3tog, PSSO. The right stitch is the one that remains and it slants toward the left.
D4L *Decrease over the next 4 stitches as follows:*
K3tog, return stitch to the left needle. Pass the second stitch on the left needle over the stitch just returned. Return the first stitch on the left needle to the right needle. The stitch that remains slants toward the right.
This pattern is equally attractive with or without a knob worked in the center of each pattern. The knob should be worked on the bold-faced knit stitch in Row 7.

Cast on 23 stitches.

Row 1: AP1, K1, O, D4R, O, K1, O, D4L, O, K1, AP2.
Row 2 and all even-numbered rows: Sl, K4, P13, K5.
Row 3: AP1, K3, O, RLD, K3tog, pass the 2nd stitch on the right-hand needle over the first, thereby casting it off, O, K3, AP2.
Row 5: AP1, *RLD, K1, LRD*, O, K1, O, *-*, AP2.
Row 7: AP1, *RLD, K1, LRD*, O, **K1**, O, *-*, AP2.
Row 8: Repeat Row 2.

Repeat rows 1-8 for desired length.

Curious Fan Edging

Special Instructions:
O2 is the basis for 2 stitches on following row.
O3 is the basis for 3 stitches on following row.
K12-O3 means wrap yarn around needle three times when knitting each of these 12 stitches.

Cast on 13 stitches and knit 1 row.

Row 1: K2, LRD, O2, LRD, K7.
Row 2: K9, P1, K3.
Rows 3 and 4: Knit 13.
Row 5: K2, LRD, O2, LRD, K2, O2, (K1, O2)3x, K2.
Row 6: K3, P1, (K2, P1)3x, K4, P1, K3.
Rows 7 and 8: Knit 21.
Row 9: K2, LRD, O2, LRD, K15.

Row 10: K12-O3, O3, K5, P1, K3.
Row 11: K9, K1, P1, K1, slip the next 12 stitches to the right needle, dropping two wraps from each stitch. Return the 12 long stitches to the left needle and knit all twelve together. Return stitch to the left needle and knit it again.
Row 12: Knit 13.

Repeat rows 1-12 for desired length. Cast off following Row 12.

Curious Fan Edging was worked with size 5 perle cotton on size 0 needles.

Scalloped Edging

Cast on 12 stitches and knit 1 row.

Row 1: Sl, K2, (O, LRD)2x, K2, O, K1, O, K2.
Row 2: Sl, K1, P3, K3, (O, LRD)2x, K2.
Row 3: Sl, K2, (O, LRD)2x, K7.
Row 4: Repeat Row 2.
Row 5: Sl, K2, (O, LRD)2x, K2, (O, K1)3x, O, K2.
Row 6: Sl, K1, P7, K3, (O, LRD)2x, K2.
Row 7: Sl, K2, (O, LRD)2x, K11.
Row 8: Repeat Row 6.
Row 9: Sl, K2, (O, LRD)2x, K2, (O, K1)7x, O, K2.
Row 10: Sl, K1, P15, K3, (O, LRD)2x, K2.
Row 11: Sl, K2, (O, LRD)2x, K19.
Row 12: Repeat Row 10.
Row 13: Sl, K2, (O, LRD)2x, K2, (O, K1)15x, O, K2.

Row 14: Sl, K1, P31, K3, (O, LRD)2x, K2.
Row 15: Sl, K2, (O, LRD)2x, K35.

On all subsequent repeats, work Row 15 as follows to connect the scallops neatly: Sl, K2, (O, LRD)2x, K34, slip the last stitch, pick up and knit the 9th stitch of the previous scallop (counting from you), pass the slipped stitch over the picked-up stitch, turn and work Row 16 as usual.

Row 16: Cast off 30 stitches, P2, K3, (O, LRD)2x, K2.

Repeat rows 1-16 for desired length. Cast off all stitches on next row.

The Scalloped Edging sample (shown three-quarter size) was knit with size 5 perle cotton on size 0 needles.

Scotch Lace

Special Instructions:
AP1 *Abbreviated Pattern #1 is worked as follows:*
Slp, K1, O, LRD.
AP2 *Abbreviated Pattern #2 is worked as follows:*
O, RLD, O, K2.
AP3 *Abbreviated Pattern #3 is worked as follows:*
K1, O, LRD, K1.
AP4 *Abbreviated Pattern #4 is worked as follows:*
Slp, K1, O, (LRD)2x.

Cast on 14 stitches.

Row 1: AP1, K1, (O, LRD)2x, O, K1, AP2.
Row 2: O, LRD, P10, AP3.
Row 3: AP1, K2, O, LRD, K1, O, K3, AP2.
Row 4: O, LRD, P12, AP3.
Row 5: AP1, K1, (O, LRD)2x, O, K1, O, D3, O, K1, AP2.
Row 6: O, LRD, P14, AP3.
Row 7: AP4, O, LRD, *K1, O, K3*, O, *-*. AP2.

Row 8: O, LRD, P17, AP3.
Row 9: AP4, O, D3, O, (P3tog)3x, (O, LRD)2x, K1.
Row 10: O, LRD, P10, AP3.
Row 11: AP1, K1, O, LRD, K1, O, P3tog, (O, LRD)2x, K1.

Row 12: O, LRD, P9, AP3.
Row 13: AP1, K1, O, D3, (O, LRD)3x, K1 .
Row 14: O, LRD, P8, AP3.

Repeat rows 1-14 for desired length.

The Scotch Lace sample (shown two-third size) was knit with size 5 perle cotton on size 0 needles.

Knob Fluted Border

Cast on 70 stitches and purl 1 row.

Row 1: Sl, K2, P5, K19, P5, K38.
Row 2: P35, turn.
Row 3: Sl, K34.
Row 4: P35, K4, *(O, LRD)2x*, K20, *-*, K3.
Row 5: Repeat Row 1.
Row 6: Repeat Row 2.
Row 7: Repeat Row 3.
Row 8: K40, O, LRD, K22, O, LRD, K4.
Row 9: Sl, K2, P5, K19, P5, K3, P34, PK1.
Row 10: K36, turn.
Row 11: Sl, P34, PK1.
Row 12: K41, *(O, LRD)2x*, K9, Knob, K10, *-*, K3.
Row 13: Sl, K2, P5, K19, P5, K3, (O, P2tog)18x, P1.
Row 14: K42, O, LRD, K22, O, LRD, K4.
Row 15: Sl, K2, P5, K19, P5, K3, P35, P2tog.
Row 16: K36, turn.
Row 17: Sl, P33, P2tog.
Row 18: K39, *(O, LRD)2x*, K20, *-*, K3.
Row 19: Repeat Row 1.
Row 20: Repeat Row 2.
Row 21: Repeat Row 3.
Row 22: P35, K5, O, LRD, K7, Knob, K5, Knob, K8, O, LRD, K4.
Row 23: Repeat Row 1.
Row 24: Repeat Row 2.
Row 25: Repeat Row 3.
Row 26: Repeat Row 18.

Row 27: Repeat Row 9.
Row 28: Repeat Row 10.
Row 29: Repeat Row 11.
Row 30: Repeat Row 14.
Row 31: Repeat Row 13.
Row 32: K41, *(O, LRD)2x*, K3, (Knob, K5)2x, Knob, K4, *-*, K3.
Row 33: Repeat Row 15.
Row 34: Repeat Row 16.
Row 35: Repeat Row 17.
Row 36: K40, O, LRD, K22, O, LRD, K4.
Row 37: Repeat Row 1.
Row 38: Repeat Row 2.
Row 39: Repeat Row 3.
Row 40: Repeat Row 4.
Row 41: Repeat Row 1.
Row 42: Repeat Row 2.
Row 43: Repeat Row 3.
Row 44: K40, O, LRD, K7, Knob, K5, Knob, K8, O, LRD, K4.
Row 45: Repeat Row 9.
Row 46: Repeat Row 10.
Row 47: Repeat Row 11.
Row 48: K41, *(O, LRD)2x*, K20, *-*, K3.
Row 49: Repeat Row 13.
Row 50: Repeat Row 14.
Row 51: Repeat Row 15.
Row 52: Repeat Row 16.
Row 53: Repeat Row 17.
Row 54: K39, *(O, LRD)2x*, K9, Knob, K10, *-*, K3.
Row 55: Repeat Row 1.
Row 56: Repeat Row 2.
Row 57: Repeat Row 3.
Row 58: P35, K5, O, LRD, K22, O, LRD, K4.
Row 59: Repeat Row 1.
Row 60: Repeat Row 2.
Row 61: Repeat Row 3.

Row 62: Repeat Row 18.
Row 63: Repeat Row 9.
Row 64: Repeat Row 10.
Row 65: Repeat Row 11.
Row 66: Repeat Row 14.
Row 67: Repeat Row 13.
Row 68: Repeat Row 48.
Row 69: Repeat Row 15.

Row 70: Repeat Row 16.
Row 71: Repeat Row 17.
Row 72: K40, O, LRD, K22, O, LRD, K4.

Repeat rows 1-72 for desired length.

Knob Fluted Border (shown two-third size) was worked with Antique Bedspread Cotton on size 0 needles.

Braided Leaf Insert

Special Instructions:
This pattern is presented in two versions, which differ only in the number of times each row is worked.
AP1 *Abbreviated Pattern #1 is worked as follows:*
Sl, K2, O, LRD.

VERSION 1

Cast on 54 stitches and purl 1 row.

Row 1: AP1, K2, LRD, (O, LRD)3x, (O, K1, O, K2, LRD, K4, LRD, K2)2x, (O, LRD)3x, O, K3, O, LRD, K2.

Row 2: Sl, K6, P39, K8.

Row 3: AP1, K1, LRD, (O, LRD)3x, [O, K3, O, (K2, LRD)2x, K2]2x, (O, LRD)3x, O, K4, O, LRD, K2.

Row 4: Sl, K7, P39, K7.

Row 5: AP1, LRD, (O, LRD)3x, [O, K5, O, K2, (LRD)2x, K2]2x, (O, LRD)3x, O, K5, O, LRD, K2.

Row 6: Sl, K8, P39, K6.

Row 7: AP1, K2, (O, LRD)3x, (O, K2, LRD, K4, LRD, K2, O, K1)2x, (O, LRD)4x, K3, O, LRD, K2.

Row 8: Sl, K7, P39, K7.

Row 9: AP1, K3, (O, LRD)3x, [O, K2, (LRD, K2)2x, O, K3]2x, (O, LRD)4x, K2, O, LRD, K2.

Row 10: Sl, K6, P39, K8.

Row 11: AP1, K4, (O, LRD)3x, [O, K2, (LRD)2x, K2, O, K5]2x, (O, LRD)4x, K1, O, LRD, K2.

Row 12: Sl, K5, P39, K9.

Repeat rows 1-12 for desired length.

VERSION 2

Repeat each pair of rows twice as follows:
1, 2, 1, 2, 3, 4, 3, 4, 5, 6, 5, 6, 7, 8, 7, 8, 9, 10, 9, 10, 11, 12, 11, 12.

Repeat this 24-row sequence for desired length.

The Braided Leaf Insert samples (shown two-third size, with Version 1 above and Version 2 below) were worked on size 5 perle cotton on size 0 needles.

Fan and Cable Insert

Special Instructions:
This pattern uses a 5-stitch cable in which 3 stitches always cross in front of 2 stitches.
CF5 *Work a front cross cable on the next 5 stitches as follows: Slip 3 stitches to a cable needle and hold in front of work. Knit 2 stitches, then knit the 3 stitches from the cable needle.*
CB5 *Work a back cross cable on the next 5 stitches as follows: Slip 2 stitches to a cable needle and hold in back of work. Knit 3 stitches, then knit the 2 stitches from the cable needle.*
AP1 *Abbreviated Pattern #1 is worked as follows:*
K1, P1, K9, P2, K1, LRD.
AP2 *Abbreviated Pattern #2 is worked as follows:*
K1, P1, K1, CF5, K3, P2, K1, LRD.
AP3 *Abbreviated Pattern #3 is worked as follows:*
RLD, K1, P2, K9, P1, K1.
AP4 *Abbreviated Pattern #4 is worked as follows:*
RLD, K1, P2, K3, CB5, K1, P1, K1.
The sample is worked on 47 stitches: 45 pattern stitches, with a 1-stitch garter border on each side. The border stitches are not included in the directions.

Cast on.

Row 1: AP1, O, K2, LRD, *O, K1, O*, D3, *-*, RLD, K2, O, AP3.
Row 2 and all even-numbered rows: K2, P9, K2, P19, K2, P9, K2.
Row 3: AP2, K3, O, LRD, O, K3, O, RLD, O, K3, AP4.
Row 5: AP1, (K2, O)2x, LRD, K1, RLD, (O, K2)2x, AP3.
Row 7: AP2, K1, *O, K3, O*, LRD, K1, RLD, *-*, K1, AP4.
Row 8: Repeat Row 2.

Repeat rows 1-8 for desired length.

Fan and Cable Insert was knit with size 5 perle cotton on size 0 needles.

Buttonhole Border

Special Instructions:
AP1   Abbreviated Pattern #1 is worked as follows:
Slp, K4, O, LRD.

Cast on 16 stitches using LCO.

Row 1: AP1, K3, LRD, O, K1, O, LRD, K1.
Row 2: O, K2, P9, O, P2tog, K3.
Row 3: AP1, K2, LRD, O, K3, O, LRD, K1.
Row 4: O, K2, P10, O, P2tog, K3.
Row 5: AP1, K1, LRD, O, K5, O, LRD, K1.
Row 6: O, K2, P11, O, P2tog, K3.
Row 7: AP1, LRD, O, K1, cast off 5 stitches, O, LRD, K1.
Row 8: O, K2, P2, LCO5, P5, O, P2tog, K3.
Row 9: AP1, K1, O, RLD, K5, O, K1B, O, LRD, K2.
Row 10: O, K2, P14, O, P2tog, K3.
Row 11: AP1, K2, O, RLD, K3, LRD, O, K3, O, LRD, K1.
Row 12: O, K2, P15, O, P2tog, K3.
Row 13: AP1, K3, O, RLD, K1, LRD, O, K5, O, LRD, K1.
Row 14: O, K2, P16, O, P2tog, K3.

Row 15: AP1, K4, O, D3, O, K1, cast off 5 stitches, O, LRD, K1.
Row 16: O, K2, P2, LCO5, P10, O, P2tog, K3.
Row 17: AP1, K3, LRD, O, K1, O, RLD, K5, LRD, O, LRD, K1.
Row 18: O, LRD, P17, O, P2tog, K3.
Row 19: AP1, K2, LRD, O, K3, O, RLD, K3, LRD, O, LRD, K1.

Row 20: O, LRD, P16, O, P2tog, K3.
Row 21: AP1, K1, LRD, O, K5, O, RLD, K1, LRD, O, LRD, K1.
Row 22: O, LRD, P15, O, LRD, K3.
Row 23: AP1, LRD, O, K1, cast off 5 stitches, O, D3, O, LRD, K1.
Row 24: O, LRD, P4, LCO5, P5, O, P2tog, K3.
Row 25: AP1, K1, O, RLD, K5, D3, O, LRD, K1.
Row 26: O, LRD, P12, O, P2tog, K3.
Row 27: AP1, K2, O, RLD, K3, LRD, O, LRD, K1.
Row 28: O, LRD, P11, O, P2tog, K3.

Row 29: AP1, K3, O, RLD, K1, LRD, O, LRD, K1.
Row 30: O, LRD, P10, O, P2tog, K3.
Row 31: AP1, K4, O, D3, O, LRD, K1.
Row 32: O, LRD, P9, O, P2tog, K3.

Repeat rows 1-32 for desired length.

The Buttonhole Border sample was worked with size 5 perle cotton on size 0 needles.

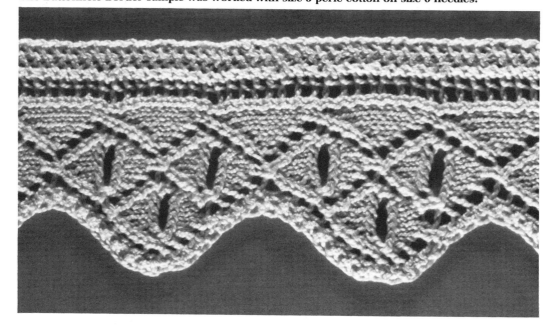

Diamonds and Vines

Special Instructions:
AP1   Abbreviated Pattern #1 is worked as follows:
Slp, K1, O, LRD.

Cast on 41 stitches.

Row 1: AP1, LRD, (O, LRD)2x, O, K5, O, RLD, K1, LRD, O, K5, (O, LRD)2x, O, D3, (O, LRD)4x, K1.

Row 2: O, LRD, P34, K4.

Row 3: AP1, K2, (O, LRD)2x, *O, RLD, K1, LRD*, O, K5, *-*, (O, LRD)2x, O, K3, (O, LRD)3x, O, K2.

Row 4: O, LRD, P35, K4.

Row 5: AP1, K3, (O, LRD)2x, O, D3, O, K7, O, D3LR, (O, LRD)2x, O, K5, (O, LRD)3x, O, K2.

Row 6: O, LRD, P36, K4.

Row 7: AP1, K1, LRD, O, K1, (O, LRD)2x, O, RLD, K2, O, D3, O, K2, LRD, (O, LRD)2x, O, K1, O, RLD, K1, LRD, O, K1, (O, LRD)3x, O, K2.

Row 8: O, LRD, P37, K4.

Row 9: AP1, LRD, O, K3, (O, LRD)2x, O, D3, *O, K3, O, D3LR*, (O, LRD)2x, *-*, O, K3, (O, LRD)3x, O, K2.

Row 10: O, LRD, P38, K4.

Row 11: AP1, K3, LRD, O, K1, (O, LRD)2x, O, RLD, K3, LRD, (O, LRD)2x, O, K1, O, RLD, K5, LRD, O, K1, (O, LRD)3x, O, K2.

Row 12: O, LRD, P39, K4.

Row 13: AP1, K2, LRD, O, K3, (O, LRD)2x, O, RLD, K1, LRD, (O, LRD)2x, O, K3, O, RLD, K3, LRD, O, K3, (O, LRD)3x, O, K2.

Row 14: O, LRD, P40, K4.

Row 15: AP1, *K1, LRD, O, K5*, (O, LRD)2x, O, D3LR, (O, LRD)2x, O, K5, O, RLD, *-*, (O, LRD)3x, O, K2.

Row 16: O, LRD, P41, K4.

Row 17: AP1, K3, *O, RLD, K1, LRD*, (O, LRD)2x, O, K3, (O, LRD)2x, O, RLD, K1, LRD, O, K5, *-*, (O, LRD)4x, K1.

Row 18: O, LRD, P40, K4.

Row 19: AP1, K4, O, D3LR, (O, LRD)2x, O, K5, (O, LRD)2x, O, D3, O, K7, O, D3LR, (O, LRD)4x, K1.

Row 20: O, LRD, P39, K4.

Row 21: AP1, LRD, O, K2, LRD, (O, LRD)2x, O, K1, O, RLD, K1, LRD, O, K1, (O, LRD)2x, O, RLD, K2, O, D3, O, K2, LRD, (O, LRD)4x, K1.

Row 22: O, LRD, P38, K4.

Row 23: AP1, K2, O, D3LR, (O, LRD)2x, O, K3, *O, D3, O, K3*, (O, LRD)2x, *-*, O, D3LR, (O, LRD)4x, K1.

Row 24: O, LRD, P37, K4.

Row 25: AP1, K2, LRD, (O, LRD)2x, O, K1, O, RLD, K5, LRD, O, K1, (O, LRD)2x, O, RLD, K3, LRD, (O, LRD)4x, K1.

Row 26: O, LRD, P36, K4.

Row 27: AP1, K1, LRD, (O, LRD)2x, O, K3, O, RLD, K3, LRD, O, K3, (O, LRD)2x, O, RLD, K1, LRD, (O, LRD)4x, K1.

Row 28: O, LRD, P35, K4.

Repeat rows 1-28 for desired length. Cast off after Row 2.

Version 1 above and Version 2 below were worked on size 5 perle cotton on size 0 needles.

Oakleaf and Acorn Border

Special Instructions:
Every even-numbered row begins with O2. The second loop should be dropped on the following row.

Cast on 40 stitches and knit 1 row.

Row 1: K3, O, LRD, K1, O, B1, O, K2, LRD, P1, LRD, K3, O, LRD, O, K2, P1, LRD, K1, O, LRD, O, K3, O, K4, (O, LRD)2x, O, K2.
Row 2: O2, P2tog, P18, (K1, P9)2x, K4.
Row 3: K3, O, LRD, K1, O, (KP1)3x, O, K2, LRD, P1, LRD, K3, (O, LRD)2x, P1, LRD, O, LRD, (O, K5)2x, (O, LRD)2x, O, K2.
Row 4: O2, P2tog, P20, K1, P8, K1, P13, K4.
Row 5: K3, O, (LRD)2x, *O, K6, O*, K2, LRD, P1, LRD, K3, **O, LRD, O**, D3, **-**, K7, *-*, (LRD, O)2x, K2.
Row 6: O2, P2tog, P30, K1, P13, K4.
Row 7: K3, O, (LRD)2x, O, K6, O, K2, LRD, P1, LRD, K3, O, RLD, D3, transfer the last two stitches on the right needle back to the left needle, then LRD over these same 2 stitches, O, K4, P1, K4, O, K4, LRD, O, K1, (O, LRD)2x, O, K2.
Row 8: O2, P2tog, P17, K1, P11, K1, P13, K4.
Row 9: K3, O, (LRD)2x, O, K6, O, K2, LRD, P1, LRD, K2, O, LRD, O, K3, LRD, P1, LRD, K3, O, K3, LRD, O, K3, (O, LRD)2x, O, K2.

Row 10: O2, P2tog, P18, K1, P10, K1, P4, (KP1)6x, P3, K4.
Row 11: K3, O, (LRD)2x, O, P12, O, K2, LRD, P1, LRD, K1, O, LRD, O, K3, LRD, P1, LRD, K3, O, K4, O, RLD, K3, (O, LRD)2x, O, K2.
Row 12: O2, P2tog, P19, K1, P9, K1, P4, (LRD)6x, P3, K4.
Row 13: K3, O, (LRD)2x, O, P6, O, K2, LRD, P1, K2, O, LRD, O, K3, LRD, P1, LRD, K3, O, K4, O, RLD, K1, LRD, (O, LRD)3x, K1.
Row 14: O2, P2tog, P18, K1, P9, K1, P4, (LRD)3x, P3, K4.
Row 15: K3, O, LRD, (K1, O)2x, P3tog, O, K2, LRD, P1, K2, O, LRD, O, K3, LRD, P1, LRD, K2, O, KP1, O, K5, O, D3, (O, LRD)3x, K1.
Row 16: O2, P2tog, P19, K1, P9, K1, P10, K4.
Row 17: K3, O, LRD, K1, O, K3, O, LRD, O, K1, LRD, P1, K2, O, LRD, O, K3, LRD, P1, LRD, K2, O, (KP1)3x, O, K7, LRD, (O, LRD)2x, K1.
Row 18: O2, P2tog, P22, K1, P9, K1, P11, K4.
Row 19: K3, O, LRD, K1, O, K5, (O, LRD)2x, P1, (LRD, O)2x, K3, LRD, P1, LRD, K2, O, K6, O, LRD, K3, LRD, (O, LRD)3x, K1.
Row 20: O2, P2tog, P21, K1, P8, K1, P12, K4.
Row 21: K3, O, LRD, K1, O, K7, O, LRD, O, D3, O, LRD, O, K3, LRD, P1, LRD, K2, O, K6, O, LRD, K2, LRD, (O, LRD)3x, K1.

Row 22: O2, P2tog, P20, K1, P21, K4.
Row 23: K3, O, LRD, K1, O, K4, P1, K4, O, RLD, D3, transfer the last two stitches on the right needle back to the left needle, then LRD over those same 2 stitches, O, K3, LRD, P1, LRD, K2, O, K6, O, LRD, K3, (O, LRD)3x, K1.
Row 24: O2, P2tog, P10, (KP1)6x, P4, K1, P11, K1, P7, K4.
Row 25: K3, O, LRD, K1, O, K3, LRD, P1, LRD, K3, O, LRD, O, K2, LRD, P1, LRD, K2, O, P12, O, LRD, K3,(O, LRD)3x, K1.
Row 26: O2, P2tog, P10, (LRD)6x, P4, K1, P10, K1, P7, K4.
Row 27: K3, O, LRD, K1, O, K3, LRD, P1, LRD, K3, O, LRD, O, K1, LRD, P1, LRD, K2, O, P6, O, LRD, K1, LRD, (O, LRD)3x, K1.
Row 28: O2, P2tog, P9, (LRD)3x, P4, K1, P9, K1, P7, K4.
Row 29: K3, O, LRD, K1, O, K3, LRD, P1, LRD, K3, O, LRD, O, K2, P1, LRD, K2, O, P3tog, O, K1, O, K3, (O, LRD)3x, K1.
Row 30: O2, P2tog, P16, K1, P9, K1, P7, K4.

Repeat rows 1-30 for desired length.

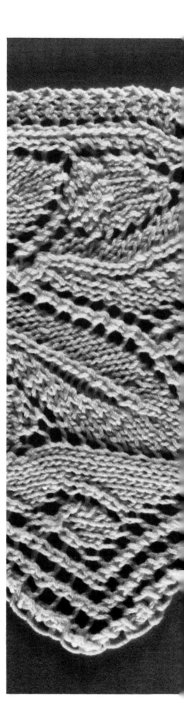

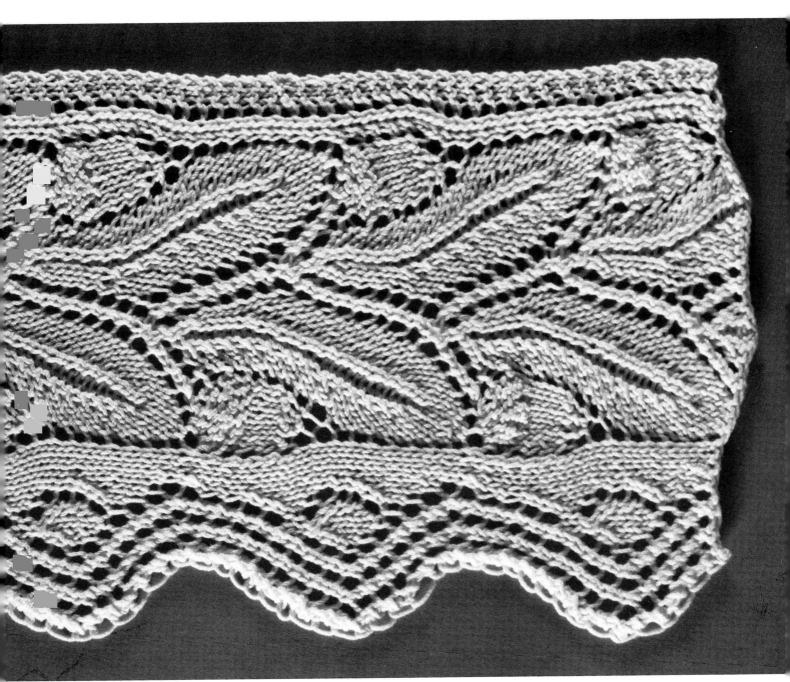

Oakleaf and Acorn Border was worked with Parisian Cotton on size 1 needles.

Sources of Supply

Yarns

The companies listed below generously provided the yarns needed to make the samples for this book. If these yarns are not available in your local stores, the companies can supply you either with their products or with addresses of nearby stores carrying them.

B. Blumenthal & Co., Inc.
c/o Newark Dressmaker Supply, Inc.
6473 Ruch Rd.
Lehigh Valley, PA 18001

Lily cotton carpet warp, perle cotton and Antique Bedspread Cotton, the first two of which are available in a variety of colors.

Bucilla Yarns
c/o Artworks
31 Liberty St.
Newton, NJ 07860

Wondersheen Cotton, which is also available in colors.

Coats and Clark
P.O. Box 1010
Dept. CS
Toccoa, GA 30577

Knit-Cro-Sheen J & P Coats, which is available in colors and is sold in many variety stores.

Frederick J. Fawcett, Inc.
1304 Scott St.
Dept. W
Petaluma, CA 94952

10/2 linen, which is also available in colors.

Joseph Galler Yarns
27 W. 20th St.
New York, NY 10011

Parisian Cotton and Marisa Swiss Cotton, which are also available in many knitting and needlework shops.

Needles and Knitting Accessories

Needles in the small sizes needed for counterpane knitting are sometimes difficult to find locally. The following stores and mail-order sources carry small-sized needles, and some have sets of five double-pointed needles. Many also carry yarns, knitting books and other knitting supplies. Those noted with an asterisk (*) provided needles and accessories to produce the samples for this book. The conversion chart on the facing page indicates comparable sizes for U.S., metric and British knitting needles and crochet hooks.

Abel Morall Ltd.*
Box #2
Edward St.
Redditch
Worcestershire B96 6HB
England

Manufacturer of Aero needles, to whom I owe a debt of gratitude for sending me these needles during the early years of research for this book, before they were distributed in the United States.

Arlene Mintzer
The Sensuous Fiber®
P.O. Box 44
Parkville Station
Brooklyn, NY 11204

Needles, books and yarn.

Bernat Yarn & Craft Corp.*
Depot and Mendon Sts., P.O. Box 387
Uxbridge, MA 01569-0387

U.S. distributor of Aero needles from England; other knitting accessories.

Boye Needle Company*
4343 N. Ravenswood Ave.
Chicago, IL 60657

Needles in small sizes and sets of five double-pointed needles.

Lacis
2982 Adeline St.
Berkeley, CA 94703

Needles in small sizes, sets of five needles, knitting books and, additionally, a full line of supplies for lacemaking.

Schoolhouse Press*
6899 Cary Bluff
Pittsville, WI 54466

Needles, including sets of five, other knitting equipment and yarn. Also specializes in knitting books.

Straw into Gold*
3006 San Pablo Ave.
Berkeley, CA 94702

Needles, including those made of bamboo and sets of five double-pointed needles; hard-to-find knitting equipment, yarns and books.

Susan Bates*
212 Middlesex Ave.
Chester, CT 06412-0364

Needles, crochet hooks and other knitting accessories, which are sold in most needlework and knitting shops.

Out-of-Print Book Dealers

Many of the books listed in the Bibliography on pp. 176-177 are long out of print. Sometimes copies of these books can be found through dealers who specialize in such books. Often these dealers carry current books as well.

Betty Feinstein Books
96 Roundwood Rd.
Newton, MA 02164

Black Cat Books
1 Granby Rd.
Edinburgh EH16 5NH
Scotland

Books in Transit
2830 Case Way
Turlock, CA 95380

Willow House Books
58 Chapel St.
Chorley, Lancs. PR7 1BS
England

Wooden Porch Books
Rte. 1, Box 262
Middlebourne, WV 26149

Conversion Chart for Counterpane Knitting

		U.S.	Metric	U.K.
Knitting Needles		0	2.00mm	14
		1	2.25mm	13
			2.50mm	
		2	2.75mm	12
			3.00mm	11
Crochet Hooks		B/1	2.00mm	14
		C/2	2.50mm	12

Counterpane Collections

The following museums, historical societies and historic sites have interesting counterpanes and other knitted pieces in their collections.

France

Musée Alsacien
23 Quai Saint-Nicolas
67000 Strasbourg
France

Musée de l'Oeuvre
Notre Dame
3 Place du Château
67000 Strasbourg
France

Musée d'Unterlinden
1 Place d'Unterlinden
6800 Colmar
France

Switzerland

Bernisches Historisches
Museum
Helvetiaplatz 5
3000 Berne
Switzerland

Gewebenmuseum
Spalenvorstadt 2
4000 Basle
Switzerland

Schweizerisches
Landsmuseum
Museumstrasse 2
8023 Zurich
Switzerland

United Kingdom

Australia
Como Historic Melbourne
House
Como Ave.
South Yarra, Melbourne
Australia

The Van Diemen's Land
Museum
103 Hampden Rd.
Battery Point
Hobart, Tasmania
Australia

Canada
National Museum of Man
Metcalfe and McLeod Sts.
Ottawa, Ontario
Canada K1A 0M8

McCord Museum
690 Sherbrook St., W.
Montreal, Quebec
Canada H3A 1E9

Royal Ontario Museum
100 Queen's Park
Toronto, Ontario
Canada M5S 2C6

England, Scotland, Wales
Bradford Art Galleries and
Museums
Bolling Hall Rd.
Bradford, West Yorkshire

National Museums of
Scotland
Chambers St.
Edinburgh, EH1 1JF
Scotland

Strangers' Hall Museum
Charing Cross Norwich
Norfolk, NR1 4AL
England

The Victoria and Albert
Museum
Cromwell Rd.
South Kensington, S.W.
London, England SW7 2RL

Welsh Folk Museum
St. Fagans
Cardiff, Wales CF5 XBX

New Zealand
Auckland War Memorial
Museum
The Domain
Auckland, New Zealand

Broadgreen House
Nelson, New Zealand

Canterbury Museum
Rolleston Ave.
Christchurch, New Zealand

Ewleme Cottage
14 Ayr St.
Parnell, Auckland
New Zealand

Glorat, Clark Home
Wanganui
Maxwell Town
New Zealand

The Hawkes Bay Art
Gallery and Museum
Herschel St.
Napier, New Zealand

Historic Alberton
Mt. Albert
Auckland, New Zealand

Kemp House
Kerikeri
New Zealand

Larnach Castle
Dunedin, New Zealand

Manawatu Museum
Pioneer Cottage
Palmerston North,
Totaranui
New Zealand

Museum and Arts Center
Wyllie Cottage
Stout St.
Gisborne, New Zealand

Otago Early Settlers
Museum
Lower High St.
Dunedin, New Zealand

United States

The Baltimore Museum
of Art
Museum Dr.
Baltimore, MD 21218

The Brooklyn Museum
200 Eastern Pkwy.
Brooklyn, NY 11238

Colonial Williamsburg
Williamsburg, VA 23185

D.A.R. Museum
1776 D Street, N.W.
Washington, D.C.
20006-5392

Hennepin County
Historical Society
2303 Third Ave.
Minneapolis, MN 55404

Hillwood
4155 Linnean Ave., N.W.
Washington, D.C. 20008

Historic Cherry Hill
South Pearl St.
Albany, NY 12202

Hotel de Paris
Museum of the National
Society of Colonial Dames
of America
Georgetown, CO 80444

Lowie Museum of
Anthropology
University of California
Kroeber Hall
Bancroft Way
& College Ave.
Berkeley, CA 94720

Minnesota Historical
Society
690 Cedar St.
St. Paul, MN 55101

National Museum of
American History
Smithsonian Institution
12th and Constitution, N.W.
Washington, D.C. 20560

Newark Museum
49 Washington St.
Newark, NJ 07101

The Margaret Woodbury
Strong Museum
700 Allen Creek Rd.
Rochester, NY 14618

The Museum of Art
Rhode Island School
of Design
224 Benefit St.
Providence, RI 02903

The Nott House
White Columns
Kennebunkport, ME 04046

Shelburne Museum
Shelburne, VT 05482

Witte Museum
3801 Broadway
San Antonio, TX
78209-2601

Bibliography

Entries marked by an asterisk (*) were not used in my research for this book, but they are important suggested sources of related information.

Books

Nineteenth-Century Books:

Beeton's Needlework. London: Wark, Lock & Tyler, 1870. Reprint. London: Chancellor Press, 1986.

Mrs. Beeton's Book of Household Management. London: S.O. Beeton, 1859.

Butterick. *The Art of Knitting.* London: The Butterick Publishing Co., Ltd., 1892.

———. *Fancy and Practical Knitting.* London and New York: The Butterick Publishing Co., Ltd., 1897.

Caufield, S.F.A., and Blanche C. Saward. *The Dictionary of Needlework.* London: L. Upcott Gill, 1882.

Cupples, Mrs. George. *A Knitting-Book of Counterpanes.* Edinburgh: Johnstone, Hunter & Co., 1871.

Dillmont, Thérèse de. *Encyclopedia of Needlework.* Mulhouse, France: Editions Th. de Dillmont, 1886. Reprint. New York: DMC Library, Crescent Books, 1987.

———. *Knitting,* Series 1-5. Mulhouse, France: Editions Th. de Dillmont, DMC Library, n.d.

Dorinda [pseud]. *Needlework for Ladies.* London: Swan Sonnenchein, Lowrey & Co., 1886.

Mlle de Lorette, comp. *The Ladies' Daily Companion, or Guide to Plain and Useful Knitting.* London: Thomas Gill, 1847.

Eureka Silk Manufacturing Co. *What to Make with Eureka Silk: Knitting, Crochet, Embroidery, Etching.* Boston & New York: The Eureka Silk Manufacturing Co., 1893.

Eyre, Jane. *Needles & Brushes and How to Use Them: A Manual of Fancy Work.* Chicago: Clark and Co., 1887.

Florence Knitting Silk: How to Use. Boston: Nonotuck Silk Co., 1885.

Hartley, Florence, compiler. *The Ladies Hand Book of Fancy and Ornamental Work.* Philadelphia: G.G. Evans, 1859.

June, Jenny [Jane Cunningham Croly]. *Knitting and Crochet.* Lynn, Mass.: A.L. Burt, J.F. Ingalls, 1886.

Kelly, F.G. *The Lady's Knitting Book.* Dublin: J. M'Glashan, 1848.

The Knitted Lace Pattern Book. Kilmarnock, Scotland: Thomson Brothers, 1850.

The Ladies Knitting and Netting Book. 3rd ed. London: John Miland, 1837.

Miss Lambert. *The Hand Book of Needlework.* New York: Wiley & Putnam, 1842.

———. *My Knitting Book.* 5th Edition. London: John Murray, 1844.

Masters, Ellen T., ed. *The Work Table Companion.* London: Ward, Lock & Bowen, Ltd., 1893.

Mee, Cornelia. *Manual of Needlework.* London: Alyott & Co., 1854.

The New Knitter or Lady's Worktable Companion. London: Darton & Co., 1848.

Niles, Eva Marie. *Fancy Work Recreation.* Minneapolis, Minn.: Buckeye Publishing Co., 1884.

Rules & Directions for the Use of Finlayson, Bousfield & Co.'s Real Scotch Linen Crochet Thread. Boston: Finlayson, Bousfield & Co., 1887.

The Young Ladies Journal: Complete Guide to the Worktable. London: E. Harrison, 1884.

Twentieth-Century Books:

Abby, Barbara. *The Complete Book of Knitting.* New York: The Viking Press, 1971.

*———. *Knitting Lace.* New York: The Viking Press, 1974.

Anchor Manual of Lace Crafts. London: B.T. Batsford, Ltd., 1961.

Anchor Manual of Needlework. London: B.T. Batsford, Ltd., 1958.

Compton, Rae. *The Complete Book of Traditional Knitting.* New York: Charles Scribner's Sons, 1983.

Finley, Ruth E. *The Lady of Godey's, Sara Josepha Hale.* Philadelphia: J.B. Lippincott Co., 1931.

Freeman, Sara. *Isabella and Sam: The Story of Mrs. Beeton.* New York: Coward, McCann & Geoghegan, Inc., 1977.

*Kinzel, Marianne. *First Book of Modern Lace Knitting*. London: Artistic Needlework Publications, 1954. Reprint. New York: Dover Publishing Co., 1972.

*———. *Second Book of Modern Lace Knitting*. London: Mills & Boon Limited, 1961. Reprint. New York: Dover Publishing Co., 1972.

*Lorant, Tessa. *Collection of Knitted Lace Edges*. Somerset, England: The Thorn Press, 1981.

*———. *Knitted Quilts and Flounces*. Somerset, England: The Thorn Press, 1982.

*Macdonald, Anne L. *No Idle Hands: A Social History of American Knitting*. New York: Ballantine Books, 1988.

Norbury, James. *Traditional Knitting Patterns*. London: B.T. Batsford, Ltd., 1962. Reprint. New York: Dover Publishing Co., 1973.

Norbury, James, with Margret Agutter. *Odhams Encyclopedia of Knitting*. London: Odhams Books Lts., 1957.

Nylén, Anna-Maja. *Swedish Handcraft*. New York: Van Nostrand Reinhold, 1977.

Peake, Miriam Morrison. *The Wise Book of Knitting and Crochet*. New York: Wm. H. Wise & Co., Inc., 1949.

Phillips, Mary Walker. *Creative Knitting*. New York: Van Nostrand Reinhold, 1971. Reprint. St. Paul, Minn.: Dos Tejedoras Fiber Arts Publications, 1986.

———. *Knitting*. New York: Franklin Watts, 1977.

———. *Step-by-Step Knitting*. New York: Golden Press, 1967.

———. *Step-by-Step Macrame*. New York: Golden Press, 1970.

Rutt, Richard. *The History of Hand Knitting*. London: B.T. Batsford, Inc. 1987.

Thomas, Mary Hedges. *Mary Thomas's Book of Knitting Patterns*. London: Hodder and Stoughton, Ltd., 1943. Reprint. New York: Dover Publications, Inc., 1972.

———. *Mary Thomas's Knitting Book*. London: Hodder and Stoughton, Ltd., 1938. Reprint. New York: Dover Publications, Inc., 1972.

*Walker, Barbara G. *Charted Knitting Designs: A Third Treasury of Knitting Patterns*. New York: Charles Scribner's Sons, 1972.

*———. *A Second Treasury of Knitting Patterns*. New York: Charles Scribner's Sons, 1970.

*———. *A Treasury of Knitting Patterns*. New York: Charles Scribner's Sons, 1968.

Warren, Geoffrey. *A Stitch in Time: Victorian and Edwardian Needlecraft*. New York: Taplinger Publishing Co., Inc., 1976.

*Zimmermann, Elizabeth. *Knitters Almanac*. New York: Charles Scribner's Sons, 1974. Reprint. New York: Dover Publications, Inc., 1981.

Periodicals

Nineteenth-Century Periodicals:

Godey's Lady's Book and Magazine [1830-1898], selected issues.

Home Needlework Magazine. Boston [1899-1917], selected issues.

Madame Weigel. Melbourne, Australia [1880-1950], selected issues.

Modern Priscilla Magazine. Boston [1887-1930], selected issues.

New York Tribune Extra. Nos. 62, 75 and 82 (supplements devoted to needlework), [1880-1882].

Weldon's Practical Needlework and *Weldon's Practical Knitter*. London [1886-circa 1930], selected issues.

The Worktable: A Supplement to The Lady's Newspaper & Pictorial Times. London: *The Lady's Newspaper*, 1856.

Twentieth-Century Periodicals:

Needlecraft: The Magazine of Home Arts. Augusta, Maine [1909-1941], selected issues.

Paragon Art and Needlecraft. Booklet #21. New Zealand: Art and Needlecraft, Inc., n.d.

Articles

Davidson, Hughla. "The Development of Knitting as a Craft." *Craft Australia* 1 (1977): pp. 41-51.

Nylander, Jane C. "Counterpanes." *Early American Life* (April 1986): 62-65.

Potter, Esther. "English Knitting and Crochet Books of the 19th Century." *The Library*, 3rd series, 10 (March 1955): 25-40 and (June 1955): 103-119.

Index of Patterns

Editor: Christine Timmons
Designer: Ben Kann
Art Director: Deborah Fillion
Layout artist: Richard Erlanger
Art assistants: Cindy Nyitray, Iliana Koehler
Copy/production editors: Victoria Monks, Ruth Dobsevage
Editorial assistant: Maria Angione
Darkroom supervisor: Robert Marsala
Darkroom assistants: Monica Bulson, Lisa Carlson,
  Priscilla Rollins
Typesetter: Margot Knorr
Print production manager: Peggy Dutton

Photos, except where noted: Cathy Carver
Drawings: Lee Hov

Typeface: ITC Zapf Book Light
Paper: Sterling Litho Satin, 70 lb., neutral pH
Printer and Binder: Ringier, Olathe, Kansas